The Political Economy of Hawai'i

Ibrahim G. Aoudé
Guest Editor

Social Process in Hawaii
Volume 35, 1994

Department of Sociology
University of Hawaii at Manoa

Contents

Foreword v

Preface vii

Introduction xi

Native Hawaiian Struggles and Events, A Partial List 1973-1993
    Luciano Minerbi 1

Foreign Investment in Hawai'i
    Marion Kelly 15

The Political Economy of Foreign Investment in Hawai'i
    Karl Kim 40

The Potential for High Tech in Hawai'i
    Paul A. Herbig and Hugh E. Kramer 56

Hawai'i: the Housing Crisis and the State's Development Strategy
    Ibrahim G. Aoudé 71

Internationalization of Capital, Migration, Reindustrialization, and Women Workers in the Garment Industry
    Joyce Chinen 85

Kaua'i: Between Hurricanes
    Jon K. Matsuoka and Davianna Pomaika'i McGregor 103

A Green Economy for Hawai'i
    Ira Rohter 124

Sustainability Versus Growth in Hawai'i
    Luciano Minerbi 145

Why There Are No Asian Americans in Hawai'i: The Continuing Significance of Local Identity
    Jonathan Y. Okamura 161

The End of the American Age of Abundance: Whither Hawai'i?
    Noel Jacob Kent 179

Missionaries, Polynesians, and Tourists: Mormonism
and Tourism in Laʻie, Hawaiʻi
 T. D. Webb 195

Traversing Inter-Ethnic Social Orders: Native Hawaiian
Song Collections
 Jeffrey J. Kamakahi and Albert B. Robillard 213

Contributors 231

Foreword

This issue on the political economy of Hawai'i, Volume 35, follows on an earlier issue, Volume 31. This work continues the legacy of participation by a full and diverse range of faculty, students, and other parties exploring the wide range of populations and processes that involve life and society in and around this archipelago. Romanzo Adams, Andrew W. Lind, Bernhard L. Hormann, and Douglas S. Yamamura, former sociology professors or students involved in the first issues of this journal, were committed to the view that understanding Hawai'i's peoples requires many social science perspectives and approaches. The papers in this issue reflect on aspects of life and work in Hawai'i and draw upon more contemporary thinking on topics which have received attention in earlier study and research.

Kiyoshi Ikeda

Preface

It was gratifying to see the large number of submissions to this volume of *Social Process In Hawai'i*, which proved the need for a forum to discuss issues of political economy in the state. The Editorial Board decided to include 13 of those submissions: A list of the Native Hawaiian land struggles and events, and 12 articles that deal with various aspects of Hawai'i's political economy.

Luciano Minerbi's list is not a chronology in the strict sense of the word. Dates are listed chronologically for each event, e.g., dates for the anti-geothermal struggles are listed from 1987-1993. These are followed by dates for the Makalawena, West Hawai'i project from 1988-1990. Events were further listed by Island with a section created for statewide events.

Two articles, Marion Kelly's and Karl Kim's, discuss directly foreign investment in Hawai'i. Several others, e.g., Jonathan Okamura's and Ira Rohter's deal with foreign investment and/or tourism in developing their central arguments. On one level, all of these articles reinforce one another, and each, in its own way, is a testimony to the proposition that any societal issue rests ultimately on the same macro basis as any other. Finally, the emphasis on foreign investment varies from one article to the next.

T.D. Webb's article on Mormonism and tourism in La'ie represents a neglected part of Hawai'i's history that the Editorial Board decided to include in this volume.

The article by Jeffrey Kamakahi and Albert Robillard contributes to this volume by demonstrating the way in which post-structuralist/post-modernist language may be integrated with political economy to analyze the development of Native Hawaiian culture in a capitalist setting.

Hawaiian words are only italicized (and defined) on first mention. Glottals are used with Hawaiian words except in cases where the author's reference does not use them, e.g., Bank of Hawaii. Glottals are kept in references depending upon how they were submitted by the authors. However, in cases where it was clear that a glottal should be inserted, the editor has exercised his editorial privilege.

The term *high-tech* instead of *high technology* is used, especially in Paul Herbig's and Hugh Kramer's article for two reasons: (1) it was the authors' preference; and (2) it does no harm to the English language or the topic.

Government documents in imbedded notes are indicated by source, e.g., (Hawaii, 1993) for State of Hawai'i documents, or (Honolulu, 1992) for City of

Honolulu documents. Only if there is more than one reference with the same date is the source identified further; e.g., (Honolulu. Department of General Planning, 1991). Obviously, complete references are given at the end of each article.

It is important to state that this volume only tackles some of the current important issues to Hawai'i by way of initiating a sorely needed debate. Our hope is that more research will be done in the very near future on other pressing issues not covered in this volume.

I would like to thank Professor Kiyoshi Ikeda, Executive Editor of *Social Process In Hawaii,* for his support in publishing this volume. My thanks also go to Professor Michael Weinstein, General Editor of *Social Process In Hawaii,* and the Department of Sociology at UHM for agreeing to publish a volume on the political economy of Hawai'i.

Many thanks to Professor Franklin Odo, Director, Ethnic Studies Program at UHM, for asking me to be the Guest Editor.

I am indebted to the University of Hawai'i at Manoa Commission on Diversity; Dean Richard Dubanoski, College of Social Sciences; the Ethnic Studies Program Enrichment Fund; Rudolph Schmerl, Director, Office of Research Administration; and Women Campus Club for their grants in support of this project. In addition, Professor Kiyoshi Ikeda was gracious enough to extend a modest loan from the *Social Process In Hawaii* Fund. Finally, thanks to Jonathan Okamura for helping to secure the UHM Commission on Diversity grant.

I was so fortunate to work with superb individuals on the Editorial Board: Professors Beverly Keever (Journalism Department), Peter Manicas (Director of the Liberal Studies Program), Robert Stauffer (Professor Emeritus, Political Science Department), and Franklin Odo (with whom I kept in touch constantly while he was on Sabbatical). It was a real pleasure working with these scholars. Special thanks go to Beverly Keever for her incisive comments on and many suggestions for revising the submitted articles. Finally, Peter Manicas and Robert Stauffer were ready to help at short notice. Their commentaries on the many articles submitted and knowledge of political economy were extremely valuable to this volume.

Freda Hellinger must be commended for her excellent copy-editing work. Mark Santoki has my gratitude for volunteering to prepare the groundwork for computer entry of the copy-edited material. My thanks to Dean Minakami for his hard work in entering copy-edited articles into the computer. Thanks to Marie El-

Zir and Mark Hamamoto for their clerical support. Many thanks to Janet Heavenridge, Production Manager, U.H. Press for her valuable assistance on this project. Finally, thanks to my wife, Liana, for editing the introduction to this volume.

Ibrahim G. Aoudé

Introduction

This volume of *Social Process In Hawai'i (SPIH)* seeks to initiate a progressive debate on Hawai'i's political economy. Classical Political economy originated with William Petty and was further developed by Adam Smith and David Ricardo in the eighteenth and nineteenth centuries. Karl Marx and Frederick Engels also made contributions, especially with Marx's discovery of "surplus value"—roughly, the remaining part of the value of a commodity appropriated by the capitalist after the laborer's wage and other costs are paid and the commodity sold. In the twentieth century, especially its second half, political economy began to be utilized in the West as a theoretical framework for the radical critique of capitalist society, mostly in the Marxist vein that included political economy as one of the three component parts of Marxism (the other two being Dialectical materialism, and socialism). However, the framework became so fashionable in the 1970s and 1980s that even non-Marxists made use of it. Political economic analysis sought to relate the political component to the economic and show how both interacted to yield a particular outcome, say a public policy decision, or the effect of the Vietnam War on U.S. indebtedness.

Major development theories critical of mainstream modernization theories fall within the political economy tradition. The most celebrated of these is Dependency theory (Frank). Marxists, neo-Marxists and even non-Marxists all wrote under the rubric of Dependency theory and were also referred to as political economists.

Political economy is an analytical framework that relates politics to economics in an integral way and consequently rejects the existing spurious separation between these two "disciplines" in the dominant literature. Ironically, mainstream economics, in its neo-Keynesian and monetarist varieties, has often been referred to as "political economy" by eminent figures in the literature such as Paul Samuelson and Milton Friedman.

SPIH had dedicated the 1984-85 volume (number 31) to the political economy of Hawai'i. Ten years later, this volume has appeared. Why the renewed interest in the political economy of Hawai'i? A cursory look would quickly reveal the ongoing problems in both the political and economic arenas. Foreign investment has traditionally concentrated on tourism and real estate. From 1986 till the end of 1989, tourists and investments from Japan boosted the Hawaiian economy in unprecedented ways

Tourism, the mainstay of the Hawaiian economy, is in the doldrums. For over a decade we have been subjected to a barrage of discussions (by leading figures in both the public and private sectors), papers, newspaper articles, and conferences promoting diversification of the economy. And yet, the policy makers and planners in both the public and private sectors have nothing significant to show for diversification. Valiant attempts to develop a high technology sector and diversified agriculture yielded feeble results. Commitments to diversification were not sufficient to change the realities of the Hawaiian economy. In fact, the policy makers were forced by the economic structures to further promote tourism as though it was imprinted: NO WAY OUT. Hawai'i remains heavily dependent on tourism.

The state continues to depend on major construction projects to keep the economy and its mainstay, tourism, going. In the past several years the political arena has witnessed fights and debates regarding the building of a convention center and mass transit system. The fight heated up between 1991-1993. The results were the demise of the mass transit, fixed guideway system and the decision to build a convention center.

This continued dependency on tourism is occurring within a qualitatively different global political economy. The heady days of Japanese investment are all but over, and the decline in tourist arrivals and expenditures in Hawai'i reflects the deep global recession/depression. Still, the gurus of tourism are gambling upon the yet undefined Asia-Pacific market for Hawaiian tourism. Their argument seems quite "logical": Tourism is growing worldwide. Eventually, Hawai'i is bound to get its share of this growth. What is needed, they maintain, is an aggressive campaign to promote Hawai'i, especially in those Asian countries (e.g., South Korea, Taiwan, China, and Singapore). The danger of the "build-it-and-they- will-come" mentality gaining control among the planners and special tourism interests is very much in evidence.

Hawai'i is being subjected, as usual, to the vicissitudes of the world market but it does not have the wherewithal to respond on the same level. Hawai'i remains a small actor on the global scene that is subject to the international division of labor over which it has no control. Hawai'i's economic structures and its dependency on tourism developed over the past 40 years, especially with statehood and the advent of the jet plane. The great success of the tourist industry precluded Hawai'i from pursuing an independent path to development.

The 1993 bickering in the State Legislature over the Senate Presidency is but one manifestation of Hawai'i's economic problems in the political arena. This is not politics as usual—although bickering has occurred several times in the past. What makes it different this time is the dramatically changed global political economy that is not in Hawai'i's favor. A local political crisis is unfolding before our eyes written with the material generated by a global economic crisis.

The Democratic Party does not have a vision or a Program to pull the economy out of the doldrums. Republicans are quick to attack the track record of the Democratic Party in education, economic development, crime, and so forth. In a gubernatorial election year, the Republicans are promising Nirvana. If elected, we are told, their policies would dramatically change Hawai'i's situation for the better.

These are specious claims. While it is true that the Democrats have been in control of the State Government uninterruptedly since 1962, a coalition of business people (Democrats and Republicans alike) and Democratic politicians (and sometimes a coalition of Democratic and Republican politicians) were running the affairs of the state. A classic example of this wedding on the local level was Democrat George Ariyoshi and Republican Hebden Porteus in the 1960s. Another example was the transformation that occurred in the Big-Five Republican-run companies that became international and wielded enormous economic power in this state. These international companies have done well under Democratic Governors and Democratic majorities in both Houses of the State Legislature. Democrats as well as Republicans have participated in building Hawai'i's economic structures. Neither party can dissociate itself from the current political economic mess. Both parties will find it difficult to extricate us out of this crisis.

While both elite Democrats and Republicans had been busy cashing in on the economic good times, Native Hawaiians were reeling under the effects of maldevelopment. Evidence of this is available in statistics on Native Hawaiian health, education, prison population, and homelessness. The Native Hawaiian sovereignty movement, in many ways, can be attributed to this maldevelopment. Struggles for land, housing and against evictions in the late 1960s and early 1970s were instrumental in giving shape and direction to the now politically significant Native Hawaiian movement. Native Hawaiians had to fight hard to achieve tangible results such as stopping the bombing of Kaho'olawe, or having the United States apologize for its part in the overthrow of the Hawaiian Monarchy. It should be pointed out here that some of those who have actively participated in the general deterioration of the Native Hawaiian condition are now supporting the Hawaiian cause for their own self-aggrandizement. Some businesses are more eager than ever to incorporate Hawaiian culture through a "genuine" portrayal of Hawaiiana to tourists. A realization of the centrality of the Native Hawaiian issue has set in among Hawai'i's multi-ethnic elite. But one suspects that it is not so much out of concern to do justice to the cause as it is to maintain political stability, the sine *qua non* for a healthy economy. Both Democrats and Republicans are trying to play the Native Hawaiian card in preparation for the 1994 elections.

Again, why the renewed interest in the Hawaiian political economy at this juncture? The above discussion maintains that the global economic crisis is exacerbating politics on the local level. Various political trends within the Hawai'i elite have detected an opening through which they can enter or dominate local politics. Democrats and Republicans want to "restructure" we are told. The Republicans more so, perhaps, than the Democrats. But the question remains: Restructure what and how and in whose interest?

This restructuring argument explains in large measure the impetus behind the two volumes of *The Price of Paradise* whose ideological bent is quite clear: free enterprise. All that is essentially lacking in this view is sound public policy that promotes privatization.

This volume of *SPIH* is timely. It intends to show that the problems we face in Hawai'i today have historical roots that the free enterprise approach cannot solve. It also addresses salient problems of the political economy on the macro level. Micro cases, which are expressions of the macro problems, are dealt with as well. Volume 35 is critical of Hawai'i's development and also tries to point out some alternative solutions.

This volume will not be sympathetic to the positivist, free-market solutions espoused by works such as T*he Price of Paradise*. It is difficult to fathom the notion of free markets at this stage of the development of the global economy, let alone the "actual" free market since no such thing exists. Free market pronouncements and presumed remedies are utterly unconvincing in an age of international finance and the transnational corporation. The presence of competition among economic actors is not a necessary and sufficient condition for "free enterprise" or "free markets." The airline industry is a case in point. Since 1979, deregulations (presumably to make that industry "free" from government intervention regarding routes and fares to serve the consumer more efficiently) have resulted in the concentration of the market in the hands of fewer airline companies. Whatever "advantages" may have accrued to consumers, the presumed remedy resulted in a more "efficient" oligopoly situation.

At this late stage of the twentieth century, small business exists as a consequence of the global economy, not in spite of it. Many small businesses in

Hawai'i, for example, are part of the tourist industry that is internationally driven (e.g., finance and corporations). Due to cost-benefit considerations those businesses occupy a niche left for them by the big corporations. It is important to note that the tendency among small businesses is to grow (witness, for example, the pervasiveness of the *ABC* stores in Waikiki). In addition, those businesses that cater primarily to the local population can only exist because of enough personal income generated by an economy that is primarily based on tourism.

This volume of *SPIH* begins and ends with articles dealing with Native Hawaiians. Significantly, it includes a list of Native Hawaiian struggles and events contributed by Luciano Minerbi. The inclusion of this list is in recognition of the centrality of Native Hawaiian rights to events in Hawai'i. It is a statement that the Native Hawaiian issue is not merely one among many that Hawai'i policy makers have to take into account—this is positivist a-historical thinking—but that it should be at the core of public policy.

Marion Kelly's article provides an historic base and extension of the scope to the way we ought to look at foreign investment. The article makes clear that foreign investment is not new to Hawai'i. Foreign merchants built trading stores and warehouses; whaling and agricultural activities generated investments (constructing irrigation ditches, dams, and mills). Earlier experiences with the sandalwood trade reveal a direct relationship between foreign investment and indebtedness of both the *Ali'i* (chiefs) and the Hawaiian Government.

Hawai'i's experience with foreign investment clearly demonstrates the ultimate relationship between investment and politics. Politically influential h*aole* (foreigners) led the charge against the old land tenure system and instituted the *Mahele* (land division). After Annexation in 1898, American capital was no longer considered foreign. Kelly's article adds detail and specificity to the other articles in this volume that deal with foreign investment. Kelly asks: "Is racism an issue?" She then discusses the impact of tourism on Native Hawaiians and Hawai'i's resources concluding that the impact has been negative. Finally, she points out that some advocate independence for Hawai'i as the solution "to soften the often disastrous results of roller coaster, economic swings ..." This solution may seem unworkable to many. However, it is important to note that more Hawaiians are espousing it.

Karl Kim's article on foreign investment begins by recognizing a "direct connection between capital and colonialism." His central argument is that evidence of colonialism may be perceived if one looks at the pattern and magnitude of foreign investment, especially from Japan. Kim describes Japan's interests in Hawai'i and offers an explanation of foreign investment by way of regression analysis. He then describes the impact of that investment. Kim argues that Hawai'i's loss of control has been exacerbated by Japanese investors selling to other international buyers. In addition, Kim decries the "growth coalition" and its effects in widening the gap between the haves and the have-nots. He further accuses this coalition of heavily contributing to "loss of community."

Kim then advances strategies for managing foreign investment. His concern for representative democracy, leads him to see Hawaiian sovereignty as a "savior." Perhaps this argument needs to be taken up in another volume of S*PIH* that could show the interest of non-Native Hawaiians in supporting Hawaiian sovereignty.

It could be argued that Hawai'i had lost control over its political economy long before the foreign investment waves that began in the 1950s. In fact, it is plausible to argue that Hawai'i had lost effective control over its political economy since the Mahele in 1848.

Another point to be made in connection with Kim's article is that there may be no significant difference between Japanese and other international investors so far as control is concerned. One would also have to ask if the strategies Kim advances would work to alleviate the problems that Hawai'i is reeling under from foreign investment.

The article by Paul Herbig and Hugh Kramer on the potential for high technology in Hawai'i discusses the elements necessary for a high-tech industry. The authors' argument is essentially technical and its meta-theoretical commitment is mainstream. They identify Hawai'i's strengths in high tech: ocean thermal energy, and space/astronomy research. Herbig and Kramer politely conclude that it would require a long-term commitment (about 40 years) for Hawai'i to develop a viable high-tech industry.

If the broader political economy argument is pursued, one could conclude, on the basis of the evidence provided by Herbig and Kramer, that it may be too late for Hawai'i to become a high-tech center given the existing global competition. The recent scramble to save the faltering tourist industry demonstrates in a real way that the policy makers are cognizant of this fact. Policy makers are also aware that even if Hawai'i were to become a high-tech center, the industry would only be able to employ an insignificant number of a growing labor force given the capital-intensive nature of high-tech.

Housing is another area where public policy has consistently failed. The article that I contributed argues that the current crisis in housing has been in the making for 30 years. I identify the state's development strategy as the culprit. Private developers and financiers have benefited from this strategy. This article takes issue with "free market" solutions as unworkable in an age where a "free market" does not exist.

The article draws upon the history of land and housing struggles in Hawai'i and suggests a growing potential for a political mass movement that could form alongside the Native Hawaiian sovereignty movement. The article further argues that a political mass movement is an essential element in securing systemic changes to resolve the housing crisis.

Joyce Chinen's article examines the garment industry in Hawai'i in the context of global shifts, particularly in labor migration. The industry has traditionally employed women workers from various ethnic backgrounds (most of whom are Filipina). The situation of immigrant women workers is examined in relation to those of two other subgroups of workers ("old timers" and "young locals") in the garment industry. Chinen, compares the domestic and working conditions of these subgroups to understand how impediments may be overcome in building a coalition committed to labor organizing within the local garment industry and perhaps for the building of a more inclusive feminist movement. Age, generation and ethnic characteristics are identified as obstacles to workers' unity. Finally, Chinen suggests "bridging" across ethnic boundaries.

This topic represents an important period of labor and immigration history. Furthermore, the organizing strategies advanced by Chinen are relevant today and still have implications for organizing women workers in the garment and other similar industries.

Jon Matsuoka's and Davianna McGregor's article reflects a measure of public opinion on environmental and socio-cultural issues on Kaua'i in the period between Hurricanes Iwa and Iniki. Public opinion surveys can be significant inputs in future land use and economic development decisions. While opinion surveys may not be the best way to analyze what the optimal development for Kaua'i might be, decision makers ignore public opinion at their peril. It must be noted that the survey was conducted in response to community and government groups that wanted to know what the public thought on a multitude of social and other issues.

The article includes an interesting discussion on the contradictions among the people of Kaua'i based on class, ethnicity, age, area of residence and history of the subgroups under consideration. It also points out the need to listen and act according to the community's desires and to learn from past mistakes. Matsuoka and McGregor question the wisdom of rebuilding a Kaua'i tourist-based economy along the old lines. They point out that politics, economics, and planning are inseparable.

In contradistinction to this presentation, the Bank of Hawaii and its analysts maintain that the Kaua'i economy will experience high rates of growth. Their observations also suggest that business is rebuilding along the same old lines. In addition, the Tourism Congress of December 1993 demonstrated that the old ideology is deeply ingrained in the social and political culture of the decision makers. Regrettably, despite the survey's findings, there seems to be little hope for Kaua'i to retain what is left of its description as "the last local place."

Ira Rohter rejects the "any-kind-of-growth-is-good" strategies for Hawai'i. Instead, he argues for "sustainable development" based on "Green tourism" where "small is beautiful." Tourism should become a localized activity supporting a multi-cultural society. In opposition to mass tourism, eco-cultural tourism is supportive of Native Hawaiian culture. Furthermore, sustainable agriculture is part of this type of development. Why should people in Hawai'i pay more for agricultural products?

The "free market" answer to Rohter's question is: it is not cost-effective to grow locally most of what we consume. Hawai'i's comparative advantage lies in tourism. While this is true under the current economic organization of society, a Green economy proposes to restructure the economy in a manner that would reorder economic priorities and values (e.g., less emphasis would be put on profitability). Rohter's arguments imply that in a Green economy, the opportunity cost (the highest valued alternative foregone in order to pursue a certain course of action) calculations would take into account hidden social costs that are not presently considered in determining comparative advantage. Presumably, a Green economy would restructure the land tenure system to make it feasible for small farmers to own or lease land. The "highest and best use" notion, on which the restructuring of the Hawaiian economy in the 1950s and 1960 had rested, could conceivably be redefined by changing the values imbedded in this term. The free marketeer might not like upsetting the apple cart. But why not?

This sustainable development argument is refreshing in that it is at odds with the dominant Hawai'i development model that has brought serious problems to the economy in general and disaster to the lower sections of the multi-ethnic working class, especially the Native Hawaiians. The Green model is one alternative future among several that can be envisioned for Hawai'i. Its value lies in its practical challenge to the dominant model of mass tourism.

Luciano Minerbi's article with its "carrying capacity" argument is sympathetic to Rohter's. However, Minerbi, suggests radical reform to the present system. He examines the growth-led model for Hawai'i to see whether people's basic needs are being met and the Islands ecology is being protected. The article focuses on O'ahu where sustainable development and carrying capacity are analyzed at various levels. Minerbi, argues for a development model that is not based on population growth through in-migration as is the current one.

He also discusses outside control that makes the objectives he is advocating more elusive. Restructuring of the magnitude that both Minerbi and Rohter suggest, would require a social movement and a political party to lead it. Such power shifts would not come easily. The models advanced in those two instances (Minerbi and Rohter) offer a vision of hope for the future of Hawai'i.

Jonathan Okamura's article posits that there is an unfamiliarity with the concept "Asian American" rather than a "disavowal" of it. One element in this unfamiliarity is the presence of "localism" as a pan ethnic identity. Okamura reviews the past decade's political and economic developments arguing that they have contributed to the continuing significance of local identity in Hawai'i. Specifically, the increased marginalization of Hawai'i's people, due to Japanese investment and tourism development, continues the affirmation of local identity in opposition to outside control.

In Okamura's view, local identity derives its significance from structural more than cultural factors. The structural dimension of local identity is based on the categorical opposition between "local" and "non-local" groups.

Okamura also points out the paradox of separate ethnic organizations (e.g., Japanese, Chinese, and Filipino) alongside local identity. He recognizes differences even within the Asian American community on the basis of "local" versus "immigrant" and "refugee."

Okamura believes that the concept, "Asian American," can also be adopted in Hawai'i, particularly as a collective means to foster the socioeconomic adjustments and mobility of Asian American immigrant and refugee groups. While Okamura does not discuss the impediments to adopting the new term and how to overcome them, he has answered the question why there are no "Asian Americans" in Hawai'i. Finally, Okamura also demonstrates the complexities and integral nature of our politics, economy, culture, and ideology.

Noel Kent's article argues that "the American Age of Abundance is being succeeded by the Age of Downsizing and Insecurity." This structural transformation in labor markets and income are undermining Hawai'i's tourism base. Kent's discussion of the 1980s in the United States, Hawai'i's boom years, and the subsequent erosion of the economy show the integral relationship between foreign investment, high tech, and politics. The "twin dynamos" (Japan and the United States mainland) of growth in Hawai'i are rapidly losing power.

Kent attributes the uneven economic growth that has been occurring in Hawai'i to the alliance of foreign investors, big-landed estates, financial institutions, and local political figures. This alliance has been operating with impunity due to the absence of a real social and political opposition to the tourism- land-development model. Boom-time Hawai'i is a relic of the past. Also, an important constituency for the political economic elite, the upper middle fifth income level, has been decimated in the 1990s. Band-aid solutions and other "gimmicks" will not extricate Hawai'i from its long-term downward economic motion. Finally, Kent, argues for a new kind of politics to deal with the deteriorating state of affairs.

T. D. Webb's article traces the development of the Polynesian Cultural Center (PCC), a precursor to the current cultural tourism craze. A whole section of the article is dedicated to "The Manipulation of Religiosity," a fascinating discussion that points out the relationship of the Mormon Church to the PCC. Webb, also deals with "The Consequences of Profit" for a nonprofit institution and the ten-year battle with the Internal Revenue Service that ended essentially in the PCC's favor. Recently, however, Hawai'i's First Circuit Court ruled that the PCC is not a museum but a tourist attraction. Litigation could drag on for years regarding the PCC's tax exempt status. Webb, believes that the Hawai'i Court is accurate in depicting the PCC a tourist attraction subject to taxation. But this does not diminish the "peculiar relationship" of religion and commerce. Neither does it take away from the PCC's success due to the intertwining of Mormonism with the PCC's operation.

Jeffrey Kamakahi's and Albert Robillard's article studies social change in Hawai'i through an examination of the texts of Native Hawaiian folk songs. Their concern is with how Hawaiian songs were transformed under influences of the changing political economy. "It was only in the nineteenth century that texts of Native Hawaiian folk songs and song collections could emerge." The article points out the role played by tourism in the commodification of Hawaiian culture. Its focus is on mass commodification and Native Hawaiian folk songs that "express the mixture of assimilation and peripheralization of Native Hawaiians." These folk songs played their part in a Hawaiian cultural resurgence that was only possible because of Native Hawaiian socialization into the dominant Eurocentric code.

Kamakahi and Robillard show the relationship between political and economic changes and cultural transformation. It is an attempt to close the gap in our understanding of social transformation beyond what is imprecisely perceived by many as strictly political economic.

Ibrahim G. Aoudé

Native Hawaiian Struggles and Events
A Partial List 1973-1993

Luciano Minerbi

Native Hawaiians are under many types of stress. Native Hawaiian groups, often supported by other local people, have been involved for many years in struggles throughout the Hawaiian islands, particularly the rural areas.[1]

Many of these confrontations result because of public and private development that adversely impacts on Native Hawaiian lifestyle, tradition, customs and practices, and the natural environment, so important to Native Hawaiians. Other events are due to alleged government mismanagement, inaction or breach of indigenous trust and issues of Native Hawaiian sovereignty. Many issues involve land ownership and use, access to private lands, and management of Ceded Lands and Hawaiian Home Lands. All these struggles are precipitated by decisions external to local communities. These confrontations indicate a need for more home rule and local autonomy in a highly centralized state such as Hawai'i. The struggles involve outright eviction, physical displacement, economic dislocation, cultural debasement, and Native rights.

The resulting physical and emotional stress has implications for the good health, safety, and welfare of Native Hawaiians and local people, who have divergent values from the political-economic interests that carry out the projects Native Hawaiians object to. Particularly when living conditions are such that family life does not function, people are economically emarginated, households become crowded, or families are homeless because of evictions, tension and conflicts arise and break-up of families and family violence may occur.

Native Hawaiian groups involved in these actions often attempt to protect ancient religious and burial sites, sacred places and *mauka-makai* (inland-ocean) natural resources. They promote cultural restoration projects, perpetuation of rural lifestyle, fishing practices, and community-based development.

Reporting and monitoring these events are important for proper planning and risk assessment. For example, in 1985 the State of Hawai'i Legislature requested that the state develop a system to monitor the adverse impact of tourism on the people and on the natural environment in Hawai'i. In addition, the Legislature authorized in 1989 a carrying capacity study of tourism.[2] The monitoring system was supposed to include quality of employment, cultural and environmental integrity, and a community journal.

Events in this list are broken down by island. The last section includes events statewide.

Island of Hawai'i (Big Island)

- 1974—Grass-roots Native Hawaiians at Kuka'ilimoku in Kona, Hawai'i, occupy a shoreline area and constructed a traditional fishing village as a cultural action against resort development.

- 1979—A land claim demonstration was held at the Hilo airport, built on Hawaiian Homes Lands.

- In the 1980s Native Hawaiians of Malama Ka 'Aina settled at King's Landing on Hawaiian Home Lands in Keaukaha Tract II outside of Hilo in Puna. A plan for subsistence lifestyle for ten families was developed, but not acted upon by the Department of Hawaiian Home Lands.

- 1985—Native Hawaiians of the Pele Defense Fund opposed geothermal development in Wao Kele O Puna Forest (in part of the Natural Area Reserve System) because it encroaches on the land of the volcano goddess Pele. The Pele Defense Fund also opposed the "public trust" land swap between the state and Campbell Estate to open the way to drilling. The State Supreme Court approved the land swap in its September 28 1992, but ruled that Native Hawaiian rights for subsistence, and cultural and religious needs must be honored in the Wao Kele O Puna Forest.

- 1986—The Miloli'i Native Hawaiian fishing village obtains long-term residential leases from the state to legitimize residency, after waiting 66 years.

- December 1987—Rural residents object to sign forbidding access to Kulani prison. Twelve groups representing geothermal opponents sue state and county and request an environmental impact statement of the geothermal project.

- November 1989—The Puna Community Council enters as a party in the contested case hearing regarding the alignment of the power line from the proposed Pohoiki plant to the Kea'au substation. Geothermal opponents win in Federal Court and obtain that a federal impact statement be done to assess geothermal development.

- October 28, 1989—A demonstration against geothermal to stop the delivery of drilling equipment ends in five arrests.

- November 3, 1989—50 people protest the two billion 500 megawatt and sea cable proposal.

- December 15, 1989—39 geothermal opponents are arrested for trespassing at the site during a demonstration.

- December 17, 1989—Seven arrests are made at a "Hawaiian Court" held outside the site.

- March 24, 1990—Demonstrations are held by the Big Island Rainforest Action Group against geothermal at the site.

- August 1991—The State Department of Health moves a family away from the geothermal blast area because of health problems caused by the June's blowout of a well.

- March 18, 1992—The State Supreme Court shuts down some geothermal drilling until the State Department of Health establishes specific rules for determining hydrogen sulfite emission levels.

- March 21, 1992—A blowout takes place at Puna Geothermal Venture Site.

- April 18, 1992—A geothermal leak forces a test to end.

- May 7, 1992 —Foes and supporters clash for 8 hours at a hearing to set hydrogen sulfite emission standards.

- February 9, 1993—The state shuts off Puna Geothermal until it solves its technical and communication problems.

- 1988—Local people speak in opposition to the resort proposed by Bishop Estate in West Hawai'i at Makalawena, "the glowing place cleansed from defilement," noted for its fishing resources and as a pu'uhonua, and succeed in convincing the state and county government to deny the permit to build the project which would have destroyed the anchialine ponds near the sea, where Hawaiian birds, including the sit and coot, have their habitat, and which would have encroached on a white sandy beach, important to the public.

- 1990—The Pa'a Pono Miloli'i demonstrate in Honolulu against the project encroaching on their fishing grounds and village.

- January 1989—The Hawai'i county testifies against the Riviera Resort development at the State Land Use Commission. The Land Use Commission approves scaled down plans for the Hawaiian Riviera Resort in May 1991.

- 1989—Residents formed the Ka 'Ohana O Ka Lae to protect natural and cultural resources of the Ka'u district from the planned spaceport to launch missiles at Kahilipali or Palima sites approved by the U.S. Transportation Department. In May the state and Lockheed agree to develop a commercial site.

- July 1992—The Big Island Court sends the project back to the Land Use Commission, to assess the impact of the proposed marina on Miloli'i fishermen and their fishing grounds. The same month the developer gives up the resort plan and a bank takes over the land.
- October 14, 1993—At a public presentation by the State of Hawai'i Office of Space Industry, Native Hawaiian groups oppose the space port project encroaching on their fishing grounds. The same month Lockheed pulls out from the project.
- July 25, 1990—Governor John Waihee stops the auction to sell Hamakua Sugar land at the rim of Waipi'o, Hawai'i, a valley most important and sacred to Native Hawaiians.
- 1991—A national hiking organization and hiking magazine names the Big Island's Ala Kahakai Trail one of the nation's 10 most endangered trails because of encroaching private development.
- August 12-18, 1991—The Pu'ukohola heiau and Spencer Beach Park are closed to the public to allow Native Hawaiian ceremonies to take place for the 200-year celebration.
- 1992-Efforts are made to stop a 500 acre South Kohala resort to be built by Mauna Kea Property of Seibu Railway Co. at Hapuna Beach, which is considered the Island's best public beach.
- August 1993—State officials evict an ohana group and destroy their pavilion at an informal beach park on land administered by the Department of Hawaiian Home Lands at Puhi Bay. The Native Hawaiians, most of whom are from Keaukaha, rebuild the pavilion and construct an ahu, or stone monument, on the site. On September 22 state agents raze the ahu and the pavilion again and arrest 12 demonstrators.
- October 10, 1993—Supporters of the pavilion at Puhi Bay protest the lease of the Prince Kuhio Plaza to non-Hawaiians by the Department of Hawaiian Home Lands. The group Aupuni O Hawai'i wants the land turned over to Native Hawaiians for farms, pastureland or housing.

Island of Kaho'olawe

- 1976—Protect Kaho'olawe 'Ohana is formed to stop military bombing of that island, which has been going on since 1941. The island was transferred to the federal government on February 20, 1953 under presidential executive order 10436, which also stipulated its possible restoration and return to the Territory of Hawai'i.

- 1990— A presidential order halts the bombardment of the island. For many years this organization works to stop military bombing of the island and to promote its cultural and environmental restoration as a Native Hawaiian cultural center.

- 1991—The Protect Kaho'olawe 'Ohana brings 3,000 visitors and students to engage in religious, scientific, cultural, and educational activities on the island of Kaho'olawe.

- March 31, 1993—The Kaho'olawe Island Conveyance Commission, created by Congress, submits to Congress its recommendation on returning the island once used for bombing practice by the military.

- October 1993—The U. S. Senate authorizes return of the target island to Hawai'i and $400 million to clear the island from unexploded ordinances and for revegetation.

Island of Kaua'i

- 1973—The Niumalu-Nawiliwili Tenant Association opposes eviction and resort development at Niumalu with a petition signed by 20% of the adults on Kaua'i. The resort proposal is then shelved by the County Council.

- 1974—The Nukoli'i property is zoned urban by the State Land Use Commission. The Kaua'i Planning Commission and the Council classifies the parcel for resort use with the support of the Mayor, although a 15-member Citizen Advisory Committee established to give input in the Lihue Development Plan does not appear to favor resort development at Nukoli'i. Political confrontation follows; demonstrations, civil disobedience, arrests, bomb threats and explosions, assassination threats, and some damage to the construction site. Local opposition to the project mounts in 1977 because some island residents use the area for camping, surfing, ocean gathering and net fishing.

- 1978-79—The Nukoli'i zoning bill passes, but the development is scaled down to one-third the size of the original proposal. The Committee To Save Nukoli'i conducts a petition drive signed by more than 20% of the registered voters on Kaua'i for a referendum to overturn the zoning to be held during the 1980 election. Meanwhile the property has gone through various changes of ownership. The last buyer, Hasegawa Komuten, obtains the building permit for the hotel the day before the election in which Kaua'i voters by a 2-1 margin reject resort zoning for Nukoli'i.

- 1981—The Kaua'i Circuit Court rules that the developer has vested rights to continue construction in spite of the referendum.

- October 1982—The Hawai'i Supreme Court overturns the Kaua'i circuit Court decision on the basis that the referendum was certified before the last discretionary county permit for shoreline management area (SMA) was issued, thus halting the development. The U.S. Supreme Court declines to hear the Nukoli'i case. Kauaians for Nukoli'i undertake a petition drive, financed by the developer, to certify an initiative to re-establish resort zoning. After the devastation of Hurricane Iwa in 1982, 58% of the voters in a special election, promoted and financed by the developer approve Nukoli'i resort zoning.[3]

- Since 1987 the Hawaiian Farmers of Hanalei with community-based projects at Waipa and Ka Wai Ola seek to protect the shoreline of Hanalei from commercial tour boat over-exploitation.

- September 1989—A U.S. federal magistrate rejects a claim that Native Hawaiians have a right to kill the endangered Hawaiian monk seal for food on Hawaiian Home Lands because it is a violation of the Federal Endangered Species Act. The case refers to the slaying of a monk seal on Kaua'i in March.

- 1989—The Office of Hawaiian Affairs opposes the land sale by the federal government of Makahuena Point on Kaua'i to a Native Alaskan Corporation.

- 1989—Burial dunes are surveyed and dug to build the Keoneloa Bay Villas at Poipu on Kaua'i. The Native Hawaiian group E Makakaka Kakou considers the land sacred ground and in need of protection.

- 1991—The Hui O Mahaulepu of Kaua'i requests the Smithsonian Institution in Washington DC to return 133 ancient Native Hawaiian remains.

- July 15, 1991—14 Native Hawaiians are arrested in Anahola and their structures on the beach are demolished. Filmaker Nichaolas Rozsa documents the event in the video "Anahola," which is aired on Cable TV the same month.

- August 1991—Environmentalists and Native Hawaiian groups rally against the Polaris rocket launches from the Pacific Missile Range Facility at Barking Sands. They oppose encroachment on burial grounds, on Ceded Lands, on Hawaiian Home lands and the pristine ahupua'a at Mana.

Native Hawaiian Stuggles and Events 7

- March 17, 1993—60 people protest the arraignment of 21 people arrested for trespassing in February while demonstrating against the launch of the Polaris rocket.
- May 1993—Some of the demonstrators bring their concerns to Washington, D.C.
- November 1, 1993—The Coalition for Kanaka Maoli Land Rights stages a rally at Kapa'a on Kaua'i in support of the Native Hawaiians arraigned for trespassing in connection with the Prince Kuhio controversy on the Big Island regarding the lease to non-Hawaiians of Hawaiian Home Lands.

Island of Lana'i

- 1987—An agreement is reached between Lana'ians for Sensible Growth and Castle & Cook, the owner of the island of Lana'i concerning some cultural and historic preservation and access aspects of resort development.
- 1990—Castle & Cook plans to double the size of the Manele-Hulopoe Bay to 870 acres to provide for golf course and residential development.
- January 1992—Concern is expressed at a Maui County Council meeting by local people about the adverse socio-economic impact of the proposed 634 luxury houses and apartments. The Council approves land expansion at the Lodge at Koele and the Manele Bay Hotel for golf courses, but requires a social impact study before approving the luxury homes.

Island of Maui

- Since the 1980s Hana Pohaku has been working on community-based development on their kuleana lands.
- In the 1980s Ke'anae Community Association works to keep the water flowing to their taro patches instead of it being diverted for development in Kula and Kihei or hydro-electric plants.
- 1985—Lawsuits are filed by the Hui Alanui o Makena against resort development, land exchanges, and loss of the traditional Pi'ilani trail access to fishing, gathering and recreation on Maui. A settlement agreement with the developer is reached in 1987.
- December 1988—Protest erupts at Honokahua on Maui because of the excavation of hundreds of ancient Native Hawaiian burials to build a hotel by

Kapalua Land Company. The excavation is halted. The Hui Alanui O Makena files for a contested case hearing. Eventually a plan is devised in September 1989 for the proper reburial of more than 900 Native Hawaiian bodies disinterred. The state also pays $6 million for a perpetual preservation easement and restoration of the sacred burial site.

- November 6, 1989—The geothermal underwater cable proposal is opposed at a Maui meeting by Hui Alanui O Makena and other organizations because of the impact of electro magnetic fields on whales, spinners, dolphins and other mammals in the channel and because of the cultural and historical significance of the Kahikinui area.

- 1989—Edward Kaiwi and Eric Kanakaole file a lawsuit in federal court saying that they have a right to land and water in Nahiku, Maui, because they descend from the *konohiki* (headman) of the district.

- January 1990—A federal magistrate sentences two Native Hawaiians to five days in jail for taking two protected Pacific green sea turtles off Alaelae Point on Maui in 1989.

- August 1991—The Kaeo family objects to a Hawai'i judge's decision that it accept compensation rather than their percentage of interest in land, and pickets the office of Bishop Estate because two of the estate trustees are directors of Keola Hana Maui, Inc., which is planning a resort in Hana, Maui.

- September 1991—The homeless at Ma'alaea on Maui vow to fight eviction from the property of Alexander & Baldwin. Eventually they leave to avoid criminal trespassing charges with no agreement on relocation.

- December 1991—The Maui Burial Council rejects a request from Sokan Hawai'i and instead orders that the entire burial dune be protected from golf-course development at Waihe'e.

- 1992—The Hui Malama I Na Kupuna of Maui attempts to obtain the return of ancient Native Hawaiian remains from the Berkeley Museum.

- October 1992—Hui Alanui o Makena joins environmental groups to ask for a court order to stop the runway extension at Kahului Airport.

Island of Moloka'i

- 1975—Hui Alaloa (Long Trail) is formed to protect beach and forest trail access, water use, homestead lands, fishing and taro cultivation and moratorium on resort development on Moloka'i.

- From 1970 to the 1980s on Moloka'i, the Hui Ala Loa, Ka Leo O Mana'e and Hui Ho'opakela 'Aina are community groups formed to protect natural and cultural resources for farming and fishing rather than tourist resort development.

- Since 1983 Native Hawaiians oppose the Kaluakoi Resort development at Kaiaka Rock on Moloka'i, which is approved by the county in 1986. A settlement agreement with a developer is reached in 1986 on historic sites, job training and water availability.

- 1991—The restoration of the 20 acre Ualapu'e fishpond on Moloka'i by Hui o Kuapa begins. Seaweed growing and farming of 30,000 mullet and 10,000 awa is underway. More than 70 fishponds exist on Moloka'i and a Governor's Task Force for Fishpond Restoration is formed.

- May 1992—Some Native Hawaiians object to third-party leases of Hawaiian Home Commission Lands and have access to low-cost homestead land and water. Moloka'i homesteaders say the island's largest operator is using homestead land and competing with them unfairly.

- 1993—A Governor's Task Force on Moloka'i Subsistence undertakes a survey and conducts focus groups to establish the importance of subsistence on the island and comes up with policy recommendations to protect subsistence.

Island of O'ahu

- 1970—Kokua Kalama was formed to stop eviction of farmers to make way for upper-income housing in Kalama Valley on O'ahu. It subsequently changes its name to Kokua Hawai'i to deal with statewide displacement issues, such as the attempt to displace people at Coconut Grove in Kailua to build hotels and condominiums.

- 1973—Kuleana land-owners on Windward O'ahu organized as Hui Malama 'Aina o Ko'olau to stop development of their agricultural land.

- 1973—The Waimanalo People's Organization fights eviction by the state to obtain long-term leases and funds to construct affordable homes.

- 1974—The Waiahole-Waikane Community Association (a multiethnic group) fights eviction and private housing development in the valleys. Waiahole Valley is eventually bought by the state for $6 million dollars.

- 1975—The He'eia Kea residents fight eviction by Hawaiian Electric on the Windward side of O'ahu.

- 1975—In an effort to evict Native Hawaiians from Mokauea Island at Keehi Harbor on Oʻahu, the state unlawfully burns down their homes. The state then settles by granting a 65-year low rent lease on the islet to allow four families of the Mokauea Fishermen's Association to stay provided they conduct cultural programs for schoolchildren.

- 1977—Leprosy patients at Hale Mohalu resist relocation by the state to Leʻahi Hospital away from land originally dedicated to them. They are eventually evicted.

- 1980—150 Native Hawaiian families who want to establish a live-in cultural park fight eviction. The state demolishes their homes at Sand Islands Fishing Village on Oʻahu. Ahahui ʻOhana Moku Avenue fights the eviction. More than 90 homeless camping on the island because of lack of affordable housing are evicted in March 1992.

- 1983—After the destruction of Hurricane Iwa, the state demolishes structures, establishes roadblocks, evicts families, and arrests those Native Hawaiians who assert their right to live on the shoreline in a traditional way at Makua Beach on the Leeward Coast of Oʻahu. Kokua Makua ʻOhana is formed in solidarity against eviction.

- 1984—House Resolution no. 304 calls for a study of the feasibility of Subsistence Lifestyle on state lands stemming from the arrest of a Native Hawaiian growing taro on state lands in Waiʻanae.

- 1985—Native Hawaiians are evicted from the City and County beach park in Waimanalo (which is leased from the Department of Hawaiian Home Lands) and arrested by police for having erected a Hawaiian Hale on the site.

- 1987—The state approve a 65 year lease for residents of Kahana Valley in connection with the establishment of a "cultural living park" in the valley. On May 1, 1993, after 20 years of planning, resident families sign 65-year leases to live at the park.

- 1987—The Waiʻanae Land Use Concerns Committee, which fought the West Beach Resort Development on Oʻahu, enters in a Settlement Agreement concerning certain aspects of environmental and historic site protection. Kaʻala Farms, the ʻOpelu Project and NaʻHoa ʻAina O Makaha continue to pursue community-based economic development projects in the district.

- 1988—Some Native Hawaiians claim ownership and occupies Makapuʻu point on Oʻahu and are evicted by the state in 1990.

Native Hawaiian Stuggles and Events 11

- 1989—Windward residents pressure the military to stop live-fire training in Makua Valley.

- 1989-90—The Kamaka family of Waikane Valley on the Windward side of Oʻahu and requests restitution of and clean up of the land of ordinances from the military, who leased the valley and then decided to take it by condemnation to avoid the clean up costs.

- 1990—The Temple of Lono claims Kualoa district and county park as a place of refuge, a puʻuhonua, and very sacred place for the god Lono and followers.

- 1990—Native Hawaiians halt the H3 Highway project from being built on what they believe is the Kukui o Kane, heiau (place of worship) complex on the windward side of Oʻahu.

- 1990—Hui Malama ʻAina ʻO Laiʻe of Kuleana landowners and Hawaii's Thousand Friends sue and settle out of court with the Mormon Church at Laiʻe on Oʻahu for dumping raw sewage on kuleana lands against Federal Clean Water Act regulations since perhaps 1982. Hawaiʻi Laiʻe Ikawai Association is formed to conduct educational programs on Native Hawaiian and environmental issues by using the proceed of $2.25 million won in the lawsuit.

- 1990—The Concerned Residents of Waiahole-Waikane opposes the two golf courses and beachfront development proposal by Hoyu Construction Co. on the Marks' property threatening the agriculture use of the valleys.

- February 1990—Native Hawaiians are evicted from state controlled land in Waimanalo, Oʻahu.

- 1992—At Aala Park in Honolulu the remaining 120 people of various ethnic background face eviction.

- 1992—Residents oppose transportation and open burning of ammunition and would like that the Army leaves the Makua valley. Native Hawaiians claim for the return of Makua Valley and Lualualei on Oʻahu.

- May 1992—The H3 Highway is realigned in Halawa Valley on Oʻahu to skirt two ancient Native Hawaiian sites after strong protests, marches, and vigils by Native Hawaiian groups against desecration of Native Hawaiian ancient sites, including a possible women heiau (hale o Papa). On April 4, 1993 a commemorative march is held by the Halawa Coalition at the Halawa Valley ancient sacred sites.

- August 1992—Nine families are evicted from the Maunawili property owned by Y.Y. Valley Corp. In October 1992, the Hawaiʻi Supreme Court lifted its month long stay for the eviction of the remaining five families at Maunawili on Oʻahu. They are evicted by Yasuda development to build two golf courses.

- December 1992—Native Hawaiians and environmental activists protest the shipping of oil-contaminated soil from Oʻahu to the Marshall islands.
- On January 28, 1993 Native Hawaiians counter-demonstrate the march on city hall and on Bishop Estate offices which was conducted by those protesting the fee price for lease to fee conversion.
- May 1993—Representative Abercrombie calls for the restitution of Bellows Air Force Station to serve the interests of Native Hawaiians because it is located on Ceded Lands.

Statewide

- 1988—A conference is organized in Honolulu with the support of international ecumenical groups to look at the impact of tourism on Native Hawaiians and call the attention of the churches to their problems.
- 1990—Five schools conduct Hawaiian Language Immersion Programs for kindergarten children so that Hawaiian is taught as the first language. The intent is to prevent the extinction of the language and to perpetuate Hawaiian culture.
- February 1992—The 2nd Circuit Court of the State of Hawaiʻi rules on whether the county has authority to enforce rules of the Department of Hawaiian Home Lands.
- 1991—Hui Naʻauao receives $364,000 from the Administration of Native Americans to carry out its sovereignty education project.
- 1991—The U.S. Justice Department states that funding for Native Hawaiian programs are illegal benefits for a selected racial class, is spite of the fact that Congress recognizes its trust obligation in 1921 by passing the Hawaiian Homes Commission Act to provide lands for Native Hawaiians.
- September 9, 1991—*The Wall Street Journal* publishes an article entitled "Broken Promise: Hawaiians Wait in Vain for Their Land," bringing the land claim issue and mismanagement of trust obligations to national attention.
- December 12, 1991—A study by the Hawaiʻi Advisory Committee to the U.S. Civil Right Commission entitled "A Broken Promise: How Everyone Got

Hawaiian's Homelands Except the Hawaiians" by Susan Faludi, indicating that The Hawaiian Home Lands program denies civil rights to Native Hawaiians, is released at Iolani Palace. One of the issues is that 89,833 acres of general leases are leased to non-Hawaiians.

- September 1991—The 9th U.S. Circuit Court of Appeal rules that Native Hawaiian, unlike Native Alaskan, have no legal rights to hunt and fish protected species.

- 1991—Homeless people in Hawai'i are estimated at 9,000. Seven out of ten are Caucasian or Hawaiians. The state submits a plan to create seven homeless villages. A 1992 study finds that 21% of the homeless are Native Hawaiians. Social workers estimate their number to 2,000, twice the number counted in the survey. Native Hawaiians are without homes or live in crowded conditions. The safety net of the Native Hawaiian extended family is stretched at the breaking point, according to experts. Ninety people of various ethnic backgrounds are homeless at Sand Island.

- 1993—The state agrees to pay the Office of Hawaiian Affairs $111.8 million for back rent owned from 1981-1990.

- 1993—The Chairman of the Office of Hawaiian Affairs calls for a constitutional convention.

- January 13, 1993—The five days Centennial Observance 1893-1993 'Onipa'a of the overthrow of the Hawaiian monarchy is held in Honolulu on Iolani Palace grounds.

- January 17, 1993—The General Synod of the United Church of Christ national policy making body issued an apology at Kaumakapili Church because some of the early members of its forerunner, the Hawai'i Evangelical Association, were directly involved in the overthrow of the Hawaiian monarchy and Queen Lili'iokalani. The Hawai'i Conference is divided on this matter.

- January 20, 1993—Native Hawaiian groups petition the Legislature for a moratorium on the use of lands held in trust for the Native Hawaiian by non-Hawaiians, for a referendum and a bill to return 1.6 million acres of ceded and Hawaiian Homelands to Ka Lahui.

- February 1993—The State's Hawaiian Claims Office begins accepting individual claims from Native Hawaiians who suffered out-of-pocket losses through breaches of the Hawaiian Home Lands trust from 1959 to 1988.

- June 1993—Five Native Hawaiian representatives testify at the U.N. World Conference on Human Rights on Native Hawaiian concerns.

- August 12-21, 1993—The Peoples' International Tribunal Hawai'i 1993 is convened to look at the alleged crimes of the U.S. government against the Kanaka Maoli people and nation.

Notes

1. Appendix B. in Luciano Minerbi, Davianna McGregor and Jon Matsuoka, eds. June 1993. *Native Hawaiian and Local Cultural Assessment Project: Phase I Problems/Assets Identification.* Honolulu: University of Hawai'i at Manoa. Daily Newspapers: the Honolulu Advertiser and the Star Bulletin.

2. State of Hawai'i Legislature. 1991. Act 160. H.B. no. 2296.

3. George Cooper and Gavan Daws. 1985. *Land and Power in Hawa'i.* Honolulu: Benchmark Books.

Foreign Investment in Hawai'i

Marion Kelly

Foreign Investment in Hawai'i: 1778-1954

Foreign Traders Exploit Natural Resources

Foreign investment is no stranger to Hawai'i. Long before sugar or pineapple plantations were developed by foreign capital to exploit the natural and human resources of Hawai'i, traders from foreign countries stopped by as early as 1786. They were on their way to China loaded with furs that they had obtained from the Native Americans of the Northwest Coast in exchange for items of far less value than the furs they received. They gave Hawaiians nails and pieces of metal cut from barrel hoops in exchange for firewood, food, and fresh water.

Early in the nineteenth century traders found sandalwood, a limited natural resource of Hawaiian forests. Its discovery set off a frenzy of the worst possible exploitation of the natural resources and the people of the Islands. Hawaiians spent weeks in the mountains cutting sandalwood trees into manageable lengths, stripping the bark, and carrying the logs to waiting ships (Ellis 1963:286-287).

Through trading, Hawaiian chiefs accumulated an arsenal, but most items received, such as bolts of cotton, and embroidered silk, woolen uniforms, underwear, teak furniture, horse carriages, and many other China trade items had little use value for Hawaiians. They were deposited in chiefs' storehouses, representing new wealth and status (Morgan 1948:63-65).

The most expensive items offered by traders for sandalwood were old ships, which were no longer useful, and were sometimes unseaworthy. For such ships traders demanded tons of sandalwood.

Sandalwood and the National Debt

The ship Thaddeus, that brought the first missionaries to Hawai'i, was riddled with sea worms when sold to the chiefs for "four thousand piculs of sandalwood valued at eight dollars a picul" (Kuykendall 1938:91). Each picul was 133 1/3 lbs. Resident merchant James Hunnewell was responsible for collecting the payments.

> ... full settlement was not made until twelve years later. The "Thaddeus" did not prove satisfactory to her purchasers. They repeatedly offered to return the vessel to Hunnewell, Captain Blanchard's representative, if he would cancel the balance due. Hunnewell.... felt the justice of their offer; but, nevertheless, in

the interest of the owners, he was obliged to insist on a compliance with the letter of the contract. (Sullivan 1926:14)

This and other similar situations led to a series of unpaid I.O.U.s in the 1820s and threats to take over the country. Traders and merchants called on their countries' gunboats in the Pacific Ocean to provide "Gunboat Diplomacy," intimidate native peoples, and assist colonial merchants in the exploitation of resources and peoples of the Pacific (Morgan 1948:65-66).

In 1822 the chiefs owed a debt estimated at "something between 22,500 and 23,000 piculs...but in the fall of 1826...the *claims* of the traders totaled $200,000" (Kuykendall 1938:91). The U.S. gunboat captain submitted a list of claims, demanded payment, and threatened that the United States "has the will, as well as the power to enforce..." (Jones to Kauikeaouli, Nov. 4, 1826, cited in Bradey 1968:108). During "negotiations," a re-evaluation adjusted the amount of the debt to $150,000, or approximately 15,000 piculs of sandalwood, to be paid by September 1, 1827 (Bradey 1968:109).

This agreement, known as the "Convention of 1826," between Commodore Thomas AP Catesby Jones on behalf of the United States and Kauikeaouli (Kamehameha III), King of the Hawaiian Islands and his guardians, was signed December 23, 1826. It was the first treaty between the Hawaiian Kingdom and the United States of America. Article I claims, "peace and friendship subsisting between the United States and their Majesties the Queen Regent and Kauikeaouli, King of the Sandwich Islands, and their subjects and people, are hereby confirmed and declared to the perpetual." The debts of the chiefs and king became the national debt (Kuykendall 1938: Appendix D).

Thus, the very earliest experiences of the Hawaiian Nation with the sandalwood trade reveal a direct relationship between foreign investment and local indebtedness. The value of the goods received by the Hawaiian chiefs had been paid for, perhaps several times over. With sandalwood resources exhausted, recovery from debt within any foreseeable future was impossible.

Whaling and Resident Merchants

The next foreign investment adventure in Hawai'i was part of American whaling activities. Before private ownership of land was recognized in Hawai'i, foreign resident merchants built trading stores and warehouses in port villages on land for which they had only use-rights from the *ali'i nui* (king), or *konohiki* (chiefs). Traditionally, upon the death of the ali'i nui all assigned use-rights to land were returned to the heir for reassignment among the heir's supporters. Use-rights to the farmers usually continued generation after generation, as long as they wished and were productive.

During the whaling trade, foreign merchants pursued their profitable commerce in whale oil and other ships' products. Merchants also stored ships' chandlery.

Occasionally merchants "sold" their businesses and sites to other foreigners, contributing to conflicts between foreigners and Hawaiian chiefs. New occupants refused to return the land, claiming they had purchased it. In one case the British, backed up by naval power, illegally occupied Hawai'i for five months, an example of colonial tyranny experienced by Hawaiians (Kuykendall 1938:206-219).

Commercial Agriculture

As whaling disappeared, agriculture was tried by foreigners wishing to carry on commercial activities. Sugarcane plantations required large acreage of land with water. Capital invested in cultivating the land, and building dams, ditches, and mills required protection. In the opinion of foreign investors, the Hawaiian system of land use-rights was inadequate; they had to own the land outright. The traditional system of use-rights controlled by the chiefs was an obstacle that foreigners were dedicated to overcome.

By the mid-1840s, having gained authoritative positions within the Hawaiian government, two American missionaries and their friends developed a scheme to retire the Hawaiian use-rights land system. In its place they proposed to adopt a system of private ownership that would serve the needs of the foreigners and any industry they might pursue.

Private Ownership of Land and Foreign Investment

The mechanism developed by foreigners within the Hawaiian government to change the land system was called the "Great Mahele" (Great Division). Essentially a land registration program, the Mahele transformed use-rights into private ownership through a series of quit-claims and gave private ownership of 38% of all land in the Islands to approximately 250 chiefs, and 24% to the King. Lands turned over to the Hawaiian Kingdom as Government Land amounted to approximately 37%. Less than 1% of the total land available went to the *hoa'aina* (farmers). Once these land laws were enacted, and the scheme carried out in the mid-nineteenth century (1845-1855), foreign capital investment in Hawai'i increased dramatically.

Not only was land made a commodity, to be bought and sold, the market, but Government Land could be obtained with cheap long-term leases. Missionaries and foreigner friends within the Government serve the best interests of the planters. Interestingly, these changes were made when American missionaries were asked to reduce their dependency on the Boston office and to support themselves.

In 1837, before the Mahele, there were five known sugar plantations. By 1861 (24 years later) there were twenty-two. Most owed their existence to foreign capital (Lind 1938:71).

Exploiting the Rainforests

Some resident merchants found other exploitable resources. For a while they again used the Hawaiian people as a means of exploiting the native forests, this time the tree ferns of the upland rain forests.

Pulu is the Hawaiian word for the soft fibers that grow at the base of tree fern leaf stalks. Western merchants paid Hawaiians 1/2 cent per pound for pulu they collected. The merchants sold pulu in Australia, New Zealand or California and British Columbia for 10.5 cents a pound (Thrum 1876:58, cited in Kelly 1980:97, footnote). To motivate Hawaiians to spend months in the rain forest collecting pulu, and to carry bags of it down to the seaports, the merchants encouraged Hawaiians to charge items from their stores and when they had run up a large bill, to pay their debt with pulu. The market for pulu eventually disappeared when it was discovered that the fern fibers, used in mattresses and pillows, irritated the lungs. By this time, however, large portions of the indigenous tree-fern rain forests had already been destroyed.

Reciprocity, "Bayonet Constitution" and Annexation

The biggest increase in foreign investment capital in the nineteenth century occurred subsequent to the signing of the 1876 Reciprocity Treaty with the United States willing to admit duty-free raw sugar from Hawai'i. A market for Hawaiian sugar was secure, at least for seven years, the life of the treaty. Numbers of sugar mills and plantations grew rapidly. "There were 20 plantations in 1875; five years later there were already 63" (Morgan 1948:215). The largest sources of foreign capital were Great Britain, Germany, and the United States.

The Reciprocity Treaty lapsed in 1883, and the planters tried desperately to get it renewed. King Kalakaua finally had to promise the United States sole use of Pearl Harbor for a coaling station and ship-repair facility. Although the scheme was unpopular among Hawaiians, Kalakaua was forced to acquiesce due to pressure from the sugar barons, to whom he owed his throne in the contest of 1874. Amid many objections brought by his chiefs. Kalakaua agreed to give exclusive use of Pearl Harbor to the U. S. in return for signing a "supplementary convention" that extended the Reciprocity Treaty for seven years, to 1894.

Ignoring the treaty, the United States, under the McKinley Tariff Act of 1891, ended all duty charges on raw sugar imports, thus removing any advantage to Hawaiian raw sugar over other foreign-produced sugar entering the U.S. In effect, the U.S. unilatterly cancelled its part of the Reciprocity Treaty three years before it was to have ended. The agreement regarding U.S. use of Pearl Harbor might also have been cancelled, except for the control of the Hawaiian Government by American interests and subsequent events.

Pearl Harbor was not the only concession made by King Kalakaua. In 1887, members of the Missionary Party, then called the Hawaiian League and supported by the Honolulu Rifles, forced the King to sign a new, highly restrictive constitution. Many Party members were sugar planters, or had investments in sugar and other Island industries. For good reason the new constitution is called the "Bayonet Constitution." It disfranchised the great majority of the Hawaiian people by placing large property or money income requirements on otherwise eligible voters. It gave foreigners control over the legislature and over the King's cabinet, while maintaining the outward appearance of an independent Hawaiian government.

With the death of King Kalakaua in January 1891, and with his sister and heir, Lili'uokalani, becoming Queen, the sugar planters and their fellow industrialists and merchants feared they might lose control over the government. She was not obligated to them as was her brother, Kalakaua.

This time, calling themselves a "Committee of Safety," these foreigners, primarily Americans and missionary descendants, moved quickly to obtain U.S. support for a takeover of the Hawaiian government. They were successful in getting American marines to illegally invade Honolulu on January 16, 1893, in support of their acts of treason against the Hawaiian government. Under U.S. military protection, the Committee of Safety took over the government of the Hawaiian Kingdom, temporarily calling themselves, the Provisional Government. When annexation failed to materialize, as they had wished, they adopted the name of Republic of Hawai'i (1894).

Thus, the Hawaiian people had the ultimate experience of "foreign investment." That is, when mere economic control seem insufficient to achieve these desires, the agents of foreign investment capital resorted to direct political control by force. (Not just an option, rather, it became the action of preference.)

After some reluctance by a racist U. S. Congress, military priorities prevailed and sugar industry advocates finally achieved annexation in 1898. The Islands had become an important coaling station for American troopships (on their way to destroy Philippine independence and take over those Islands. This was yet another act of U.S. colonialism in the Pacific, as were take-overs of Guam and what is today known as "American" Samoa. With passage of the 1900 Organic Act, Hawai'i became officially a Territory of the United States . An elected "delegate" sent to Congress had a voice, but no vote. Thus, since 1898, U.S. capital investments in Hawai'i were no longer identified as "foreign investments."

Primarily as a result of consolidation and mergers, twenty-one plantations without mills in 1890 declined to six by 1930 (Lind 1938:181). Meanwhile, land planted in sugarcane increased from 64,149 acres in 1890 to 199,460 acres in 1906, and to 235,100 acres by 1938 (Lind 1938:75). By 1900 there were 52 sugar plantations. By 1930, there were 47 plantations with 225,000 acres under cultivation. As a result of cannibalization and expansion, the number of plantations dropped rapidly after 1930, but the acreage continued to increase. In more recent years this action represents the consolidation of economic power in the hands of a few sugar "factors," locally called "the Big Five." These are: Castle and Cook, Alexander and Baldwin, C. Brewer and Co.; Theo. H. Davies (British capital), and American Factors, formerly Hackfield and Company (German capital). Hackfield was taken over by the U. S. government in 1918, subsequently sold to American interests, and renamed (Morgan 1948:186). By the 1930s, over "90 percent of the small retail stores distributed over the Islands purchased their supplies through one or another of the sugar factors" (Lind 1938:183).

In the early stages, capital for the sugar industry came from overseas, primarily Great Britain, Germany, and the United States. The California and Hawaiian Sugar Refining Corporation at Crockett, California, to which all the unrefined sugar was sent, was owned by 33 Hawaiian sugar plantations. The directors consisted of the managers of the sugar factors in Honolulu (Lind 1938:183).

As with the development of the pineapple plantations in the Territorial period during the 1920s and 1930s, most of the capital came from the United States, thus, it was not identified as "foreign" capital. Capital was generated locally by exploiting Hawaiian land and cheap imported labor. Libby McNeil and Libby and California Packing Corporation both invested heavily in Hawaiian pineapple plantations. The pineapple industry cultivated approximately 600 acres in 1900, and by 1930 it had approximately 79,000 acres in cultivation (Lind 1938:75).

The majority of field laborers for both sugar and pineapple plantations were imported from Asia: first from China, Japan, and Korea and later from the Philippines. Foreign capital invested in the cheapest labor resources, and held the workers to oppressive contracts, poverty wages, and poor living conditions. Some additional labor was imported from Portugal, Spain, Puerto Rico, and a few from Norway, Scotland, and countries on the European continent. By far the majority of workers were from Asia.

Tourism Replaces Agriculture

The tourist industry in Hawai'i began during World War I, circulating broadsides (brochures) in Europe, and inviting affluent people to escape the war by visiting Hawai'i. In the summer of 1914, World War I was seen as "Hawaii's Golden Opportunity!" by the Hawaii Promotion Committee. The Committee expected the war in Europe to have a positive effect on Hawaii's "tourist crop" (Kuykendall 1928:91). A *Honolulu Star-Bulletin* editorial was effusive: "Hawaii now faces a golden, a stirring, an unprecedented and never-to-be-repeated opportunity to go after and get a large share of the world's tourist traffic" (cited by Kuykendall 1928:91). The chance to capitalize on the war was not missed by the committee members. A. P. Taylor, secretary of the Hawaii Promotion Committee announced:

> A very large part of the $200,000,000 spent for tourist travel in Europe will be directed to the Pacific coast.... This augurs well for our own business, as Hawaii is now the only safe tourist resort in the world, as I am advertising. (Kuykendall 1928:91)

The Honolulu Ad Club moved into high gear to support the Hawaii Promotion Committee:

> "Hawaii's Golden Opportunity is at hand and must be grasped...the proper time to strike is NOW. (Kuykendall 1928:91-92)

Sensitive to the connection between profits and the blood shed by soldiers fighting the war in Europe, Mr. Theodore Richards, editor of *The Friend*, suggested that Hawai'i could promote itself by organizing a large community effort in support of volunteers for the American Red Cross and by placing some of the "blood money" in the hands of the Red Cross. The article continued: "it will be the best advertising idea for Hawaii ever put forth. Hawaii the great Peace center! HAWAII THE SYMPATHETIC, with gifts extended to war-cursed suffering and homeless ones. We submit that here most signally is HAWAII'S GOLDEN OPPORTUNITY" (cited in Kuykendall 1928:95).

The growth of the tourist industry in Hawaiʻi, from World War I to World War II had some problems, expanding when the world economy was on an upswing, and slowing down when it slumped. It began to increase substantially after the Islands were endowed with statehood in 1959. As a result, the possibilities increased for obtaining greater returns on dollars invested than could be obtained in commercial agriculture.

The expansion of industrial unions in Hawaiʻi during and after World War II, the reduction in available labor during World War II and several postwar strikes forced sugar and pineapple plantations to mechanize and reduce hand labor. Survival plans after World War II included purchasing and leasing large acreage of land where there was a more-than-adequate supply of cheap labor. Cheap labor and land in the Philippines, Southeast Asia, and Central America increased agricultural production on overseas landholdings, and reduced the number of sugar and pineapple plantations in Hawaiʻi. As additional capital became available, primarily from foreign sources, what were formerly agricultural lands in Hawaiʻi were urbanized. Numbers of resort-hotels and golf courses increased.

Initially, some capital spent on the tourist industry was financed by local or U.S. capital. Additional capital was made available as a result of profitable World War II contracts and lucrative partnerships. Dillingham and Rockefeller (Dilrock) built the luxury resort Maunakea Hotel in South Kohala, Hawaiʻi Island in the mid 1960s. Land-rich and capital-poor corporations negotiated "marriages" with land-poor and capital-rich foreign investors, most of whom, at least for a while, came to Hawaiʻi from Japan.

An important element in the success of investments from Japan was the ability of the Japanese investors to fill their resorts with thousands of visitors willing to spend large amounts of money on vacations in Hawaiʻi.

Foreign Investment in Hawaiʻi: 1954-1990

Osano and Kokusai Kogyo Co.

Beginning in the early 1950s, the most prominent new foreign investor in Hawaiʻi was a banking corporation in Japan. It provided some of the capital to establish the Central Pacific Bank of Hawai'i in 1954 (State of Hawaii 1991:26). By 1972 it held 13.7 percent of the shares (State of Hawaii 1991:32). Full advantage of Hawai'i as an investment attraction was not taken until after statehood in 1959. In the early and mid-1960s Kenji Osano purchased three primary Waikiki hotels: Princess Kaiulani, and Moana and Surfrider in 1963 (State of Hawaii, 1991:27). The purchase price for the Princess was $8.7 million and for the last two, $10.7 million (State of Hawaii 1991:27). His arrival in the tourist industry woke up the community.

Osano founded the Kokusai Kogyo Co., which became owner of the three hotels with a total of 1,070 rooms, as well as of several other Waikiki properties (State of Hawaii 1991:27-28, 68). In 1972 the International In-Flight Catering Co. was founded at the "Honolulu Airport, with Osano as minority owner and Japan Air Lines holding 51 percent control" (*Honolulu Advertiser (HA)*, 7/21/77). Osano already was the largest individual stockholder of Japan Airlines, with 2.6 per cent of its stock (*HA*, 7/21/77). In 1974 Osano purchased the Sheraton-Waikiki, Royal Hawaiian and the Sheraton-Maui Hotels, adding 2,500 hotel rooms to his holdings, making Osano-Kokusai Kogyo owner of more than a third of the hotel rooms in Waikiki, just eleven years after the first big purchase.

Not All Purchases Bring Additional Income to Hawai'i

Hotel purchases by other Japan interests eventually brought the ownership of Waikiki hotel rooms by investors from Japan up to well over 50%. The purchase of already-in-place hotels added nothing new to the capital investment in the state. It merely replaced one source of capital for another. New capital from a foreign source also tends to move the important aspects of social responsibility and community concern by the corporate structure out of the reach of the community that is affected by the foreign investments.

The addition of new floors, new wings, and the refurbishing of the old portion of a hotel however, add to the capital investment, provide some short-term construction jobs and some long-term, low-pay service jobs within the hotel as well as some tourist-dependent service industry jobs in the community, such as laundry services, etc.

According to available records, Japan-owned capital investments in Hawai'i, from 1970 to 1984, totaled approximately $1.5 billion. In the following three years (1985-1987) the total invested in Hawai'i from Japan, was over $2.2 billion, bringing the grand total to over $3.7 billion. By the end of December 1990, Japan's investment in Hawai'i was over $9.3 billion (State of Hawaii

1991:129). These totals do not include those purchases with "undisclosed" prices, and are therefore minimum totals.

In the 1980s, Hawai'i experienced new dimensions in foreign investment. Already, some investments were being made in the service industries. Osano had already purchased a company providing food services in Honolulu for Japan Airlines. Also, purchases were made of already-existing tour-bus companies that provide transportation from the airport to, and between, hotels in Waikiki.

These types of purchases add no new capital, nor do they necessarily add new jobs. In fact, to properly service the visitors from Japan, which was one of the motivations for these purchases, the tour buses were furnished with drivers and attendants who spoke Japanese and were trained in and comfortable with Japanese social etiquette. This kind of foreign capital investment replaced local labor with foreign labor. Locally owned service industries that had in the past reinvested their profits in their companies, or in other local industries were also replaced with foreign capital that sent its profits back to investors in its home country. Thus, all foreign investments do not necessarily expand the local economic base.

It must also be remembered that the tourism industry as a whole pays one of the lowest wages in Hawai'i (*Labor Area News*, Sept. 1993:4). Considering also that workers are laid off when hotel rooms are empty, tourism may indeed actually be the lowest-paying industry.

We must acknowledge, also, that the tourists from Japan spend their money on round trip air fares on Japan Airlines, are taken by tour buses owned by investors in Japan, to resort hotels owned by investors in Japan, purchase their golf course memberships in Japan from resort owners, and make expensive purchases of foreign-produced items at hotel gift shops that are owned by investors paying rent to Japan-owned hotels in Hawai'i. How much of the tourist trade from Japan sloughs off and stays in Hawai'i is debatable, and these facts suggest that only a very minor part of the income from the industry remains in Hawai'i.

Japanese investments are worldwide, and will continue to be. It comes as no surprise that profits made on investments in Hawai'i may very well end up being invested elsewhere in the world. Of course, this route of Japanese capital investments is not theirs alone. As David Ramsour points out:

> When Broken Hill Proprietary of Australia bought PRI, the thousands of U.S. and international holders of PRI shares received payment from Australia into

their bank accounts throughout the world. When David Murdock bought Castle & Cook, the transfer occurred with few funds coming into Hawaii. (Ramsour 1990:1)

Beyond Resort Hotels

However spectacular the investment history in Hawai'i by corporations from Japan may appear, as in the beginning with Osano's large purchases of hotels, there was even more to come in the late 1980s. Figures available provide totals for capital investment by corporations in Japan in the period January 1987 to March 1988, are reported to have been over $890 million within those 15 months. Over 1,800 properties were purchased or leased by investors from Japan and nearly 50% of these occurred in Waikiki, primarily in hotels, condominiums and commercial properties, and in Kahala, a residential community on O'ahu.

During this 15-month period, purchases of $288 million were made in single-family homes and $264 million in condominiums, plus an additional $114 million in resort properties. By March 1988, 51% of the office space in downtown Honolulu was foreign owned, and of that 51%, capital from Japan owned half (National Association of Realtors, Dec. 1988 Report). During those 15 months, over 32% of the properties that changed hands were improved residential properties, nearly 30% were apartments or hotels, over 14% were commercial property, and over 12% were resort hotels (Ramsour, 1990:1).

Reaction in the communities focused on two aspects. One centered on those who saw the Japanese buyers as presenting the opportunity of a lifetime to make a fortune—to get more money than they had ever dreamed of by selling their properties. Offers to purchase were considerably higher than the estimated value of those properties at that time.

A second reaction was that of fear. People who did not wish to sell their homes, who were settled for the rest of their lives and had no desire to move elsewhere, were suddenly afraid. With sales of properties all around them climbing into the multi-millions, the taxes of some older residents began skyrocketing and they, unable to pay, feared being forced to sell, and becoming middle-class victims of this rush of foreign investment money.

The aggressive style of the foreign buyers failed to win many friends. There were, however, real estate agents and lawyers who catered to the new clients and, for a price, furnished updated lists of desirable properties available and assisted in consummating purchases for the new foreign real estate speculators (*Honolulu Star-Bulletin and Advertiser*, 4/8/90).

Another interesting outcome of these foreign investments is that the landowner in Kahala, Bishop Estate, revised upward the prices it offered to lessees through the "lease to fee" actions in which this community was engaged at that time. The prices asked by Bishop Estate for the purchase of the land under the lessees' houses were so much higher than the previous value of the land that the new prices were seen by many as gouging. Bishop Estate revised the land-purchase price upward, based on the new inflated land valuation that resulted primarily from the high purchase prices paid by investors from Japan in the past few years. In such an indirect way, some landowners made money from local lessees.

Are Controls Available, and Adequate?

The roots of the rush by investors from Japan to purchase property in Hawai'i have been analyzed and presented to the residents as having been caused by events that were controlled by international forces. Thus, they were completely out of the control of anyone in Hawai'i. Among the most effective of these forces were the rise in the value of the yen over the dollar, the cheap interest rates available to real estate speculators in Japan, and the high cost of real estate in Tokyo. These elements, and others, combined to drive Japanese capital overseas.

The first big investments settled on resort/hotel properties, which were perceived as the sure money makers. With their easily obtained capital Japanese investors bought already-built hotel/resorts at the start, then renovated and enlarged them. They also connected with large landowners who were anxious to sell raw land, which they purchased and built their own luxury resorts. Development of golf courses and development and sale of condominiums, and commercial properties served as back-up industries for their primary hotel/resort developments. They also purchased residential properties.

Particularly in the nineteenth and early twentieth centuries, heavy investment came from the U.S., Germany, and Great Britain. Investors from China elsewhere were involved to a lesser degree; their investments in Hawai'i focused on commercial agriculture. Beginning in the mid-1950s and continuing through 1990, 23 countries contributed substantially to capital investments in Hawai'i (State of Hawaii, 1991). Not including the "undisclosed" investments, the remaining investments for the period 1954 through 1990 for the top five foreign countries are shown in Table 1.

These five countries own over 95% of the total amount of known (disclosed) foreign investments made between 1970 and 1979, and they owned 97% of the total between 1980 and 1990 (State of Hawaii 1991:127).

Table 1.
Investments of Top Five Foreign Countries in Hawai'i: 1954-1990

	Pre 1971	1970-1979	1980-1990	Grand Total
Japan	31,900,000	593,429,000	8,659,085,000	9,284,414,000
Australia	100,000	16,500,000	634,031,000	650,631,000
Hong Kong	—	101,300,000	202,045,000	303,345,000
United K.	—	101,600,000	92,201,000	193,345,000
Canada	3,000,000	96,370,000	80,200,000	179,570,000
	$35,000,000	$909,199,000	$9,667,562,000	$10,611,761,000

Source: *Foreign Investment in Hawaii,* Department of Business and Economic Development 1991. Honolulu.

In addition, corporations from Japan owned by far the largest share of all foreign investments, according to the data gathered by the DPED, starting in 1954. In fact, Japan owned 86.8% of the known (disclosed) amount invested by these top five foreign countries. Australia ran a weak second with only $650.6 million since 1954. Investments from Japan in the period 1980 to 1990 are 98% of the total of all foreign investments for that decade (State of Hawaii 1991:129).

One important aspect of the hotel/resort investment is the golf course. No resort should be without one, or two, or perhaps even three 18-hole golf courses. The big advantage of having golf courses attached to a resort was that the developers were selling golf club "memberships" in Japan, and at one point the reported going rate was $200,000. The number of memberships that could be sold by any single resort was phenomenal, given the fact that a "member" was not likely to travel to Hawai'i from Japan any more than three or four times a year to play golf. Thus, many memberships could be sold without fear that the golf course would become over-crowded.

In some cases membership money was being used to build the golf courses. Memberships sold early in the development of a resort could be used to pay for much of the actual construction of, not only the golf course, but also the resort. The case of Ken Mizuno, a Japanese investor in Hawai'i, is a good example. He was tried in Japan on fraud and tax charges. "Between 1988 and 1991, KI (Ken International, Inc.) and Sanki Finance Lease Co., Ltd. "sold approximately 52,000 [golf club] memberships at $15,000 each—amounting to 120 billion yen or $800 million" (*Honolulu Star-Bulletin (HSB)*, 10/5/93; *HA*, 10/6/1993:A3). Neither the golf courses nor the club facilities, to which these new "members" now belonged, were ever finished. As a result of these practices, Japan authorities changed the rules. Memberships can no longer be sold for nonexisting golf courses. The result in Hawai'i is that some resort developments that had depended on this source of income are now in financial trouble.

A recent headline revealed, "Lavish Maui links development floundering: Waikapu country club shaken by downturn." (*HA*, 8/15/93). The main cause was reported to be "sales of golf country club memberships are languishing because the Japanese no longer are able to buy and sell memberships for very high prices" (*HA*, 8/15/93). The resort had planned two golf courses on its 600-acre area that was bought back in the heyday of big-spending investors for $9.1 million (*HA*, 8/15/93).

Once built, a golf course is relatively inexpensive to maintain: a dozen groundskeepers with equipment to keep the greens properly, an expert nursery keeper with a helper, and a staff to service the players, perhaps no more than 30 or 40 people altogether, could maintain a 300-acre golf course, serve refreshments at the "nineteenth-hole" bar and manage the cash register.

Golf course accouterments usually include a private clubhouse with a restaurant and bar and perhaps special cottages for golfers. Necessary, of course, is the resort hotel to tie everything together. The only proper site for such a resort is the seashore with an inviting beach and safe swimming. This leads to conflict of use by local communities that will have their access restricted or cut off completely. The state and county governments often allow shoreline property for private development. The state controls the coastal activities of a large portion of the population with selected park space that is usually inadequate. Waikiki hotels have taken over much of the coastal area they front, and few local residents are seen using that area of Waikiki beach. Parking is restricted, and buses will not allow passengers to bring along their surfboards or boogie boards. Ocean-related activities for the local population are restricted by over-development of the shoreline. At one time the state planned to take over Ala Moana Park for hotels (Ala Moana Master Plan, 1959).

The Magnitude of Foreign Investment

The Hawai'i State publication, *Foreign Investments in Hawaii* (1991) contains a total of 123 pages of listings, of which 85 pages are devoted to listings that involve capital investment from Japan. Seven of the 85 pages list what are called "future investments," which range from $207,000 to $600,000,000. The top figure is the price that Asahi Jyuken, owner of the Kuilima Resort, will commit when it begins construction on a 4,000-unit resort hotel project and an 18-hole golf course and the 383-room Kawela Bay Hotel. The project will also include "two golf courses, a variety of sports clubhouses, private and public parks, a shopping village, a 97-acre wildlife preserve, an equestrian center and condominiums" (State of Hawaii 1991:107). Estimated cost is between $600 and $800 millions.

In contrast, among the 123 pages of listed foreign investments there are only 7 pages of listings for Canada, with the largest listing being $32 millions by "Grosvenor International (Hawaii), Ltd. completing construction of the first of two business towers of Grosvenor Center in downtown Honolulu" (State of Hawaii 1991:12).

The biggest year for Japan capital investments in Hawai'i was 1989. One writer claims that in 1989 "Japanese investors purchased a record $2.629 billion in Hawaii real estate and started development on projects worth hundreds of millions of dollars more" (*Honolulu Advertiser and Star-Bulletin*, 4/8/90). This estimate is approximately double the 1988 investment in Hawai'i by Japan capital.

Another estimate claimed that investors from Japan "poured $4.44 billion into real estate purchases in Hawaii" in 1989 (*HSB*, 3/12/90). As much of this investment was in raw land, the 1990s investment total was expected to continue escalating. To help accomplish all this, the Japanese investors hired "top attorneys, accountants, banks, appraisers, real estate brokers, engineers, construction companies, public relations agencies, translators and others" with the claim that this generates "millions of dollars for the state of Hawai'i" (*Honolulu Advertiser and Star-Bulletin,* 4/8/90). However, the list developed by the Department of Business and Economic Development and Tourism indicates that the Japanese have bought into, or purchased entirely, banks, real estate agencies, printshops, and dozens of other local industries related to tourism. In addition, many of the big-time Japanese investors have their own lawyers, translators, accountants, engineers, and construction companies. The largest thrust of Japanese investment is tourist related. "More than 90 per cent of Hawaii's 'deluxe-class' hotels are Japanese-owned" (*HA*, 3/23/90).

Is Racism an Issue?

The policy of the state administration is to support foreign investment, particularly tourism. Waikiki is, of course, the "traditional" crown jewel of the state's tourist industry, although some people prefer terms like "tarnished" or "faded." As the figures on the massive purchases by foreign investors got to the legislators, some had second thoughts about all-out support for foreign investment in Hawai'i. However, bills introduced into the state legislature relating to controlling the purchase or ownership of real estate by aliens did not succeed. Such bills are derided by select members of the local Japanese community accusing the supporters of "scapegoating" and claiming that they will "add fuel to dangerous racial tensions" already in existence as a result of Hawai'i's history of exploitation of the Japanese laborers who were brought to Hawai'i to work in the fields (Odo, n.d.). Franklin Odo, then president of JACL (Japanese American Citizens League), was responding to a legislative effort to prohibit purchase of residential, agricultural or preservation lands by nonresident aliens.

The complaint went on to point out that the real reason for the high cost of land and housing today dates back to the Mahele or division of land carried out in the mid-nineteenth century when the land was alienated from the majority of Hawaiians and made a commodity (Odo, n.d.).

It is true that after 1850, thousands of acres of the best lands were purchased by sugar plantations, or acquired on cheap, long-term leases from the government's holdings. Sugar plantations in Hawai'i were the object of the "foreign" investors of the nineteenth and first half of the twentieth century. Land court laws facilitated the further alienation of land, particularly the *kuleana* (small holdings) of Hawaiian farmers within the larger parcels. The result has been that by the mid-1960s, 75 major landowners (including the state and the federal governments) exercised ownership over 95.5% of all the land in the State (Horwitz and Finn, 1967).

The policy of the largest landowners in Hawai'i to lease rather than sell their land, maintained their concentrated land ownership intact. This concentration of land in the hands of very few owners caused an extreme scarcity of land available for housing and also made land very expensive. This condition long preceded the recent arrival of Japan capital investment in land in Hawai'i.

Land purchases in Hawai'i by investment capital from Japan cannot be held entirely responsible for the inflated prices of Hawaiian real estate today. Still, they must bear part of the burden—their fair share, and from the figures available, it would seem that their share is a considerable amount. The irony of all this is that, because of the greatly inflated price of land (much of it due to recent highly inflated prices paid by investors from Japan and the willingless of the major private landowners in Hawai'i to sell), the children of most local Japanese-American families, along with the children of most of the rest of the local population, will not be able to purchase homes for themselves and their families.

An example of how some land prices are inflated is the Kohanaiki case in Kona, Hawai'i. Gaining approval from the County Council for a 470 acre resort was essential. Once the permit was granted, the land "changed hands several times, frequently for large profits that drove the land value from $13.3 million to a new high of $54.2 millions, all without the land even being cleared" (*HSB*, 1989).

Impact of Tourism on Hawai'i's Resources

Other equally serious impacts of this very high level of investment in tourism and tourist-related businesses are discussed. What are the environmental costs of tourism? Tourism is an industry that exploits whatever it can in order to produce profits and stay in business. Tourism uses large acreage's of the precious little land we have in Hawai'i — only 4.2 million acres in all (approximately 6,400 square miles) and much of the land is mountainous. (In contrast, San Bernadino County, California, contains 20,000 square miles of land). Thousands of acres of golf courses are being planned for Hawai'i. One writer claimed that Hawaii's tourist industry needs 46 more golf courses, 27 of them on O'ahu (*Honolulu Star-Bulletin*, 1990). Each 18-hole golf course uses 300, or more acres of land and millions of gallons of precious fresh water daily. In addition, the use of pesticides and herbicides threatens the ground water supply and the nearby ocean resources. We do not have an endless supply of water. In fact, it is estimated by some water specialists that we are presently pumping out of the deep recesses of our mountains, water that was stored there millions of years ago, and that we are pumping out much more than is being put back by present rainfall, our only source of replenishment.

One writer revealed that there are five resort-related boat harbors planned for the leeward coast of the island of Hawai'i (Clark, 1990). These will use hundreds of acres of Hawai'i's shoreline primarily to enhance the profits for the owners of the big resorts. Three resorts are owned outright by Japan capital, and one is a joint venture of Japan and American capital. Exploitation of Hawai'i's resources for profits that end up elsewhere is the pattern. The excavation of boat harbors destroys inshore fisheries and other ocean resources that are an important source of food for many local residents.

Tourism and the Native Hawaiians

Tourism is an industry. The primary purpose of an industry is to make a profit, no matter what the source of the capital is. In Hawai'i this means the tourist industry is profiting from Native Hawaiian land. They use and abuse the resources of the land and the surrounding sea. The tourist industry uses enormous amounts of water. Not only do hotels require tremendous amounts of water, but golf courses are even greater consumers of fresh water. Because the islands are small, they have a limited supply of water storage space in the ground-water lens. Overdrawing the ground water can cause infiltration of salt water into the lens. So, there is a water resource problem, as well as a land resource problem. Part of the land-use problem is that local residents, many of them the indigenous people, are being evicted and traditional access rights are impaired. Part of both of these problems—land and fresh water— is the tremendous size of the tourist industry—30 tourists for every resident; six million tourists a year (Trask, 1993). Dr. Haunani-Kay Trask, Director of the Center for Hawaiian Studies at the University of Hawaii at Manoa, has expressed her opinion that tourism has not only done nothing good for Hawaiians, it has exploited them, evicted them and demeaned them (Taped Interview, 1989).

Many tourists come to see Hawaiian culture. This results in the exploitation by the tourist industry of Hawaiians and their culture. The people become "artifacts" to be viewed. Hawaiians become ornaments for the tourist industry, items to be displayed and bought. Hawaiians become poorly paid servants, serving the needs of the wealthy tourists, dancing for the tourists, and indeed fulfilling the tourists' every fantasy. The commercialization of Hawaiian culture and the demeaning of the Hawaiian people is what tourism means to many Hawaiians today (Taped Interview, 1989).

Trask points out that the impact of this subservient role on Hawaiians is disastrous. Hawaiians begin to see themselves as they are depicted in the posters. They are colonized in their minds by seeing themselves as they are depicted by the colonizers. They begin to see themselves only as servants whose lives are lived to make the tourists happy. They are there to dance for the tourists, smile for them, serve them; never express their own thoughts, just keep the tourists happy and serve the tourist industry. This becomes an extremely difficult psychological problem to overcome (Taped Interview, Trask, 1989).

The tourist industry destroys what Trask calls the "Hawaiian cultural alternative," much of which depends on (1) the availability of agricultural land on which to grow traditional food crops, and (2) access to coastal waters and an unpolluted sea where Hawaiians can fish, and develop traditional aquaculture to provide themselves with needed protein (Taped Interview, Trask, 1989).

Of all ethnic groups that live in Hawai'i, Hawaiians, the indigenous peoples of these islands, have the worst health, the poorest educational record, the largest in prison population; they are landless and houseless, living on the beaches, unemployed, in abusive relationships and the list continues.

It can be argued that in one way or another, all residents of Hawai'i are impacted negatively by the overindulgence of investments in tourism, in which investment capital from Japan played the lead role for a time and is still extremely influential. A few examples of the ability or inability of the present system to provide adequate housing for its residents will bear this out. In 1990, single-family homes in Honolulu had the highest median price nationwide for the third consecutive quarter: $290,400 (*HSB*, 5/8/90). "The median price of a single family home on O'ahu was 25% higher at the end of 1989 than at the end of 1988" (*HA*, 2/8/90). By September 1993, the median price for a one-family home on the Island of O'ahu rose 11% to $385,000, which is 8.5% higher than September 1992 (*HSB*, 10/5/93). Mortgages take half of the income from resident islanders. Even after a 20% down payment, 52.5% of a family's gross monthly income goes to buy their home (*HSB*, 3/27/90). In 1989 condominium prices increased by 18% to a median of $135,000. Property taxes have soared, and as early as 1990, the Mayor of Honolulu was warning people to "brace themselves for the worst" (*HA*, 4/16/90). If the tax rate remains the same as last year for O'ahu property owners, the city could collect as much as $375 million more this year.

In addition, as a result of increased urbanization, there are about 4,500 more residential land parcels and condominiums from which to draw taxes this year (*HA*, 4/16/90). As an argument against using the market value as a basis for taxes, it was pointed out that the market value is inflated only because "the Japanese can borrow money for less, they can afford to pay 57 percent more for the properties than can U.S. buyers. Therefore, the prices they pay should not be taken as market value" (*HA*, 4/16/90).

At the peak of foreign investment announcements, the Tokyo stock market exploded. By March 1993, Hawai'i was reporting that investment from Japan was off by 80% (*HA*, 3/91/93).

Some Consequences of Foreign Investment

The situation appears serious. Residents of Hawai'i who are not making money because of the inflated prices— and that includes 90% of the residents—

Table 2.
Japanese Real Estate Investment

Year	Hawai'i Total	Percent of total U.S. Investment
1992	$328,000,000	41%
1991	$1,660,000,000	33%
1990	$2,860,000,000	22%
1989	$4,437,000,000	30%
1988	$1,830,000,000	11%
1987	$3,330,000,000	26%
Pre-1987	$3,905,000,000	29%

Source: *Honolulu Advertiser*, 3/19/93:D1,3

are paying the bill. Many leave Hawai'i each week because they cannot afford to live where they were born. A recent headline, "Inflation outstrips Hawaii Incomes" reminds us "Local consumers' incomes rose only 2.9% last year (1992) and inflation rate rose 4.8%" (*HA*, 10/08/93).

What is happening to Japan's economy now—when it shakes and trembles, threatening disaster—is affecting us as a result of our over-dependence on the tourist industry and on capital investment from Japan, Encouraged by our political and economic leaders (the Governor and Lieutenant Governor and their advisors, the banks and their economists, etc.), it will undoubtedly cause great suffering among the people of Hawai'i, particularly the Hawaiian people, whose only homeland is Hawai'i.

As early as 1990, some analysts, were predicting an economic "crash" in Japan land prices. These and other predictions have come about. Foreclosures in Hawai'i are rampant and real estate investors are scrambling to "save" their investments by filing for protection under the bankruptcy laws. Investments may simply be sold at auction (*HA*, 10/5/93). The Hyatt Regency Waikiki is in receivership (*HA*, 10/5/93). Mitsui Trust and Banking Co. began court action for back rent due from the Azabu Building Group, owners of the hotel since 1986 as well as a number of other Hawai'i properties, including the Ala Moana Hotel, in Honolulu, Maui Marriott, and the Keauhou Beach and Kona Lagoons hotels on the Big Island and the King's Village shopping center in Waikiki (*HSB*, 10/5/93).

Shimizu Corp, part-owner of the Four Seasons Wailea, Maui, will have its interest bought out by TSA International. First, TSA's interest will be bought by Shimizu Corp, and in a separate transaction, Shimizu Corp will sell everything to TSA (*HA*, 9/30/93).

One observer commented "It is very difficult to identify the net benefits, if any in foreign investment" (Minerbi 1988:7).

There has always been a wide disparity between cost of living and wages in Hawai'i. In 1992, Hawai'i was "one of only seven states where personal incomes failed to keep pace with inflation. Hawai'i had an inflation rate of 4.8% that year, which was more than a point higher than the national rate of 3.7%, making Hawaii's gap even wider" (*HA*, 10/8/93). And the forecast for future months do not look any better.

A curious figure that nearly matches Hawai'i's inflation rate is that of the rate of increase in crime in the Islands, up 4.6% in 1992. "Theft, being a crime of opportunity, appears to be the type of crime that thrives in Hawai'i as in any tourist destination" (Green, cited by Altonn, *HSB*, 10/2/93).

One cannot help but compare the present scene with what was being written in 1987: "New owners are pumping millions into [Hawai'i's] economy" (*HSB*, 1987). When the crash came in Japan, there was nothing Hawai'i could do to change its effects locally. Money spent on inflated prices for real estate and a newspaper headline explains partially what happens when we lose control of our economy: "UH to cull staff by 463 for latest budget cut: The $3.5 million loss will be spread through the system" (*HSB*, 10/14/93). There have been "three years of budget trimming that totaled more than $23 million. Enrollment during that time jumped 6 percent" (*HSB*, 10/14/93). The President of U.H. Manoa, Mortimer, is quoted as saying, "Reduced services and fewer classes may mean students will have to stay in school longer to get into classes they need to graduate" (*HSB*, 10/14/93).

Conclusion

To have more say in determining its future, Hawai'i has to have more control over foreign investments. One suggestion being discussed by some proponents of Hawaiian sovereignty is independence for Hawai'i, which, it is believed will give Hawaiians control over such important decisions as the number of acres any single individual or business may own, the amount of investment permitted by any single foreign investor, the number of investors from any single foreign country, the amount of land any foreigner or foreign business may control, and the amount of immigration permitted each year.

Returning Hawai'i to its former sovereign nation-state status, could also provide the residents of the islands a better chance to set up their own rules to protect the Islands' environment, natural resources and people. An independent Hawai'i might be able to soften the often disastrous results of roller-coaster economic swings that result from overdependence on foreign capital followed by a large number of bankruptcies. Perhaps sovereignty could provide the Islands' peoples with a way out of the constantly-increasing, outrageously-high cost of living, and accompanying inflation. The population of the Islands could then be limited. The number of visitors could be controlled. Land and water could be assigned with the priority being given to growing food for local consumption. Land and housing rents could be controlled and homelessness made a thing of the past.

Today various groups of Hawaiians are pressing the United States for recognition of the sovereignty of the nation-state of Hawai'i and for the return of their lands. Economic and socio-cultural pressure on Hawaiians have motivated many to want to try their hand at exercising their sovereignty again.

The track record of our present federal and state governments has not been kind to the Hawaiians, nor to their environment. The fresh water of the islands is loaded with introduced pesticides, herbicides, and other poisons. In addition, the deadly leptospirosis has been introduced into the islands' fresh water streams, making the cultivation of taro in traditional terraced pondfields a hazardous occupation. Also, as shoreline dredging and other intrusions continue to disturb the coastal environment, cases of ciguetera poisoning increase. Many of the coastal fish, traditionally eaten by Hawaiians, are now poisonous. This fact reduces the availability of subsistence protein foods needed by the Hawaiian people. One might ask, "In whose interest is it to continue this environmentally destructive path?" It is certainly not in the interest of the indigenous peoples of these islands. It is only in the interest of those whose come from elsewhere and will return to elsewhere, and whose profits depend on exploiting the people and environment of these islands.

References

Arago, J. 1823 *Narrative of a voyage around the world in the Uranie and Physicienne Corvettes, commanded by Captain Freycinet, during the years 1817,1818, 11819, and 1820;* on a scientific expedition undertaken by order of the French government in a series of letters to a friend, London.

Belt, Collins & Associates and H. Bartholomew & Associates. 1961.*The Comprehensive Plan: Ala Moana Reef, Honolulu, Hawaii.* Prepared for the State of Hawaii, Department of Land and Natural Resources. Honolulu: Hawai'i.

Bradey, Harold Whitman. 1968.*The American Frontier in Hawaii, The Pioneers, 1789-1843.* First published, 1942. Reprinted 1968. Gloucester, Mass.: Peter Smith.

Bryan, William Alanson. 1915. *Natural History of Hawaii.* Honolulu: The Hawaiian Gazette Co., Ltd.

Chinen, Jon J. 1958.*The Great Mahele.* Honolulu: University of Hawaii Press.

_____. 1961 *Original Land Titles.* Honolulu: University of Hawaii Press.

Devaney, Dennis M., Marion Kelly, Polly Jae Lee, and Lee S. Motteler. 1982. *Kane'ohe, a history of change.* First published 1976. (Revised ed.) Honolulu: The Bess Press.

Ellis, Rev. William. 1963. *Journal of William Ellis: Narrative of a Tour of Hawaii, or Owhyee.* Honolulu: Advertiser Publishing Co.

Freycinet, Louis Claude de Saulses de. 1839. *Voyage autour du Monde, Entrepris par Ordre du Roi...Execute sur les Corvettes de* S. M. l'Uranie *et* la Physicienne, *Pendant les Annees 1817, 1818, 1819, et 1820,* . . . Vol. 2, Part 2, *Historique* by de Freycinet.

Honolulu Advertiser. 1993. "Inflation outstrips Hawaii incomes." October 8.

_____. 1993. "Mizuno properties seized in Japanese fraud case." October 6.

_____. 1993. "Foreclosure ahead for Hyatt Regency Waikiki?" October 5.

_____. 1993. "Four Seasons Wailea to change hands twice." September 30.

_____. 1993. "Lavish Maui links development floundering: Waikapu country club shaken by downturn." August 15.

_____. 1993. "Japan Investment here off 80%." March 19.

_____. 1990. "Foreign Investment's Impact Unclear." April 16.

_____. 1990. "Money business: Isles pocketing profits: Japanese investment a windfall for lawyers, brokers, agents." April 8.

_____. 1990. "Communities around the world risking their futures on tourism." March 23.

_____. 1990. "Oahu home prices top U.S.: Median price hits $280,900, up 25 percent." February 8.

Honolulu Star-Bulletin. 1993. "Isle crime rate up 4.6 percent in '92: FBI figures show violent crimes jump 9.3 percent here." October 21.

_____. 1993. "UH to cut staff by 463 for latest budget cut." October 14.

_____. 1990. "Hawaii needs 46 more golf courses." April 15.

_____. 1990. "Mortgages take half our income in Honolulu." March 27.

_____. 1990. "Japanese real estate buys soar in Hawaii; The $4.44 billion spent on property last year doubles that of the previous year." March 12.

_____. 1990. "Big Isle going for boats: Resort builders look beyond golf to yacht harbors." February 11.

_____. 1989. "Kona resort dealing leads to new state caution." November 27.

_____. 1987. "Japanese upgrading isle investments: new owners are pumping millions into economy." April 16.

Honolulu Star-Bulletin and Advertiser. 1990. "Money business: Isles pocketing profits: Japanese investment a windfall for lawyers, brokers, agents." April 8.

Horwitz, Robert H. & Judith B. Finn. 1967. *Public Land Policy in Hawaii: Major Landowners.* Honolulu: University of Hawaii.

Kelly, Marion. 1978. "Notes and Comments," pp. 93-120. In *Hawai'i in 1819: A Narrative Account By Louis Claude de Saulses de Freycinett.* Honolulu: Pacific Anthropological Records No. 26, Department of Anthropology, Bernice P. Bishop Museum.

_____. 1980 *Majestic Ka'Ë: Mo'olelo of Nine Ahupua'a.* Report 80-2, Honolulu: Dept. of Anthropology, Bernice P. Bishop Museum

Kuykendall, Ralph S. 1928. *Hawaii in the World War.* With the assistance of Lorin Tarr Gill. Honolulu: The Historical Commission. Printed by the Honolulu Star-Bulletin, Ltd.

_____. 1938. *The Hawaiian Kingdom, 1778-1854, Foundation and Transformation.* Vol. 1. Honolulu: University of Hawaii Press.

Lind, Andrew W. 1938. *An Island Community, Ecological Succession in Hawaii.* Chicago: University of Chicago Press.

Minerbi, Luciano. 1988. "Background and Setting of Tourism in Hawai'i." In *Alternative Forms of Tourism in the Coastal Zone: Searching for Responsible Tourism in Hawai'i.* Department of Urban and Regional Planning, University of Hawaii, Manoa. Prepared for the National Coastal Resources Research and Development Institute.

Morgan, Theodore. 1948. *Hawaii, A Century of Economic Change, 1778-1876.* Cambridge: Harvard University Press.

New York Times News Service. 1976. "The Osano-Lockheed Case." February 6.

Odo, Franklin. n.d. "JACL Statement on Legislative Attempts to Curb Foreign Investment in Hawaii." Honolulu.

Ramsour, David. 1990. "Foreign Investment and Loss of Control." In *Business Trends*. Honolulu: Bank of Hawaii.

Russ, William A., Jr. 1992. *The Hawaiian Revolution (1893-94)*. (First published, 1959). Cranbury, N.J.: Associated University Presses.

_____. 1991. *A Listing of Foreign Investments in Hawaii*. Honolulu: Department of Business, Economic Development & Tourism. Trade & Industry Development Branch. Business & Marketing Division. May 1991.

State of Hawaii. Dept. of Labor and Industrial Relations. 1993. *Labor Area News*. Honolulu.

_____. Department of Business and Economic Development. 1991. *Foreign Investment in Hawaii*. Honolulu.

Sullivan, Josephine. 1926. *A History of C. Brewer & Company Limited, One Hundred Years in the Hawaiian Islands*. Edited by K.C. Leebrick. Boston: Walton Advertising & Printing Company.

Thrum, Thomas G. 1890. "Hawaiian Maritime History: a brief sketch of noted vessels and commanders in the development of the coasting service of the Hawaiian Islands." *Thrum's Hawaiian Almanac and Annual for the year 1890*:66-79.

The Political Economy of Foreign Investment in Hawai'i

Karl Kim

Introduction

The purpose of this article[1] is to develop a political economy perspective on Hawai'i in order to discuss some of the issues associated with foreign investment in Hawai'i. After briefly outlining this perspective, some of the impacts of foreign investment in Hawai'i are described. Several alternatives for managing the political economy of foreign investment are discussed in a concluding section.

Political Economy Perspective on Hawai'i

One might regard the political economy perspective as a particular vantage point from which to view society at large as well as the forces of growth, development, and change. Central to this perspective is the question of who gains and who loses as a consequence of development. What are the effects of particular social policies and developments in terms of the distribution of wealth? What is the role of the state and the elites in the public and private sector, or, of those who have "Land and Power" in Hawai'i (Cooper and Daws, 1990). What role do the institutions, laws, zoning regulations, and, the plans and policies promulgated by those in power, have to do with who wins and who suffers in our society. Hawai'i is fertile ground for studies of this ilk. Consider the following taken in part from recent headlines: the political economy of judicial appointments, of mass transit, of the insurance industry, of geothermal, of tourism promotion. The list goes on. Political economy offers a critical perspective that challenges the conventional wisdom and many of the prevailing paradigms.

In recent years, there have been some exciting developments in political economy, with an emphasis on "urban" or "spatial" perspectives. In particular, geographers such as David Harvey (1989), urban sociologists like John Logan and Harvey Molotch (1987), urban planners such as Susan and Norman Fainstein (1986) and Ed Soja have contributed greatly to the dialogue concerning the political economy of place. Mike Davis's *City of Quartz* (1990) is one example of how this perspective has been applied to critically analyze Los Angeles. Taken together, these works provide a deeper explanation of how modern society functions in terms of the relationships between capital, modes of production, and the social and spatial distribution of the costs and benefits associated with investment and development.

Edward Said's recent book on cultural imperialism provides some useful definitions. He writes,

> [T]he term, "imperialism" means the practice, the theory, and the attitudes of a dominating metropolitan center ruling a distant territory; "colonialism," which is almost always a consequence of imperialism is the implanting of settlements on distant territory . . . (1993:9)

Note that Said refers to "dominating metropolitan centers," which in Hawai'i's case might well be Tokyo, Hong Kong, or New York. One need not look far to see evidence of both imperialism and colonialism in Hawai'i. The vestiges of Hawai'i's colonial past are still expressed through large landholdings concentrated in the hands of a few. While other states have preserved their colonial architecture, Hawai'i has gone even further in terms of conjuring new images of a colonial past in the form of new resorts and visitor plantations. The imprinting of "theories, practices, and attitudes" of distant lands and people is evident in the shape and form of Hawai'i's automobile-dependent settlements, in the patterns of consumption and lifestyles of the people, and ultimately in terms of the nature and intensity of the social problems faced in this society.

There is a direct connection between capital and colonialism. The central argument of this article is that evidence of colonialism in Hawai'i can be garnered in terms of the pattern and magnitude of foreign investment, particularly from Japan. After describing why Hawai'i has become such an attractive location for foreign investment, the magnitude and pervasiveness of Japanese interests in Hawai'i are described. Some explanations for foreign investment in Hawai'i are offered utilizing regression analysis and some of the more obvious impacts of foreign investment are described.

The Problem of Foreign Investment

Part of the paralysis with respect to the management of foreign investment in Hawai'i results from the fact that under the U.S. constitution, only the national government can make foreign policy decisions including treaties and trade agreements with foreign countries. Coupled too with the long-standing commitment to free trade, it is easy to understand why few state governments attempt to regulate foreign investment. This is a particular problem because foreign investment is concentrated in a few major states. A study in 1988 found that Japanese investment was concentrated in three states: Hawai'i with $3.3 billion, followed by California $2.98 billion, and New York with $2.34 billion (Leventhal, 1989). Foreign investment in land and real estate is not a nationwide problem, so few federal policies have been developed. Because Montana and Arkansas have not experienced what Hawai'i has under the U.S. constitution, Hawai'i has to behave pretty much like every other state in the Union.

When refering to foreign investment, the federal government typically classifies it into one of two categories (U.S. Department of Commerce, 1988). Foreign direct investment refers to holdings in which 10% or more of the value of land or real estate is owned by a foreign individual or corporation. Foreign indirect investment, sometimes called "portfolio" or "passive" investment, refers to bank accounts, bonds, and interests in companies that amount to less than 10% of the equity. While there are some limited data on investments in land and real estate, there is virtually no information on the investment in bank accounts, government securities, corporate stock, and other portfolio investments.

A great deal of national attention has beem focused on foreign investment (Glickman and Woodward, 1989; Vernon and Spar, 1989; Tolchin and Tolchin, 1988). However, relatively little research was done on Hawai'i, which is surprising given the magnitude of foreign investment.

Foreign Investment in Hawai'i

Foreign direct investment in Hawai'i has been swift, extensive, and complete. (Fig. 1). Between 1970 and 1989, investment from Japan has amounted to more than $6.8 billion of the total $8.4 billion invested by all foreign countries (Department of Business and Economic Development [DBED],1989). While there have been peaks in investment in 1973, 1979, and 1982, the strongest and most lasting wave to hit Hawai'i began in 1986 and lasted through 1990. Between 1986 and 1989, foreign investment from Japan amounted to more than $5.2 billion or 76.2% of the total investment over the 20-year period.

Dollar amounts give only a partial picture of this phenomenon. Even more revealing is the functional and spatial distribution of Japanese investment (Fig. 2). When examined by function, the tidal wave of foreign investment becomes all the more pervasive. Japanese have invested in banking, insurance, real estate firms, engineering and construction companies, warehouses, retail operations,

Figure 1.
Japanese Investments in Hawaii

	YEAR																					
	Pre-1970	1970	1971	1972	1973	1974	1975	1976	1977	1978	1979	1980	1981	1982	1983	1984	1985	1986	1987	1988	1989	Total
Banking	I			I	II	I														I	II	8
Insurance								I									I			I		3
Land development				I								I					I					3
Real estate		I	I		I															I		4
Engineering/construction		I		I	I														III	I		7
Warehouse								I	I	I								II		I		6
Wholesale	IIII	I		III		I	I			I				I					I			13
Retail	I	I		III	II	I	I				III	I	III		III		I		II	I	III	26
Manufacturing	I									I			I	I		I		II	III	I		11
Trading						I		I	I						I				II	II		8
Shopping center											I			I				I	IIII	IIII	II	13
Office building												I			I		I	IIIII	IIIIII	IIIIIIIII	III	27
Restaurant	II			I			II		II			I	I		I	I	I	IIIIIII	IIIII	II	III	30
Bakery														II	I	I						4
Communications	I											I		I						I		4
Education		I	I						I										I		I	5
New hotel/resort	II											I			I			II	II	II	IIIIIIIII	19
Hotel/resort acquisitions	I			IIII	III	IIII			I		I	I					IIII	IIIIIIIIIIII	IIIIIIIIIII	IIIIIIIIIII	IIIIII	59
Hotel/resort renovation	I	I				I					I	I	I	IIII		I	III	III	I	II	I	21
New condominium					I	I	I	IIII			III		I	I		I		I	I		I	16
Condo acquisition																			II	IIIIII		8
Golf course acquisition				II	I			I					I	II	I			III	I	I		13
New golf course									I				II									3
Land acquisition <5 acres				I	I			I							I	III	IIIIII	IIIIII	IIIIII	IIII	IIII	33
Land acquisition				III	IIII	III				I		I				I		II	IIIIIII	IIIIIIII	IIIIII	37
Agriculture					I																I	2
Subdivisions											II		I		I					II	I	7
Total Japanese investments in Hawaii (Pre 1970 - 1989)																						390

Each mark indicates an establishment or acquisition of a business.

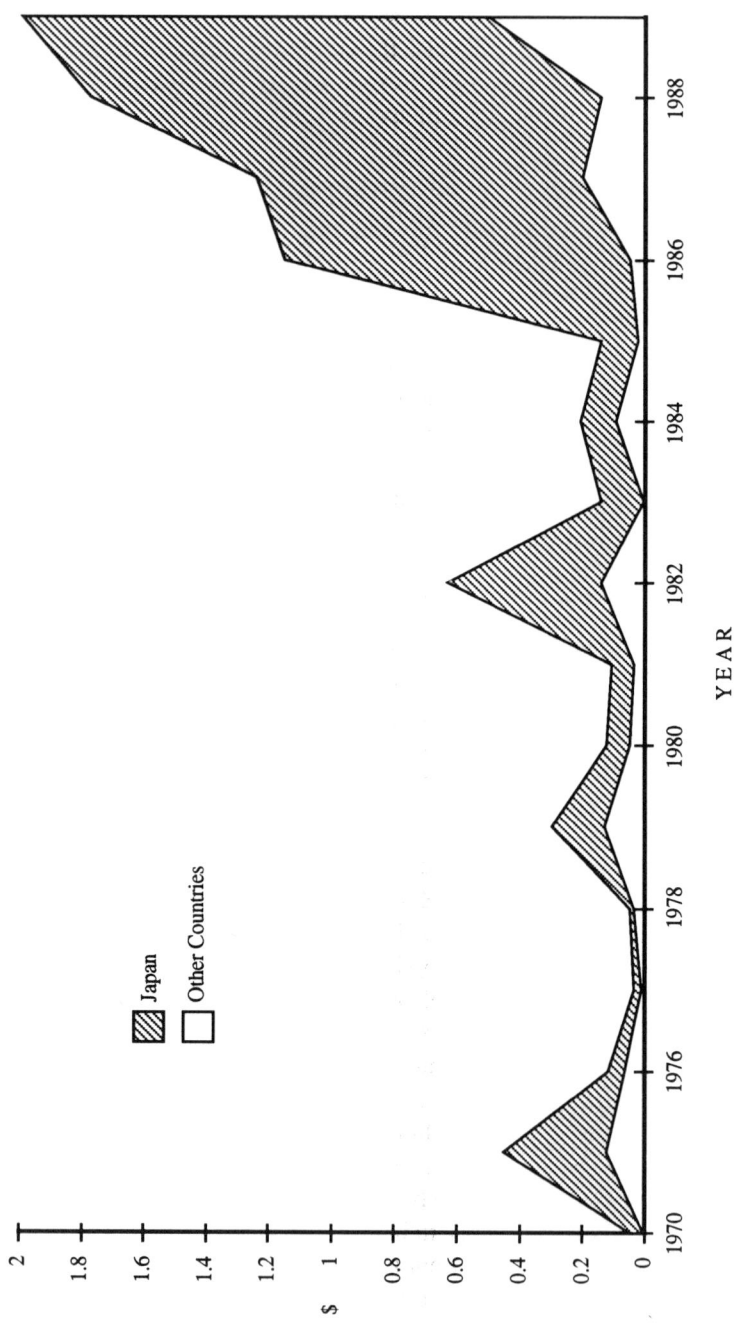

Figure 2.
Foriegn Investments in Hawaii (Billion $'s)

factories, shopping centers, office buildings, restaurants, bakeries, communications companies, hotels, resorts, condos, apartment buildings, golf courses, raw land, new subdivisions, and educational facilities. In the late 1980s, there was not only a staggering increase in the dollar volume of foreign investment, but also a mind-boggling frenzy of buying and selling of real estate in Hawai'i.

Explaining Foreign Investment in Hawai'i

What made Hawai'i such an attractive place of investment? First, Hawai'i is part of the United States, with all the security and protection of property rights that come along with being part of the Union.

Japan's interest in Hawai'i may be explained in terms of three different variables: currency exchange rates; land prices in Japan, and tourists from Japan. To test these hypotheses, three different regression equations were run utilizing annual foreign investment from Japan as the dependent variable and various explanatory variables. The results of these equations are summarized in Table 1.

Table 1.
Summary Table of Regression Results

JDIHI = 1878250 - 5119.17 ERYD
(9.183)
R^2 = .832
F-test = 84.3

JDIHI = -293062902 + 4472018.72 JCLPI
(10.415)
R^2 = .865
F-test = 108.5

JDIHI = -534885129 + 1337.86 JTHI
(6.827)
R^2 = .733
F-test = 46.6

where, JDIHI = Japanese Direct Investment in Hawaii
ERYD = Yen to dollar exchange rate
CLPI = Japanese Commercial Land Price Index
JTHI = Japanese Tourists to Hawaii

Both t-tests (in parentheses) and F-tests are all significant at the .0001 level.

The first equation utilized the yen-to-dollar ratio as an independent variable. The dollar has experienced continued erosion against the yen, dropping from 349Y to the dollar in 1971 to 139Y in 1990. The most rapid period of decline in the strength of the dollar, occurred between 1985 and 1986, when the yen-to-dollar ratio dropped from 239 to 169 in one year. Approximately 83% of the total variation in annual foreign direct investment in Hawai'i is explained by these currency changes. As the yen-to-dollar ratio declined, the amount of foreign investment in Hawai'i increased.

The second relationship concerns differences in land prices between Japan and Hawai'i. It relate investment rates in Hawai'i to land values in Japan, measured by an index of commercial land in Japan's six largest urban areas. This equation produced an even higher R-squared value, of 86.5%, suggesting that as land prices increased in Japan, places like Hawai'i became more attractive places for investment.

The third equation, relates the number of annual Japanese tourists coming to Hawai'i to the amount of foreign investment in Hawai'i real estate. It suggests a different relationship from the first two equations that show how Hawai'i has become a bargain basement by international standards. The strong relationship (R-squared of 73%-equation 1) between tourism and foreign investment is evidence that Japanese firms are establishing or purchasing businesses abroad in order to capture profits from their own citizens as well as others in the international marketplace. This suggests that Hawai'i has become an economic colony of Japan.

Taken together, these three equations reveal similar strains of a familiar tune: that because of globalization[5], Japanese investors have sought out and established new enterprises beyond the boundaries of their country; because of exchange rate differences and the price of land in Japan, the U.S. has become a bargain, and because of the huge trade imbalances between Japan and the U.S., which in 1993 have widened to over approximately $4.3 billion, the pressures to invest abroad will persist.

There is a need to expand upon these results in terms of methodology and the underlying hypotheses. There is a need for more sectoral analysis, especially to look more critically at the tourism industry and test some hypotheses regarding the "new industrial order." This order allows multi-national firms to utilize resources (land, labor, and capital) located abroad in order to produce new profits in what has increasingly become a "borderless society" (Ohmae, 1990). Hawai'i is such a rich environment to conduct research on topics such as vertical integration in the tourism industry. Vertical Integration occurs when an international firm purchases local assets such as hotels, restaurants, tour companies, rental car agencies, mu'umu'u factories. In this way, the visitor need not spend money in the host country[6] More cross-cultural comparative research between Hawai'i and other states in terms of the pattern and nature of Japanese investment is needed. Above all, there is a need for more research on the impact of these international developments on local markets and small businesses.

Impacts of Foreign Investment

Property Speculation

Foreign investment has contributed to property speculation in Hawai'i. One study done by the UH Center for Real Estate found that Japanese buyers in 1988 paid a premium of about 21% over the market price (Ordway, 1989). At that time, there was a great deal of publicity surrounding one particular Japanese billionaire who went on an apparent spending spree in Honolulu, scooping up some 75 homes and condominiums in a brazen display of purchasing power. (Yoneyama and Hooper, 1990). During the late 1980s, the average price of a single family home in Hawai'i was at or near the top of all U.S. cities (Lowry and Kim, 1990). But the connection between foreign investment and speculation is most apparent in commercial properties. Some of the most spectacular sales to Japanese companies in recent years included the Hawai'ian Regent Hotel ($207 million), Hyatt Regency Waikiki ($245 million), Maui Marriott ($150 million), Mauna Kea Resort ($315 million), Maui Intercontinental ($90 million) and Wailea Resort ($197 million). The case of the Hyatt Regency in Waikiki is a good example of the speculative nature of investment during this period. In September 1986 it was sold by VMS Realty (of Chicago) to Azabu for $245 million. Less than a year later it was resold to Kokusai Jidosha for $325 million.

Speculation is a double-edged sword. On the one hand, local buyers of real estate may resent the increased competition from international buyers in Hawai'i. On the other hand, as potential sellers of property, residents may feel entitled to "make a killing in the real estate market." Real estate speculation has become a favored local activity in a state whose residents seem to display uncanny disposition towards gambling and trips to Las Vegas. "One good real estate deal is worth a lifetime of labor" is especially true in a place like Hawai'i where the tremendous escalation in housing prices has produced many millionaires. Property speculation has produced a set of winners and losers (in terms of both buyers and sellers); it has also increased Hawai'i's dependency on Japan.

Economic Dependency on Japan

Hawai'i has become increasingly dependent on Japan in terms of capital, to sustain the engine of development, and tourists to occupy hotel rooms and purchase goods and services. It is clear that much of the expensive real estate (homes, businesses, and land) on the market is priced for the Japanese buyer. Many of the exclusive shops and boutiques in Honolulu cater to Japanese customers. Many of these establishments suffer financially when tourist arrivals from Japan decline or their spending decreases. Real estate ads are often printed in Japanese or feature services such as Japanese language translation. Moreover, a variety of trade delegations and special marketing efforts have been launched in order to encourage continued investment and travel to Hawai'i from Japan. The dependence on Japan is reflected in the extent to which downturns in Japan's economy adversely affect the Hawai'i an economy.

The dependence on Japan for capital has had implications in terms of the scale and magnitude of many development projects in the state. Many of the massive developments such as West Beach on Oahu or several of the Big Island mega-resorts were planned and developed for an international luxury market. These high-priced hotels, golf courses, marinas, and other resort developments have increased dependence on outsiders. Many local developers and businesses find that they are unable to compete on a global scale.

While the amount of foreign investment from places like Hong Kong and South Korea and other Asian countries relative to Japan remains small, Hawai'i's thirst for capital abroad may lead to even further globalization of property and other markets. Hawai'i 's loss of control over its political economy is exacerbated by the fact that Japanese companies and individuals may turn over many of the properties acquired during the last wave of investment to other international buyers.

Social and Community Impacts

Urban planners are also concerned about spatial changes which have occurred as a consequence of growth and development in Hawai'i[7.] Urban design, moreover, has long been an important topic in Hawai'i due to foreign investment. Lewis Mumford came to Honolulu in the 1930's and prepared a report for the city on how to best preserve the balance between the natural and built environment (Mumford, 1976). Although Hawai'i has strong land-use laws, special design districts, park dedications, shoreline setbacks, conservation districts, a state Environmental Impact Statement (EIS) system, some of the recently built structures may lead observers to wonder if Honolulu has any urban design ethic at all. The size, bulk, colors, building materials, and impressions created by many of the newly-built office buildings are more evocative of a design that one would associate with Tokyo or Los Angeles than a small island in the Pacific. Many of these developments have made a travesty of existing zoning and urban design codes. A real concern, given the magnitude and pace of development, heavily fueled by foreign investment, is the loss of community values and important natural and cultural resources that have been long associated with Hawai'i.

The impact goes beyond what may happen in case the height limit in Waikiki, Downtown or Kakaako is pierced. The impacts extend to farmlands and conservation districts being converted to golf courses and new resort developments. They also include what may be termed the "high wall, big dog" syndrome that has emerged in residential architecture, where the emphasis is increasingly on gated communities with security, privacy, and exclusivity. Unlike many cities on the mainland, Hawai'i has had some tradition of racially and economically integrated neighborhoods; but increasingly much of this is being lost as the polarization between haves and have-nots continues.

Another impact of foreign ownership is the real and perceived loss of control due to communication barriers. For many renters or businesses leasing properties from foreign investors, there is added uncertainty as to what the future may hold. It is difficult to have face-to-face meetings when owners are abroad and have less of a vested stake in the future of a particular small business or property.

Golf course development is another example of how foreign investment has affected land use in Hawai'i. Golf courses typically occupy 200 acres of land. There are at least 40 courses that have been proposed or are under construction on O'ahu alone (City and County of Honolulu, 1989). Often the proposed golf courses cater to wealthy and foreign clientele. Often the proposed sites are on agricultural or conservation lands. Worse yet, some golf courses have been developed around ancient Hawai'ian archaeological sites. Often, golf courses are sited to take advantage of spectacular coastal or mountain views. Many developments are linked to hotels or resorts and financed by foreign capital. At the same time, many people in the state cannot afford to play golf. There are on-going concerns and debates regarding the use of fertilizer and pesticides. Given the scarcity of land in Hawai'i, there are often competing interests in terms of potential land uses such as housing or industrial development. Some communities, such as Kilauea on Kauai have organized community and legal actions against foreign developers of golf courses. Moreover, golf courses neither directly generate much employment nor many high quality jobs. Golf course development has pitted various groups dealing with environmental concerns, agriculture, affordable housing, tourism and open space against one another. The contentious character of golf course development is evidence of the large political and economic stakes associated with land-use decisions in Hawai'i.

Debate surrounding development has often been reduced to simple binary dichotomies—golfers v. non-golfers, foreign v. local people, the haves v. the have-nots. In some cases, these dichotomies are a function of language: it is easier to talk about binary polar opposites (good versus evil, black versus white, right versus wrong). This forces everyone into a very narrow public policy trap—a "them or us" view of the world that leads ultimately to conflict or, worse, a "winner take all" mentality that is destructive to community, as well as democratic and pluralistic visions of planning.

Foreign Investment and the Growth Coalition

What is the link between foreign investment and the loss of community in Hawai'i? One way of making the link applies the notion of a growth coalition—that is, a set of elites in business, politics, and even academia, who stand to prosper because of economic growth (Logan and Molotch, 1987) We have a substantial growth coalition in Hawai'i. It is not just the tourism promoters and hotel operators who want to see their occupancy rates increase and the visitor counts continue to rise; it also includes all those engaged in real estate, banking, insurance, development, and construction who would like to see a booming economy. While Hawai'i is the thirty-seventh largest state in terms of population, it is the sixth largest in terms of licensed real estate brokers (DBED, 1990). Hawai'i has double the number of real estate brokers as teachers in the public and private school system. The state has become dependent on growth. Employment is a function of economic growth. To sustain this image of prosperity, of having a strong business climate, Hawai'i needs investment from abroad, particularly from Japan.

In the meantime, from a political economy perspective, the gap between the haves and have-nots has widened. In addition to having all this prosperity, Hawai'i has one of the lowest rates of home ownership in the nation. All of the contradictions associated with late capitalism of the 1990s exist in Hawai'i — million dollar condominiums that sit vacant while homelessness (and families living in cars) is on the increase. Plantations and agricultural operations have closed because the cost of land (among other factors) has risen to make suburban development or golf courses more profitable than farming. Families with two and three generations live together under one roof because of economic necessity. Many from the middle class have moved on to the mainland. There has been a widening gap in the economic circumstances of rich and poor, and a detoriation of the basic quality of life.

The loss of community attributable to foreign investment is difficult to measure. Certainly property speculation and changes in the physical appearance of many areas have contributed to the segregation between wealthy foreigners and lower-income residents. The feelings of loss of control due to increased uncertainties associated with foreign ownership are hard to quantify. But the hardships associated with a high cost of living and lower quality of life, which many residents must endure, undoubtedly contribute to many social tensions. Hawai'i has increasingly become a tale of two cities. One, international, cosmopolitan, and financed by foreign capital, the other the increasingly a city of growing poverty.

Strategies for Managing Foreign Investment

There is a range of different strategies for managing foreign investment. Some of these include: (1) increasing the flow and exchange of information so that we will have better data on what foreign entities are doing within our boundaries; and (2) conducting more fiscal impact assessments of foreign investment so that there can be better balancing of the costs and benefits of foreign investment. Perhaps policies might be developed to direct foreign investment towards particular industries and spatial areas. One idea might be to develop foreign investment zones in areas (such as Kahala) where the price of real estate has already soared beyond the reach of local buyers. There is a need to develop some new tax policies and increase corporate responsibility so that foreign firms that do business in Hawai'i contribute to the welfare of citizens and workers. Finally, the state could go further in terms of promoting alternative development schemes. Community development corporations, land banks, non-profit housing organizations, and other approaches to economic development are needed.

The social and economic problems engendered by foreign investment in Hawai'i have increased the need to devise some type of new social contract[8] between members of what increasingly is becoming a global village in Hawai'i. It is not just a contract between a government and its people (although that would be a good place to start), but between corporations and communities, and between rich and poor in Hawai'i. The system of representative democracy is falling apart, due in part to the tremendous differences between haves and have-nots, between the growth coalition and those shut out of prosperity in Hawai'i. Without examining the basic social relations and the responsibilities associated with citizenship, there may be no choice but allow an international market to prevail. For these reasons, the sovereignty movement in Hawai'i is a significant political development. Setting aside the enormous political, social, and managerial dimensions of the sovereignty issue, the movement has forced a much needed re-examination of what should be the rights and responsibilities of citizenship in Hawai'i. Given the failings of not just the U.S. constitution in terms of protecting the people and lands of Hawai'i, but also the increased threats from borderless, multinational firms and transnational capital, I am probably not the first (nor the last) to view Hawaiian sovereignty as at least one alternative to being an economic colony of Japan. What if, for example, Hawai'i ended up with a more democratic society under a sovereign Hawai'ian state than the present system controlled by Political Action Committees (PACs), special interest groups, and those with land and power in Hawai'i.

Notes

1. This article is adapted from the keynote address given by the author to the Hawai'i Sociological Association, at the Hilton Hawaiian Vilage, March 20, 1993.

2. Approximately 40% of the land in the state is owned by the government. Of the remaining 40%, which is privately owned, more than half is controlled by the six largest landowners in the state. The extent to which land and power is concentrated in the hands of a few is described in Cooper and Daws (1990).

3. For a more detailed discussion of constitutionality of state attempts to regulate foreign investment, see C. Tate (1990).

4. Heller (1976) has studied the earlier growth in Japanese investment in the U.S. and provides some early work on investment in Hawai'i.

5. For more discussion on these points, see Peel (1987).

6. Stern (1988) has described how vertical integration has affected the visitor industry in Hawai'i.

7. An interesting collection of essays on postmodern influences on architecture and planning is contained in C. Jencks (1992).

8. I am borrowing liberally from the French philosopher Rousseau who devised the term "social contract."

References

Cooper, G. and G. Daws. 1990. *Land and Power in Hawaii*. University of Hawai'i Press: Honolulu.

Davis, M. 1990. *City of Quartz: Excavating the Future in Los Angeles*. Verso: London.

Farrell, B. 1982. *Hawaii: The Legend that Sells*. Honolulu: University of Hawai'i Press.

Fainstein, S., N. Fainstein, R. Childhill, D. Judd, and M. Smith. 1986. *Restructuring the City: The Political Economy of Urban Development*. Longman: London.

First Hawaiian Bank. 1987. "Foreign Investment in Hawaii," Economic Indicators, January/February.

_____. 1989. "Japan's Economic Importance to Hawaii," Economic Indicators, March/April.

General Accounting Office. 1990. *Foreign Investment: Concerns in the Banking, Petroleum, Chemicals, and Biotechnology Sectors*. Washington, DC: GAO.

Gill, S and D. Law. 1988. *The Global Political Economy: Perspectives, Problems and Policies*. New York: Harvester, Wheatsheaf.

Glickman, N. and D. Woodward. 1989. *The New Competitors: How Foreign Investors are Changing the U.S. Economy*. New York: Basic Books.

_____. 1988"The Locational of Foreign Direct Investment in the United states: Patterns and Determinants." *International Regional Science Review* 11(2):137-154.

Harvey, D. 1989. *The Condition of Postmodernity*. Oxford: Basil Blackwell.

Hawaii. Department of Business and Economic Development (DBED). 1990. *State Data Book*. Honolulu: DBED.

_____. 1989. *A Listing of Foreign Investments in Hawaii*. Honolulu: DBED.

Hawley, J. 1987. *Dollars & Borders*. New York: M.E. Sharpe.

Heller, R. and E. Heller. 1976. *Japanese Investment in the United States*. New York: Praeger Publishers.

Higashi, C. and G. Lauter. 1990. *The Internationalization of the Japanese Economy*. Boston: Kluwer Academic Publishers.

Honolulu. City. 1989. *Golf Course Development on Oahu*. Honolulu: City and County of Honolulu.

Hymer, S. 1979. *The Multinational Corporation: A Radical Approach*. Cambridge: Cambridge University Press.

Jencks, C. 1992. *The Post-Modern Reader*. London: Academy Editions.

Japan Real Estate Institute. 1990. *Urban Land Price Index.* Tokyo: Japan Real Estate Institute.

Kantor, P. 1988. *The Dependent City: The Changing Political Economy of Urban America.* Glenview: Scott, Foreman and Company.

Kim, K. and K. Lowry. 1989. "Honolulu: City Profile." *Cities: International Quarterly on Urban Policy.* November.

Kent, N. 1983. *Hawaii: Islands Under the Influence.* New York: Monthly Review Press.

Kumar, Krishna. 1980. *Transnational Enterprises: Their Impact on Third World Societies and Cultures.* Westview: Boulder.

Leventhal, K. 1989. *Japanese Investment in U.S. Real Estate.* Los Angeles: Kenneth Leventhal & Company.

Logan, J. and H. Molotch. 1987. *Urban Fortunes: The Political Economy of Place.* University of California Press: Berkeley.

Lowry, K. and K. Kim. 1990. "An Assessment of Hawai'i's 60% Affordable Housing Exaction Policy." Department of Urban and Regional Planning. University of Hawaii: Honolulu.

Moki, H. 1990. Effect of Sharp Rise in Land Prices on Housing Problems in Japan. Paper presented at 12 EAROPH Congress. September 5-7, 1990, Seoul, Korea.

Mumford, L. 1976. "Report on Honolulu." Reprinted in *Hawai'i Observer.* February 3.

Ohmae, K. 1990. *The Borderless World.* New York: Harper Business

Office of State Planning. 1989. *Foreign Investment in Hawaii: An Interim Report.* Honolulu: Office of State Planning.

Ordway, N. 1989. "A Study of Foreign Investment in Real Property and its impact on the State: A Taxonomy of possible Options for Legislative Consideration." Honolulu: University of Hawaii Center for Real Estate.

Peet, Richard. 1987. *International Capitalism and Industrial Restructuring.* Boston: Allen and Unwin.

Said, E. 1993. *Culture and Imperialism.* Knopf: New York.

Stern, B. 1988. *The Aloha Trade: Labor Relations in Hawaii's Hotel Industry.* Honolulu: Center for Labor Education and Research.

Tannenwald, R. 1984. "The Pros and Cons of Worldwide Unitary Taxation." *New England Economic Review* July/August.

Tanouye, E. 1985. "1990: Jobs of the Future." *Hawaii Business.* April.

Tate, C. 1990. "The Constitutionality of State Attempts to Regulate Foreign Investment." *Yale Law Journal.* 99:2023-2042.

Tolchin, M. and S. Tolchin. 1988. *Buying into America.* New York : Times Books.

U.S. Department of Commerce, International Trade Administration, 1988. "Foreign Direct Investment in the United States." *International Direct Investment: Global Trends and the U.S. Role.* Washington, DC: U.S. Government Printing Office.

Vernon, R. and D.Spar. 1989. *Beyond Globalism.* New York : The Free Press.

Ward Research. 1990. *Attitudes Toward Japanese Investment in Hawaii.* Honolulu: Ward Research.

Yoneyama, Tom and Susan Hooper. 1990. "The Japaning of Hawaii." *Hawaii Business* January:14-77.

The Potential for High Tech in Hawai'i

Paul A. Herbig
and
Hugh E. Kramer*

Introduction

Hawai'i's economy is currently experiencing problems that could bode ill for the future. Governmental and private planners are examining alternative economic activities, one of which is to make Hawai'i the high tech East-West bridge between the United States and East Asia. This paper examines those ingredients necessary for an innovative hot spot and provides recommendations on the steps necessary if Hawai'i really does want to partake of the high tech scenario.

Hawai'i's Economic Base

Hawai'i's current economic base is built upon military expenditures, tourism, and agriculture (particularly sugarcane and pineapple). That Hawai'i has been successful is indicative in the relatively low unemployment seen in the islands. However, success could be fleeting in the decade to come. High land prices, high labor costs (as well as the inability to maintain an agricultural labor force due to other more attractive alternatives, especially on O'ahu), and lower-priced foreign competition have made agriculture a precarious proposition for the 1990s. One could almost surmise that if it were not for the price supports, sugarcane and pineapple would be marginal. Within the next decade, even with expensive price supports, long-term intensive agricultural pursuits, especially on O'ahu, could all but disappear, their economic importance minimized by the end of the decade. With the potential implementation of the General Agreement on Tariff and Trade (GATT) and the North American Free Trade Agreement (NAFTA), the disappearance of these agricultural Corporations could be hastened.

Military expenditures on O'ahu have, until recently, been increasing. With the closing of Clark and Subic Bay military bases in the Philippines, Hawai'i appears to be the only secure long-term base the U.S. has in the Pacific and it may

---

*Paul A. Herbig is deeply indebted to the East-West Center for assistance received during research.

benefit the Philippine pullback. However, with the widely acclaimed end of the cold war, overall military spending can only decrease, with the cutbacks eventually affecting Hawai'i. Even if Hawai'i's military importance were to be emphasized and the military presence increased, the effect on the local labor force would be minimal. Most of the increase would be in transient military or civilian specialists from the mainland. Additional local jobs would mainly be in service or support functions.

Tourism boomed in the 1980s. Each year since 1988 there have been over six million visitors. During the last two years, however, the numbers of visitors decreased slightly. In 1992 there were 6,513,880 visitors, down 5.2% from the previous year, according to the Hawai'i Visitors Bureau. New resorts are being planned and built at an unprecedented rate. Eastbound tourism (mainly from Japan) has, until recently, been increasing rapidly as Hawai'i becomes the major foreign destination for the Japanese (the Japanese recession, however, has deeply cut into the East-West traffic growth). Tourism is not a constant predictable force. If one major negative incident occurs (say, for example, a bombing in a Waikiki hotel), Japanese tourists may stay away in droves. Also, the build-up of the tourism industry, some local residents insist, is causing irrevocable environmental decay. If the tourists wake up one day and say "I could have stayed in Chicago (or New York) and had this same congestion, skyscrapers, and food, why come here?" they may go home and never come back. The economic health of a resort is a fragile thing as Atlantic City and many past glory spots now realize. If not kept up and in tune with tourists' expectations, those tourists leave forever.

With the three currently relatively strong legs of the Hawaiian economy displaying very fragile and weak long-term potential, it is only wise to look elsewhere to provide the necessary long-term stability and growth opportunities for the Hawaiian economy. Within the past few years, many private and public studies have been undertaken. In his March 1989 report "Hawai'i as an International Business Center," Grant Thornton of Bechtel Civil Inc., listed 21 potential business opportunities. The list included the development of Corporate Regional Headquarters, an Education/Training Center, a Pacific Islands Center, Convention and a Conference Center, and Research Centers. The report of the Governor's Congress on Hawai'i's International Role (1988) provided a similar list of potential opportunities. Included in this list was the establishment of an Asia-Pacific Institute of Business and Commerce, an International Banking and Finance center, a Honolulu Stock Exchange, a Cross-Cultural Center, a Sports/Wellness Fitness Center, and an International Training, Consulting and Research center.

High Technology and Hawai'i

One idea that has been discussed quite often focuses on Hawai'i as a research center, in particular as a high tech East-West bridge between the United States and East Asia. High tech has provided to be a growth force in other parts of the United States. Its continued viability is of national concern and often provides high-paying jobs and, by its very nature, is a growth industry. The establishment of a major high tech presence on the Hawaiian Islands would thus seem to be in its best interests.

In 1988, the High Technology Development Corporation and the Department of Business and Economic Development commissioned the Pacific International Center for High Technology Research to undertake a study and produce a Hawai'i High Tech Business Directory (Thornton, 1989). It identified 181 firms with composite revenues of more than $908 million and total employment of nearly 10,000 employees. This nearly one billion dollar industry appears to be thriving. However, this included (GTE) Hawaiian Telephone, which alone could account for upwards of almost half of the revenues. The remainder is the equivalent of the output of just a single minor player in one of the major innovative basins in the United States, such as Data General, Wang, or Prime Computer in Boston, although all were over 500 million in sales. Although these numbers are not insignificant as far as they affect the economy of Hawai'i, they are clearly indicative that Hawai'i still has a long way to go before it can achieve major league recognition as a High Tech locale.

To pursue this potential high tech utopia, the Hawai'i state government has created, staffed, and funded numerous groups. These have included the High Technology Development Corporation, the Hawai'i Information Network Corporation, the Office of Space Industry, the Hawai'i Innovation Development Program, the Hawai'i Strategic Development Corporation, and the Research and Development Industry Promotion Program. Yet despite all these programs and groups in place, the state of Hawai'i has yet to attract even one sizable company.

Why did high tech bloom in Silicon Valley near San Jose, California, and Route 128 outside of Boston, Massachusetts and not in others, say in Butte, Montana or in Wheeling, West Virginia? What is it about those areas that provided the catalyst for innovation to prosper? For purposes of comparison with Hawai'i, we are interested in reviewing conditions that have contributed to the launching of an innovative hot spot. We need to understand why they developed, where and when they did, and examine these factors in light of the current and projected Hawaiian perspectives. In addition, it is necessary to see if those conditions are met in Hawai'i and if they are not, to discuss how they might be brought about.

Hawai'i's Current Innovative Potential

In their study of the history of the development of the major innovative hot spots Herbig and Golden (1993) have compiled thirteen major factors critical in the formation of these innovative hot spots. How does Hawai'i rank when one examines these factors? What is Hawai'i's current innovative potential?

1) Leading Entrepreneur Initiator. Hawai'i has many entrepreneurs but they appear to be concentrated in the resort/travel/construction industry. At the present time there appears to be no strong entrepreneur in residence who could take over the role of a leading force in the high tech field in Hawai'i.

2) University. Each hot spot developed in proximity to a prestigious technical university, particularly private institutions of higher learning with long-established entrepreneurial spirit motivating graduates and faculty. The universities had to have a technical, engineering, and basic science focus, had to be research-oriented, and prestigious enough to allow state-of-art technology to be developed. Besides having access to major science and engineering schools, it is hardly a coincidence that all the innovative hot spots have top ranked business schools nearby (Harvard, Stanford, Texas and Duke all rank in the top ten). This combination of business acumen and scientific excellence appears to be necessary for innovation to be birthed and be managed into a successful venture.

Institutions of higher education within the state of Hawai'i include the University of Hawai'i at Manoa and Hilo branches, Hawai'i Pacific, Chaminade, Japan-America Institute of Management Science, and Brigham Young University-Hawai'i. By far, the University of Hawai'i (UHM) at Manoa is the major university in Hawaii. However, it is not yet in the same league as the Michigan Institute of Technology or Stanford. The school has some strengths, notably in oceanography, geophysics, astronomy, tropical agriculture, and Hawaiian, Asian and Pacific Studies. SHAPS (School of Hawaiian, Asian, and Pacific Studies) has more faculty and researchers covering the Pacific Rim than any other school in the world (over 300 who provide instruction in over 40 languages and have the capabilities of 40 more). Its business school is making a concerted effort to specialize in Pacific and Asian affairs and travel industry management. Although it is not part of the UH, the East-West Center provides international prominence through federal and foreign grants and focused research. One study which considers only grants for international projects ranks the University of Hawai'i merely thirteenth in the U.S. As a whole the University of Hawai'i still has a long way to go before it can be considered on par with the top universities on the mainland.

3) Physical Infrastructure. All the innovative hot spots have an outstanding physical infrastructure in terms of highways, water, sewage, airports, ports, hospitals and other medical facilities. Hawai'i's Physical Infrastructure is adequate. Road congestion and growing fresh water shortages are problems, but airports and port facilities are among the best in the world.

4) Initial low development costs for both residents and business must exist. San Jose had many square miles of orchards available for construction; Massachusetts had empty textile mills; Austin and North Carolina had cheap land and housing. Small firms are usually undercapitalized and need every break they can get; inexpensive work space could well mean the difference between success and failure.

Hawai'i's living costs are far above most mainland cities. The East-West Center provides a 30% housing differential compared to Washington D.C., which is noted to be expensive. Between 1986 and 1989 median home prices rose from three times to the unprecedented ratio of six times the Hawai'i median household income (Aoudé 1993:222). With average housing presently approaching $300,000 for a modest home on O'ahu and prime acreage increasing annually at double digit rates over the past two decades, this is and will continue to be a major problem in recruiting people and companies to Hawai'i. This problem is less noticeable on the other Islands but costs everywhere continue to escalate. Affordable housing is scant and hardly "affordable."

This situation for new businesses is made somewhat more acceptable by the low rents available through the establishment of Technology Centers and business incubator facilities: e.g., Mililani Research Park and Maui Research and Technology Center. But once a firm outgrows its incubator space, it must compete for prime land for manufacturing or proceed to source manufacturing offshore to the mainland or Pacific Rim, in which case jobs and growth opportunities are lost for Hawai'i. How can an employer convince a highly regarded scholar or engineer to leave his $100,000 spacious home with pool on several acres of land 5 minutes from work to come to Hawai'i and live in a small apartment or modest townhouse 30 to 60 minutes of rush hour commute away from his job? That is the challenge and dilemma facing firms, and key employees, who want to move to Hawai'i.

5) Attitude Towards Entrepreneurs. The predominant attitude in the innovative communities is one not only of acceptance of entrepreneurship but admiration. American culture with its appreciation of hard work and individualism encourages and provides incentives to be entrepreneurial. Entrepreneurship becomes almost a fatalistic notion in these regions. Go for it! Failure cannot be faulted, not trying is!

Does the Aloha spirit mix with the hard work ethic seen on the mainland? It appears doubtful at first glance. The Aloha Spirit involves friendliness, openness, consideration for others, sharing, a tendency to avoid confrontations, mutual respect, and caring for one's fellow men and women. The easy going Hawaiian spirit does not blend well with the workaholic entrepreneur from the mainland. The predominant attitude of the Island's leadership and people is conservative, that is to say, traditional, risk avoiders, the very opposite of the entrepreneurs, the shakers and movers, the islands would like to attract.

6) Pro-Business Attitude. In the beginning, businesses were looked upon as key to the prosperity of an innovative hot spot. Businesses were first sought after to provide answers to problems. It is not surprising that in the innovative hot spots unions are the exception not the rule. During an innovative hot spot's conception and fast growth phase, businesses were given favorable treatment and encouragement. The Islands tend to rely heavily on governmental entitlements rather than on business or private sources. Hawai'i tends to be strongly supportive of unions. Public attitudes towards business have become increasingly unfavorable. Hawai'i has a steep progressive income tax, excise tax, hotel-room tax as well as a cost of living that is near the highest in the United States.

7) Capital. Small ventures need a heavy infusion of capital to survive in high-tech industries. These funds were available and accessible during the early days and critical growth era at the innovation hot spots. In fact, the ebb and flow of innovation and small ventures seem to have a direct relationship to the ease of access and availability of venture capital. Venture Capital is very likely available from foreign funding sources, particularly Japanese firms. The availability of funds should not be a problem given the interest in and familiarity with Hawai'i by affluent business people of the Pacific Rim and the special status of Hong Kong which fosters the outflow of capital funds before 1997.

8) Government Funds and/or Support. Both Silicon Valley and Route 128 took off after World War II with heavy support from U.S. military and space programs. Many firms located near Austin and in the Research Triangle also were recipients of government funds. It is obvious that government funds,

resources, support and encouragement provide strong incentives and play the role of a catalyst for high-tech innovation. In Hawai'i, this type of funding is generally directed towards capital improvement of military bases and the infrastructure. The lack of high-tech firms with track records and the dearth of labs and research facilities (that are the offshoots of mainland or foreign firms) make the funding situation worse. Some funding is available in a few specialized areas: oceanography, space/astronomy, and geothermal.

9) Strong School Systems. Both Massachusetts and California thrive with strong school systems—particularly at the university level. In those areas, secondary and primary schools are also considered some of the nation's best. This is of importance if one realizes that the key to managing innovation is the availability and recruitment of human resources. People who make companies successful and communities prosper. These human resources are hard to find and can choose where they want to work and live. They are very concerned with quality of life and the future of their children and will often choose areas that provide cultural endowments and strong educational potential. With the exception of a few private schools such as Punahou, I'olani, the Mid-Pacific Institute, Maryknoll, Waldorf, and Kamehameha, the Hawai'i public school system is generally acknowledged to be rather poor in Hawai'i. Culturally, the Islands have numerous resort and touristic things attractions.

10) Physical Climate and Environment. For the most part all of the innovative hot spots enjoy pleasant living and working conditions such as a favorable climate, geographical proximity of the ocean or rivers and lakes, expansive woods and hills. Here Hawai'i excels, its climate is second to none in the world. Unless the continued population growth on O'ahu creates congestion and pollution that scars the natural beauty, the Hawaiian islands are truly a paradise on earth.

11) Technology Parks or Incubators. The establishment of technology parks or incubators, which allow resident companies to take advantage of university resources while providing a base for faculty contract work, has been instrumental for many successes. Eighty percent of small ventures within incubators succeed while 80% of those outside fail. The Stanford Research park is now fully leased with 90 companies, employing over 25,000 people. Many other states have begun establishing specialized research institutes (centers of excellence or advanced technology centers) to enhance particular applied research capabilities of local universities and to stimulate university industry research collaboration. The themes of these centers usually reflect both the existing program strengths of the host universities and the interests of businesses located in the state.

The Potential for High Tech in Hawai'i   63

Research parks near the core universities serve as catalysts for bringing companies to an area conveniently located near the intellectual resources and research labs of a university. They also provide faculty members with consulting opportunities and even bring rental income to the university. The number of parks initiated by universities has grown rapidly over the last few years to some 200 currently existing or being planned. Universities usually own at least some of the land on which a park is built, and they usually retain some control over tenant selection. In addition, some universities have established high-tech incubators that provide new companies with relatively low-cost office and lab space and access to related business services. In Hawai'i, such industrial parks are few: Mililani Research Park and Maui Research and Technology Center being the best known.

12) Time. In each innovative hot spot, the time lapse between the founding of the initiator firm and the rise of a full-blown innovative hot spot is somewhere between 15 and 20 years, after the proper infrastructure, attitudes, and initiator firms had all been put in place.

13) Agglomeration Effect. This is one factor that is not present at the beginning but reveals itself as the innovative hot spot, as it builds momentum and grows past a certain critical mass. Agglomeration externalities involve the spin-off of other enterprises within an innovative community, the effects that accrue to firms from close proximity to others engaged in related activities in these rapidly evolving industries. This gives impetus for other high-tech industries to locate in the same given region rather than diversify elsewhere in the country or the world. A critical mass of high tech firms is necessary to provide a sufficient number of companies and technical personnel that make staffing new ventures easy. In Silicon Valley it is reputed that one can switch jobs without ever changing parking spaces. This is the agglomeration effect, the effect of proximity and large numbers, which is totally absent in Hawai'i.

Herbig and Golden (1993) conclude the innovative hot spots spring from two major sources: they are rich in the origins of new entrepreneurs and entrepreneurs are attracted to set up shop there. Given time, devotion, attitudes, long-term orientation, and a minimum level of physical attractiveness of the area and infrastructure, many locales can become an innovative hot spot. Most employees today favor an area in proximity to the conveniences and entertainment opportunities of a major city. However, it should be close enough to an urban center to allow easy access to the center but far enough to avoid the congestion, pollution, and problems usually associated with such an urban center. Favorable temperate climates will win out over harsh extreme environments. This process involves a long-term development of 15 to 25 years or longer depending upon the current status and development of the infrastructure within the locale.

What conclusions can be drawn from the evaluation of Hawai'i for becoming a high tech innovative hot spot? Four points of agreement among the experts are:

Conclusion 1: Hawai'i is far from qualifying as a high tech innovative hot spot at this time.

Conclusion 2: Hawai'i currently does not have the necessary educational and technical infrastructure in place to start the process towards an innovative hot spot.

Conclusion 3: Hawai'i does not currently display the proper set of cultural attitudes conducive for entrepreneurs and the establishment of small high-tech ventures.

Conclusion 4: Hawai'i's excessive cost of living and costs to operate a business make it difficult to attract and maintain innovative entrepreneurs and qualified high-tech personnel and research scholars.

Can Hawai'i Become an Innovative Hot Spot?

To develop Hawai'i into a high tech paradise, will probably take 25 to 30 years and perhaps even longer. Silicon Valley and Route 128 already had the infrastructure in place prior to their incubation and critical growth years. Hawai'i must first build the requisite educational infrastructure. Or attempt to do the riskier but quicker strategy of parallel development of the infrastructure and initiator firm and its spinoffs. The government and private sector must also understand that patience, time, and constant devotion for almost a generation is necessary if a true innovation hot spot is to be produced.

The first step is to analyze and utilize Hawai'i's current strengths. High tech covers a multiple of winning combinations and Hawai'i must choose one in which it wants to be a major player. High tech has become associated with semiconductors, computers, software, telecommunications, and biotechnology. High Tech goes well beyond these areas and could represent any advanced technology or field of endeavor. Hawai'i's leaders must understand and accept the fact that the state will probably never be a major player in the semiconductor, telecommunications or computer areas. There are many other locales that have already established strengths and experience in heavy manufacturing, mining, or agriculture.

Hawai'i's decision makers must examine high tech's strengths and limitations. The industry must not take up a lot of space, endanger the environment, take away jobs or merely provide menial jobs for the local population. Hawai'i's strong existing bases include: astronomy, health, ocean sciences, genetics and evaluation, Pacific centers for education and business, alternative energies, agriculture, aquaculture, tropical environments, and travel industry management.

If Hawai'i wants to be an high tech paradise, an innovative hot spot, then it should concentrate its resources in any one of three areas that best complement its strengths and minimize potential limitations. These areas are:

1) Ocean/Marine: These include ocean mining, aquaculture, marine studies, fishing replenishment and natural balance, saltwater to freshwater conversion research and ocean/marine related geophysical studies. Existing Hawaiian facilities include: Pacific Congress on Marine Science and Technology (PACON), UH Institute of Geophysics and Marine Biology, Pacific Ocean Science and Technology Center, Hawai'i Ocean Science Technology Park at Keahole on the Big Island, DUMAND project to learn more about neutrinos from outer space by capturing them in receptions off the ocean floor near Hawai'i, the Oceanic Institute at Waimanalo (a private nonprofit research center for applied aquaculture) as well as a plentiful assortment of private sea and ocean fishing farms.

2) Renewable and alternative energy sources: These include geothermal, ocean thermal, windmills, solar, and hydropower. Existing Hawaiian facilities include the National Energy Laboratory of Hawai'i, Hawai'i Natural Energy Institute, and the proposed Geothermal development site on the Big Island.

3) Space research: includies astronomy/ observatories, commercial space launches, space research on communications, and laser space research. Existing Hawaiian Facilities include: a host of large mirror telescopes on the Big Island (especially on top of Mauna Kea) and Maui, a Canada-France-Hawai'i telescope project, Joint Astronomy Center, Planetary Geosciences Division of the Hawai'i Institute of Geophysics at the University of Hawai'i, NASA tracking stations, Hawai'i Space Authority, and the U.S. Pacific Missile Range air-sea-land test facility on Kaua'i and the Big Island.

These three areas play into the existing strengths of Hawai'i, their locale and their peoples. If any high-tech research center is to be established, emphasis should be given to these areas.

What Must Hawai'i do to Become a High Tech Innovative Hot Spot?

Recommendations on what the people, the government, and business, must do for Hawai'i to have a reasonable chance at becoming an innovative hot spot any time in the future are:

1) Recognition by the state and the people of Hawai'i of the time, resources, and support needed to make this transformation; also a willingness and dedication by the people of Hawai'i, major governmental officials, and leading private citizens to work together towards this growth.

2) The creation of an adequate educational infrastructure. This primarily entails building first-rate engineering, science, and business schools within the University of Hawai'i. Doctoral programs must be established or expanded. All possible efforts must be made, and no limits imposed, on efforts to recruit top-notch academicians and researchers to the UH, especially in the targeted areas. Sufficient funds for quality facilities, research, and human support will be required. Subsidized housing for key faculty and research employees may be in order to successfully recruit them to the University of Hawai'i or to any of the high tech centers.

3) Provide ample and consistently-funded public or privately endowed centers in those areas targeted for high tech. These include increasing funding to existing centers and creating new ones to serve uncovered but desired high tech target niches. This means providing sufficient resources, to attract and retain experts, specialists, researchers, academicians, scholars, and engineers. This also means underwriting journals, conferences, and symposiums to make the centers and Hawai'i internationally renowned in their particular high technology niche.

4) The establishment or expansion of low-cost incubator facilities for firms in the targeted high-tech areas. This includes both research and manufacturing facilities. One alternative could be for the state to secure title to a large amount of military acreage (say a valley no longer needed by the military) and use it as a high tech basin. Placing incubator facilities on the other islands is a possibility. But if the research center and expert scholars are located at the University of Hawai'i at Manoa, then one needs to either put these facilities on O'ahu or have

convenient transportation to provide access to the other Islands. Since people attracted to innovative hot spots prefer the proximity to urban areas, the best location would seem to be Oʻahu. The state has made a laudable first step by establishing an industrial area for high tech and new industries in West Oʻahu, providing seed money for a Kaimuki Technology Enterprises and ALU LIKE, Inc., a business development center charged with entrepreneurial assistance to native Hawaiians.

5) The state government and city administration of Honolulu must develop stronger pro-business attitudes to encourage and attract entrepreneurs, provide tax breaks, and create a more conducive climate for small businesses.

6) The establishment of accessible venture capital funds. The use of Japanese and East Asian financial sources could be encouraged if adequate mainland funds were not forthcoming. Amply endowed funds competing with one another have been shown to produce the best results.

7) Seek an initiator firm for each of the target niches, preferably a small entrepreneurial company or a division of a large firm.

8) An absolute need exists for the state of Hawaiʻi and City and County of Honolulu to resolve the affordable housing dilemma as well as the traffic congestion and mass transit issues. Lack of acceptable solutions to these problems may easily undo all the hard work and earlier successes. Quality of life and cost of living, no doubt, are major concerns to potential entrepreneurs and their work force.

9) Attention must also be given to improve the quality of local school systems and the cultural activities that exist on Oʻahu and the other Islands.

10) Be patient. Continue to be diligent, work hard, and consistently provide the necessary funding and support needed. Then, after 20 to 25 years, Hawaiʻi, too, could well be considered an innovative hot spot in its selected niches.

Is High Tech Even Feasible in Hawaiʻi?

Given the ever increasing levels of global competition and the economic situation in Hawaiʻi, is high tech even feasible in Hawaiʻi? We have analyzed the current innovative potential of Hawaiʻi using as a benchmark those existing hot spots of Silicon Valley and Route 128. The results are not encouraging. Of the 12 key factors, Hawaiʻi fails in ten of them with only a half for infrastructure and satisfactory for climate. At least 30 to 40 years would be required to establish

Hawai'i as a hot spot, high tech area, with adequate infrastructure land national and international prestige.

An innovative hot spot cannot be forced. Merely wishing it will not work either. Despite having dozens of committees, groups, and corporations, Hawai'i's record of securing high tech business is abysmal. Good reasons exist for this. To illustrate, one of the brightest potentials is for Hawaii to be a telecommunications intensive stepping-stone for multinational businesses between North America and East Asia. Hawai'i fares well compared with other non-U.S. locations in the Pacific Basin. Its location and climate provide major attractions for such a stepping-stone. Multinational businesses have indicated their interest in the proposition. Yet, as indicated in a new book, The Price of Paradise (Roth 1993), despite all these potentials, Hawai'i finds itself on the trailing edge of telecommunications. Reason? The cozy relationship between Hawaiian Tel (GTE) and the state government which has allowed the telephone company to continue its monopoly and not upgrade its facilities as competition would have forced it to do. If the state and the powers that be in Hawai'i are unwilling to forego present economic inefficiencies for a chance to have an industry that is almost being thrown into their laps, what chances are there for other high-tech industries that must be actively sought?

In this age of complex, highly-competitive global business, companies are being aggressively wooed by states and countries to locate their facilities there (note the heavy bidding for the Mercedes plant recently won by Alabama at a reported cost of nearly $300 million in tax benefits). Large multinationals are finding it increasingly true that they can have their pick of locales. In this regard, Hawai'i's disadvantages (cost, anti-business climate and, politics) work against it.

Innovation and entrepreneurship are the domains of small firms. New venture start-ups are the principal forces involved in job creation and innovation. The history of innovation and hot spot development indicates that local entrepreneurs were the force behind innovative hot spots. Hawai'i may have local entrepreneurs but they tend to be in real estate, development, tourism, and hotel industries. These are not high tech. The dearth of entrepreneurial high-tech new ventures in Hawai'i is not accidental. The conditions that create entrepreneurial new ventures do not currently exist in Hawai'i. Unless the proper set of incentives (as discussed earlier) are set in place, massive entrepreneurial activity of any sort is unlikely to occur in Hawai'i. Is High-Tech Feasible in Hawai'i? Yes. Is High Tech Probable for Hawai'i? No, not with the current political structure and mindset that exist in the state.

Conclusion

Can Hawai'i become a high tech paradise? Only with great patience and concentrated long-term efforts. Hawai'i's strategic development plan should cover a time horizon of 25 to 30 years and should take advantage of the state's current strengths. We have provided three industries that complement Hawai'i's strengths and that offer feasible high tech opportunities for Hawai'i over the long term. We have also reviewed Hawai'i's current high-tech potential and found it severely lacking. We have further provided Hawai'i's leaders with a set of prescriptions which must first be put in place before further consideration of Hawai'i becoming an innovative hot spot. Is it feasible to believe Hawai'i can become a high tech paradise? Yes, if its expectations are lowered to the three indicated industries and if the prescriptions are followed. Is it probable? No. With the current mindset, political structure, and conservative (meaning not conducive to change, risk avoidance) mentality of the state's leaders and populace, the likelihood of Hawai'i implementing the changes required is currently nil.

We did not address the question of whether Hawai'i even wants or needs high tech? This is a critical political question that needs to be addressed and resolved before any program is launched. The benefits of high tech include a diversified economy supplementing Hawai'i's current economic base of tourism, military spending, and agriculture; a higher standard of living for all segments of Hawai'i's population, and a stemming of the brain drain of the best of the local population.

The negatives include the prospect that some of the upper managerial and technical jobs may not go to native Hawaiians or local citizens, rather they will probably go to mainlanders or foreign nationals. The locals will likely end up with assembly, service, and support jobs. Other negatives not addressed here include the highly important basic issues such as foreign and mainland ownership, high growth, water shortages, more traffic congestion and environmental spoilage. These must clearly be examined first before the basic issue of reliance on high tech for the future development of Hawai'i's economy can be tackled.

References

Hawaii. 1988. Report of the Governor's Congress on Hawai'i's International Role.

Aoudé, Ibrahim G. 1993 "Tourist Attraction: Hawai'i's Locked-In Economy." In Peter Manicas (ed.), *Social Process in Hawaii: A Reader.* New York: McGraw-Hill, 218-235.

Bunke, Harvey C. 1987. "The Heartland from Afar." *Business Horizons.* 30(5) (September/October):3-12.

Dorfman, Nancy S. 1983. ("Route 128: The Development of a Regional High Technology Economy"). *Research Policy.* 12:299-316.

Drucker, Peter F. 1985. *Innovation and Entrepreneurship*, New York: Harper and Row.

Herbig, Paul A. and Jim Golden 1993. "Subcultural Differences in Innovation: The Rationale for Innovative Hot Spots." Working paper, Jacksonville State University.

Kirp, David L. and Douglas S. Rice 1988. "Fast Forward—Styles of California Management." *Harvard Business Review* January/February:74-84.

Roth, Randall W. 1993. *The Price of Paradise*, Honolulu: Mutual Publishing.

Sabel, Charles R.,Gary Herrigel, Richard Kazis, and Richard Keeg. 1987. "How to Keep Mature Industries Innovative." *Technology Review* 90/ 4 (April):27-35.

Scibaerras, E. 1983. "New Competition and Technical Change in the Computer Industry." *Technovation* 2:17-26.

Segal, N.S. 1986. "Universities and Technological Entrepreneurship in Britain: Some Implications of the Cambridge Phenomenon." *Technovation* 4:189-204.

Smyser, A.A. 1990. *Hawai'i: An East-West Bridge*. Working paper, East-West Center, Honolulu, Hawaii.

_____. 1990. *Hawai'i's Future in the Pacific*. Working paper, East-West Center.

Thornton, Grant. 1989. Hawai'i As an International Business Center. Paper for Bechtel Civil Inc. (March).

Wilde, Jim de. 1986. "Facilitating Innovation: Government and High Technology Industries." *Business Quarterly* (Canada) 51/1 (Spring):53-55.

Hawai'i: the Housing Crisis and the State's Development Strategy

Ibrahim G. Aoudé

This paper will argue that the current housing crisis in Hawai'i has developed over the past 33 years as a consequence of the state's development strategy. The crisis is systemic. Therefore, systemic changes need to be undertaken to resolve the housing crisis. These changes could be motivated by the development of a mass movement that is anchored in the hardest hit sections of our island society.

Background

Fifty-four percent of the state's housing stock is owner-occupied as opposed to a national average of 64% (*Honolulu Star-Bulletin (HSB)* 9/9/1991:A-1). Between 1979-1989 the number of housing units in Hawai'i increased by 21% from 324,000 to 393,354 (Dinell 1990:21). In 1990 (the latest figures available) the housing inventory was 402,644 (Bank of Hawai'i (BOH) 1991a:29). According to Locations Inc., between 1984-1989, Honolulu home prices increased from $160,000 to $275,000 (an increase of 72%) condominuim prices increased from $84,000 to $135,000 (an increase of 61%) over the same period (*HSB* 12/26/1990:B-1).

In 1986, the year in which the recent housing boom started, homes priced below $200,000 constituted two-thirds of the O'ahu market. These homes still accounted for about one-half of single family home sales up to the beginning of the 1988. By 1990, these homes were virtually nonexistent. In addition, condominuims priced below $100,000 accounted for over one-half of the O'ahu market in 1986. By 1988, these condominum prices virtually disappeared from the market (*Honolulu Advertiser (HA)*, 11/17/1991).

According to Dot Mason, the president of the Honolulu Board of Realtors, in July 1990, the median single family home on O'ahu (where 80% of the state's 1.15 million residents live) was $363,000; an increase of 41% from the previous year. Condominuim median price was $200,000 during the same period under consideration; an increase of 54% (*Honolulu Star-Bulletin & Advertiser* 8/26/1990:H-1). In 1991, a median four-person single family home on O'ahu was affordable only to families in the top 5-10% of the income distribution. Put another way, only families earning $100,000 or more per year could afford buying a house (House Majority Staff Office 1991:4). "Home affordability is defined here as the indexed ratio (1977=100) of house payments (principal and interest) to median family income: affordability worsens as the ratio rises" (BOH 1991c:1). For purposes of comparison, the indexed ratio is given for the following years: 1987, 109.4; 1989, 152.5; 1990, 183.2; 1991 (first half), 161.9. The factors responsible for the decline in 1991 are the decrease of single family home prices and a declining mortgage rate (BOH 1991c:1).

In 1990, annual median income was $43,700, an increase of 6.1% from the previous year. This, however, was a decline in income since the rate of inflation for the same period registered at 7.3%.

A buyer of a median-priced single family home would have had to pay roughly 64% of total family income. That figure does not include the down payment (BOH 1991c:1). A buyer of a median-priced single family home on Oʻahu in 1990 would have had to put $67,800 as a downpayment. Not too many Hawaiʻi residents have this amount of money in savings or in liquid assets (Hawaii 1991:4-5). "Affordable housing" is not within reach of about three fifths of Hawaiʻi's households. The 1990 Hawaiʻi State Housing Functional Plan includes in the "affordable housing" category "housing for persons or families whose incomes are identified as one hundred forty percent or less of the area median income for each of the counties of Hawaiʻi, Maui, Honolulu, and Kauaʻi, as determined by the United States Department of Housing and Urban Development (HUD) from time to time, as adjusted by family size" (Hawaii 1990:1). These families could qualify for government assistance in buying a home. There is a shortfall, however, of between 20,000 to 35,000 units in the "affordable" category (Hawaii 1989a:4; Dinell 1990:22). By the year 2000, 86,000 units will be needed statewide. Of these, 64,000 units will be needed by low- and moderate-income households. The public sector will provide 20,000 units and the private sector about 40,000; a shortfall of 24,000 units (Hawaii 1991:11).

"This deterioration in affordability was due almost exclusively to rising home prices since the slightest rise in mortgage interest rates was offset by the rise in average income" (Hawaiʻi 1991:4). Be that as it may, people who cannot afford buying their own home, with or without governmental assistance, still need a place to stay. They could rent only if rentals are available and affordable.

The Rental Market

Between 1980-1989, the number of households in Hawaiʻi had grown by 22.8% while the supply of all housing had increased by 17.7% (Hawaiʻi 1991:9). In 1987, there were 199,645 residential rental units statewide. Four thousand rental housing units would have been required to move the vacancy rate from 1% to 3%. This high rate would still have been lower than the 5% level that is the generally accepted minimum to give renters an element of choice (Hawai'i 1991:6, 10).

In 1989, 58% of all the housing stock in the state was occupied by renters. The overall vacancy rate on O'ahu was between 1-2%. "Well located and lower rent multifamily projects are estimated to have vacancy rates even lower than one percent" (Hawai'i 1991:6, 7). In 1990, the overall vacancy rate on O'ahu was 2.7% which translated to 3,717 vacant units (Department of Business and Economic Development (DBED) 1991:531).

Between 1986-1989 monthly rents on O'ahu have increased by 6-10% per year. A one-bedroom, 800 square foot apartment in Honolulu rented for $890 while the national average was $375 (Hawai'i 1991:6). In 1991, the average monthly rents for a three bedroom, one bath, 800 square foot apartment was $960 (DBED 1991:539). Rents statewide have risen faster than inflation as well as income. Over the past six years, rents in Honolulu have risen 42% making Honolulu the most expensive rental market with the lowest vacancy rate in the country (*HSB* 9/9/1991:A-1).

The average monthly rent for a two bedroom apartment in Makiki and downtown was roughly $1,093 and in Hawai'i Kai $1,400. The figures for a single family dwelling are: $1,933 in Makiki/Manoa and $1,900 in Hawai'i Kai (*HSB* 9/9/1991:A-8). Michael Sklarz, researcher for Locations Inc., attributed the sharp rise in rental rates to low vacancy rates; few newly constructed units added to the market; an expanding population base; and a growing economy. He further added that rents will increase at a steady rate of 5% per year instead of the double-digit rise that was witnessed in the past several years (*HSB* 9/9/1991:A-8). At any rate, Economist Paul Brewbaker of the Bank of Hawai'i estimates that renters pay anywhere from one-half to one-third of their take-home pay to rent (*HSB* 9/9/1991:A-8).

The military, which comprises 10% of Hawai'i's total population, puts further pressure on the rental housing market. In 1991, the military used 34,016 housing units. In 1989, the military projected deficits for FYs 1991, 1992, and 1993 of 2,287; 3,135; and 6,056 housing units respectively. These units had to be demanded in the rental housing market. About 38% of military personnel reside off-base (Hawaii 1991:10).

"Developers haven't built rental housing units for the last 20 years," said Michael Sklarz (*HSB* 9/10/1991:A-1). Paul Brewbaker, BOH economist, said that there was simply no profit in constructing rental housing units. The profit resided in building condominuims. 70% of Hawai'i's condominuims were investor-owned and were being rented (*HSB* 9/10/1991:A-8). What discourages developers from building rentals is the high fixed cost which approximates $140,000 per unit (*HSB*, 9/10/1991).

The government appears to intervene in an attempt to alleviate the housing crisis. Since 1987, the Housing Finance and Development Corporation has developed or assisted in developing 2,968 additional rental housing units with 5,086 more units to be completed by 1994 (*Honolulu Advertiser (HA)*, Friday, 12/20/1991).

On O'ahu alone, the projected demand for rental housing for the years 1989-2008 was estimated to be about 67,700 units. The contributions of private sector, federal, state and county governments were estimated to be 910 units per year or 18,200 units for the entire period; a shortfall of 49,500 units (Hawaii 1991:11). Very low income (earning less than 50% of median income) families will need about 19,500 units and lower income (earning 50-80% of median income) will need roughly 21,500 units or "35% and 36% respectively of total unmet demand for rental housing over the period 1989-2008" (Hawaii 1991:12).

At one point, rentals were perceived as a stop-over on the way to buying one's own home. As housing becomes less affordable, people continue to rent. The resulting rise in rents devours more of an individual's income thus making home ownership virtually impossible for many (Hawaii 1991:5). This situation in housing has taken its toll on the more economically vulnerable and has left them homeless.

Homelessness

SMS Research estimates the number of homeless to be between 7,023-9,417 statewide. (The figures are probably 5,000 fewer individuals than is actually the case). Those figures include 1,238 homeless families. Of the total number of homeless, 37% are Caucasians; 28% Native Hawaiians; 12% Blacks; and 12% mixed (though not Native Hawaiian). In addition, 68% of the homeless have at least a high school diploma. Many are employed. The number of employed on O'ahu and Kaua'i are 16% and 46%, respectively. Twenty-nine percent of the unemployed have looked unsuccessfully for work; 21% are disabled; and 15% have chronic health problems (Hawaii 1991:6, 43).

It is clear thus far that many Hawai'i residents have been impacted negatively by the political economy. They are either homeless or squeezed by the high rents.

Two questions arise: (1) Why is there a lack of affordable housing units? and (2) Why is the vacancy rate in the rental housing market substantially less than 5%?

Two sets of explanations exist. The first, tries to put the blame on government intervention for the problems in the entire area of housing. The second, considers bad planning to be the culprit. The first, says the problem could be resolved if the private sector is left alone by government to tackle the problems. The second, says that cooperation between the private and public sectors could solve the problem of housing.

Conventional Explanations of the Housing Crisis

The Free Marketeers

The Free Marketeers are best represented by Bank of Hawai'i (BOH) chief economist, David Ramsour, who is of the opinion that the fundamental reason for the lack of affordable housing in Hawai'i has been the creation and implementation of the strictest Land Use Laws in the country by the local government. Less than 5% of state land is available for urban use. The rest is divided into two million acres of conservation lands and two million of agricultural land (less than 15% of which is under cultivation). This situation creates an artificial scarcity.

Another major factor in the lack of affordable housing is the costly permit process, which takes anywhere from 5 to 7 years to be completed. "The capital costs alone for that time on a $50,000 piece of property will raise the cost of a house by at least $35,000 to $50,000" (BOH 1991b:1). Legal and other professional fees are even more costly. If all costs were considered, another $100,000 would be added to that $50,000 piece of property simply to complete the permit process. Those costs would then have to be added to architectural, construction, financing and other costs. It would be impossible for a developer to sell such a home at an affordable rate and break even or realize a profit (BOH 1991b:1).

Ramsour decries the governmental practice of assessing developers "affordable housing allotments" (providing a certain percentage of the units in the project below market price). He calls it "a declared circumvention of market forces... and that the goal of affordable housing cannot be reached through such a strategy" (BOH 1991b:1). This becomes all the more impossible if a developer is assessed impact fees (requiring a developer to provide a certain facility for the community).

The argument continues: even if impact fees and other assessments were to be struck down, homes would still be unaffordable. Falling demand or rising supply are the only two factors that could lower home prices. Due to government's strategies of rising personal incomes, it would be quite difficult to curb demand. It follows, then, that the only thing that could be done is increasing the supply of homes. For that to happen, the government will have to release more land for housing purposes, streamline the permit process in addition to eliminating all impact fees and assessments (BOH 1991b:4).

The free market argument appears to be quite compelling. It passes the test of fundamental economic principles. More on that later.

The Interventionist Position

The state administration recognizes that the relative unavailability of land and the permit process are major hurdles on the way to solving the housing question. Ninety-five percent of the land is owned by three major groups: the state owns 39% of the land; federally owned land is 10%; and 39 private land owners have 45% of the land. On Oʻahu large private landholders own over one-half of the land (Hawaii 1990:29).

The majority of state-owned land is undevelopable. Most federal lands are being used for military purposes. On Oʻahu alone, the military has been using 25% of the land. A relatively small group of private landowners remains with most of the potentially developable land. "Large land owners can charge whatever the market will bear or can withhold lands until favorable economic conditions can be realized" (Hawaii 1991:18). The state administration argues, that left to its own devices, the private sector cannot solve the housing crisis.

In recognition of the relative unavailability of land, the state has begun to change its policies. Between 1976-1986 the state rezoned 2,863 acres from agricultural and conservation to urban use on Oʻahu. From 1987-1990, however, the state has moved 3,947 acres on Oʻahu from the above two categories to urban, specifically for housing construction (Hawaii 1991:18).

The state administration is of the opinion that it had to intervene to solve the housing crisis in partnership with the private sector. To that end the state administration had instituted several "new" programs that will be dealt with briefly later on.

While the free marketeers (FMs) are silent on the negative effects of speculation and condominium conversion on the housing market (both rental and for-sale), the state has recently acknowledged the deleterious effects of those two practices on the market. In fact, the Waihee administration has moved to contain speculation in housing through a bill which had twice failed to pass the State Legislature (KHET-TV, 1991).

A Critique of the Free Market Position

In reality, the FMs' argument, that the private sector can solve the housing crisis if given a free hand by the state, is less than truthfull and not scientifically sound for the following reasons: (1) as stated above, they do not deal with speculation and condominium conversion perpetrated by property owners and developers as two elements that have exacerbated the crisis; (2) although they decry landownership concentration, big land-owners are part of the private sector and have much political power (Cooper and Daws 1990:passim); (3) the FMs wish to break large land concentrations through state intervention in order to deny private property rights of big estates by forcing them to sell their leased lands at lower than market prices to small, primarily Republican, haole (white) professional, free marketeer lease holders. This position constitutes an inherent philosophical contradiction added to the other contradictions in the FMs' arguments. Either the state should intervene or it should not; and (4) if the state were to release, as it has begun doing since 1987, substantial acreage designated for housing construction and virtually eliminate the cumbersome permit process and impact fees, homes would still not be affordable in relationship to household income. The median-priced home that now sells for $360,000 would go down at best to $230,000. In no way, can a family with a median income of $43,700 afford such prices. Federal government figures have put 120,000 Hawai'i residents below the poverty line (*HA*, 9/27/1991). This means that the state has to intervene to subsidize housing for thousands of people.

Interventionist Remedies

Aside from federal programs such as Section 8, the state has moved recently to address the problem. It instituted low financing rates for low- and moderate-income groups; Individual housing accounts (IHAs) for first-time buyers; Housing Finance and Development Corporation (HFDC) is directed by Section 201E-10, Hawai'i Revised Statutes to implement a Housing Information System which would deal with housing conditions, needs, supply, laws, programs, and trends (Hawaii 1991:34).

The state administration has implemented what is called "the 60% solution." Private developers are required to make 60% of the units in their development project "affordable" as a condition of getting all the necessary permits and receiving other assistance from the state or local governments. This 60% requirement was increased from 10% in 1988 (*Honolulu Star-Bulletin and Advertiser* 4/28/1991:A6). An example of how this works is the West Loch project. The city secured 491 acres for $17 million; secured all permits; spent $85 million on infrastructure; and sold the project for $93 million to Westloch Inc. to build 1,600 units. Sixty percent of these units would then sell for $89,000 to 126,000 (single family). Condominiums would sell for $72,000 and $85,000 for one and two bedrooms respectively (*Honolulu Star-Bulletin and Advertiser* 4/28/1991:A6).

Since 1987, the state administration has urbanized 12,151 acres statewide. The state is expected to release another 5,000 acres in Ewa and Central Oʻahu for housing, business and other urban use (*HA* 5/21/1992:A3).

Due to the dearth of investment capital, the state has considered changing the 60% requirement, which is now being imposed on 18 housing development projects statewide. The state has looked at relaxing this rule and rewarding developers for building low income rental units (*HA* 5/22/1992:A1).

The state recognizes that it has to move fast in its attempt to resolve the housing crisis. In its judgement, the fastest way is to go for rentals. The state hopes to lower the shortfall in rentals from the estimated 49,500 units projected in the year 2008.

Finally, since 1982 the state has moved to assist the homeless through the Homelessness Prevention Program. Thus far, the Program has assisted more than 15,000 individuals or 9,000 families. However, there remains a significant number of homeless in the state as has been observed earlier. The state has been providing shelters and has recently built "homeless villages," which are supposed to be temporary shelters. A controversy over these "villages" occurred in 1991-92. Robert Stauffer Jr., who was spearheading this effort for the state administration, was removed from his post. In addition, not all sites for these villages were approved (personal communication, 5/22/92).

The interventionist position, which claims that the private sector has been unable to solve the housing question, seems to be sound. The interventionists appear to be working hard to solve or at least alleviate the problem. Despite this, interventionist remedies have fallen short of their mark. It seems that both the FM and the interventionist explanations are incapable of facing the problem head-on and giving a deep explanation of the origins of the problem. Perhaps it is important at this juncture to begin to deal with the origins of the housing crisis.

A Glance at the Development of the Political Economy

The Hawaiian economy is highly dependent on tourism. In 1972 dollars, the Gross State Product (GSP) was 6.99 billion in 1983 and 5.9 billion in 1975. From 1959-1983, the visitor count moved from 564,000 to 4.8 million (Hawaii 1985:351;198). From 1959-1982, total tourist expenditures as a percent of GSP increased from 7 to 27 (Pai 1984:5). Table 1 represents the changing shares of the three main economic sectors in the GSP:

Table 1.
Main Economic Sectors Share of GSP, Selected Years (in percent)

Year	Agriculture	Military	Tourism
1950	18.1	19.2	3.1
1960	17.5	30.9	10.8
1970	11.2	23.4	20.6
1980	8.6	16.5	34.0
1990	3.4	9.8	45.0

Source: Bank of Hawai'i 1989, 7-9.

The GSP for 1991 is roughly $30 billion. Tourism has contributed $13 billion; defense, $2.3 billion; manufacturing (sugar, pineapple, petroleum and diversified manufacturing), $2.8 billion; and federal nondefense, $2.7 billion. The balance is contributed primarily by construction and diversified agriculture. Both of these activities are generally tied to the service economy (BOH 1991a:3). Furthermore, the service economy, based primarily on tourism, has meant low paying jobs; hence, low personal income (which is roughly $22,000- BOH 1991a:3) that has not kept up with the cost of living (Hawaii 1989:335).

It is clear from the above that Hawai'i has been undergoing a process of uneven economic development. Since 1959, the policies of the ruling circles under the Democratic regime have been in favor of overseas (both mainland and foreign) capital (Kent, 1983). Land use legislation under the Democrats was to encourage the restructuring of capitalism in Hawai'i from a plantation-based economy to one that is service based (Kent, 1983). The "Newzealand Bill" allowed for the taxation of buildings at a lower rate than it did agricultural lands. It also allowed for condemnation of land at or near assessed tax value. The "Pittsburgh Bill" was enacted so as to encourage the implementation of the "highest and best use concept." Both of these bills were passed in 1963 (Cooper and Daws 1990:37, 404-405).

The Democrats had introduced a "Maryland Bill" in 1963. It passed the State House but failed in the State Senate due to George Ariyoshi (later to become Governor from 1974-1986) voting against the bill. A version of the bill (also known as the Land Reform Act) that was satisfactory to landholders finally passed in 1967 and was ammended in 1975. The purpose of the Act was to allow people to buy in fee simple a leased lot on which their home stood. The Act went a long way to satisfy the demands of a fairly large section of the Democratic popular base (Cooper and Daws 1990:418). Ariyoshi's vote against the Act in 1963 was primarily due to his ties with the Damon Estate, First Hawaiian Bank, and other Republican figures such as Hebden Porteus. He was defending the private property rights of big landholders. In doing so, Ariyoshi was going against the Democratic Party program regarding land reform (Coffman 1973:91-103; Cooper and Daws 1990: 405-408).

The Democrats were not radical land reformers, however. They were not interested in anything beyond restructuring capitalism in Hawai'i and bolstering their Democratic popular base so they could stay in power (Cooper and Daws 1990:6). Democrat policies encouraged big-ticket development projects that were money-makers for large developers. Henry J. Kaiser, for instance, became the biggest landowner in Waikiki; he built the Hilton Hawaiian Village, established a cement plant, and developed a 6,000 acre residential project in Hawai'i Kai (Aoudé 1993:227).

The Democrats were not committed to the construction of low and moderate-income housing. In fact, their policies of encouraging big-ticket development have directly contributed to the deteriorating position of low-income people. People (many Native Hawaiians) had to be evicted from Kalama valley for Kaiser to develop his mammoth housing project to accommodate many mainland professionals who had come to take advantage of the booming economy. Evictions took place statewide to make way for development projects essential to a tourist economy (Aoudé 1993:passim).

Under the Burns and Ariyoshi Administrations speculation in land and housing was rampant. Another practice under those two administrations was condominuim conversion. From 1963-1981, 234 projects with 10,547 rental units were converted to condominiums statewide. In addition, from 1982-1988, 179 projects with 2,195 units were converted statewide (Hawaii 1991:37). These practices do not demonstrate a state commitment to solve the housing problem. Instead, they have contributed heavily to the creation of the housing crisis.

"While the U.S. economy was growing, there was not much concern by the proponents of development over its negative effects on Hawai'i's people especially those of Hawaiian and Filipino descent who in their overwhelming majority came from the lower sections of the working class" (Aoudé 1993:218).

Foreign investment, primarily Japanese, has exacerbated the housing crisis by pushing prices up in certain segments of the housing market. Foreign investors do not come to Hawai'i of their own accord. Someone invites them here. The state government, private developers, and financial institutions all have a stake in foreign capital—which is a misnomer for transnational capital—(see, for instance, Aoudé 1993:226-232 for a discussion of Japanese investment and economic growth strategy in Hawai'i).

Transnational capital is becoming relatively unavailable. A serious commitment by the state to solve the housing crisis must of necessity address the major problems with the development strategy. Structural solutions such as streamlining the permit process do not radically solve the problem. Those solutions must be elements in a much larger strategy that reorders development priorities. If capital is no longer available as it once was, it stands to reason that Hawai'i should move away from big-ticket development projects such as geothermal energy, a fixed guideway transportation system that is estimated to cost $1.7 billion, a space port, and more freeways. But the state and the private sector bigwigs, tied as they are to transnational capital, will not move away from these projects towards a real commitment to solve the housing question. For that to occur, there needs to be a mass movement to change the political system and the economic organization of society on which it is based.

A Political Mass Movement

In Hawai'i community resistance to evictions is nothing new. From Kalama valley to Mokauea Island; from Chinatown to Nawiliwili; and from Waiahole-Waikane to Mo'ili'ili people have resisted, and sometimes won, demands against great odds. Many of these struggles were intertwined with the Native Hawaiian struggle for land rights such as was the case in Kalama valley. People Against Chinatown Eviction (PACE) were in large measure successful in fighting evictions and forcing the City and state to relocate many tenants in newly constructed low income housing in Chinatown. PACE still maintains contact with many low income tenants and has been fighting against landlord abuse of tenants' rights. PACE attempts to empower tenants to fight in their own interests through helping develop tenant associations.

As the economic and housing situations deteriorate further, as the figures above suggest, people will begin to demand a serious solution to their plight. Indications exist that this has started to happen in isolated areas on O'ahu. People from various tenants' associations have also begun to meet to discuss strategy and tactics. Several meetings took place in 1992 and 1993. In attendance were representatives from tenants' associations in Chinatown, downtown, Waikiki, Waipahu, Windward and Leeward O'ahu. The goal of those meetings was to devise a strategy that would begin to effect real changes in housing policies. Rent control was considered as an element of that strategy for the City and County of Honolulu.

By organizing to reclaim their land rights, Native Hawaiians have taken an important step in dealing with housing issues statewide. Native Hawaiians are roughly 18% of the state's population. Securing their land base would give many Hawaiians affordable homes and would alleviate homelessness since many homeless are Native Hawaiian.

It is difficult to predict at this time the future direction of those two organizing efforts. But clearly a political mass movement is an essential element to eventually force real systemic changes in both the political process and the political economy of the state.

Conclusion

By its own admission the state is incapable of solving the housing question that it had created over the past 33 years. Private developers and financiers have cashed in on the development of the tourist economy and the housing crisis. The free marketeers' position on housing is inconsistent at best. Furthermore, they do not say from where or how investment capital is going to be secured. At a time of less available capital globally, transnational capital goes to areas where high profits are secured quickly. As we have seen, many of Hawai'i's people do not have the financial wherewithal to purchase homes even if the price of a single family home dropped down to $230,000. Therefore, there would be no market for affordable housing should the state decide to release more land and streamline the permit process. Looking at the problem from a technical point of view, the free marketeers ignore the political economic dimensions of the problem. This is understandable since an analysis of the political economy would indict the system itself and the profit motive on which it is based.

Finally, a mass political movement is essential in helping to change the system eventually so it can address the real problems of uneven development in the state.

References

Aoudé, Ibrahim G. 1993. "Tourist Attraction: Hawaii's Locked-In Economy." In Peter Manicas, *Social Process In Hawaii: A Reader*. New York: Mcgraw-Hill, 218-235.

Bank of Hawai'i (BOH). 1987. *Business Trends* (September/October).

_____. 1989. *Annual Economic Report*.

_____. 1990. *Annual Economic Report*.

_____. 1991a. *Annual Economic Report*.

_____. 1991b. *Business Trends*. (May/June).

_____. 1991c. *Business Trends*. (September/October).

Coffman, Tom. 1973. *Catch A Wave*. Honolulu: The University Press of Hawai'i.

Cooper, George and Gavan Daws. 1990. *Land and Power in Hawai'i: The Democratic Years*. Honolulu: University of Hawaii Press.

Dinell, Kristi. 1991. "Coping With Homelessness: A Study of the Housing Crisis in Hawai'i." Masters thesis, Department of Urban and Regional Planning.

Geshwender, James A. 1980-81. Lessons From Waiahole-Waikane. *Social Process in Hawai'i*. 28:121-135.

Hawai'i Business. 1988. "The New Big Five." Honolulu (January).

_____. 1990. "The Japaning of Hawai'i." Honolulu (January).

Hawaii. Department of Business, Economic Development and Tourism (DBED). 1989. The State of Hawai'i Data Book. Honolulu.

_____. 1991. The State of Hawai'i Data Book. Honolulu.

Hawaii. Department of Planning and Economic Development. 1985. *The State of Hawaii Data Book.* Honolulu.

House Majority Staff Office. 1991. The Widening Gap: An Overview of Housing Affordability in Hawai'i. (January).

Housing Finance and Development Corporation (HFDC). 1989a. Annual Report.

_____. 1989b State Housing Functional Plan.

_____. 1990 State Housing Functional Plan (Addendum).

Homeless Aloha. 1990. Hawai'i Homeless Interim Report.

Honolulu Advertiser (The). 1990. Various Issues.

_____. 1991. Various Issues.

_____. 1992. Various Issues.

Honolulu Star-Bulletin (The). 1990.

_____. 1991. Various Issues.

Honolulu Star-Bulletin & Advertiser (The). 1990. Various Issues.

_____. 1991. Various Issues.

Kelly, Marion. 1980. "Land Tenure in Hawai'i." *Amerasia* 2:57-73.

Kent, Noel. 1983. *Hawai'i: Islands Under the Influence.* New York: Monthly Review Press.

KHET TV. 1991. Dialog: Foreign Investment in Hawai'i. Participants: Wallace Fujiyama, Noel Kent, and Gregory Pai.

Pai, Gregory. 1984. "Long-Term Changes in the Structure of the Hawaiian Economy and Their Impact on Employment and Labor in Hawai'i. Paper prepared For: the Department of Labor and Industrial Relations." Turtle Bay Hilton.

SMS Research. 1990. Homelessness in Hawai'i Study. Hawai'i Housing Authority (July 2).

Trask, Haunani-Kay. 1984-5. Hawaiians, American Colonization and the Quest for Independence. *Social Process in Hawai'i* 31:101-136.

Internationalization of Capital, Migration, Reindustrialization, and Women Workers in the Garment Industry[1]

Joyce Chinen

Introduction

The phenomenal success of the Four Dragons (the economies of Singapore, Korea, Taiwan, and Hong Kong) over the past two decades has directed considerable attention to the effects of industrialization in Asia and the Pacific. Other Newly Industrializing Countries (NICs) in Asia, such as the Philippines, have tried to model themselves after these four nations, taking up the strategy of export-oriented industrialization, but without as much success. Critics of this strategy for economic development, which emphasizes production of goods for markets outside the country, have charged that it produces uneven development; that is, some sectors of the society enjoy high incomes and high standards of living, while other sectors are faced with poverty and social dislocation. This uneven development, in turn, has produced a greater migration, both within societies as well as internationally.

While uneven development and migration have characterized the NICs, developed countries also have been undergoing change. Deindustrialization and reindustrialization in the United States have produced regional shifts in both capital and labor, with production moving initially from the industrial North and Midwest to the South and Sunbelt, and subsequently, overseas. The result has been the large scale entrance of goods both from the offshore plants of American firms and from foreign owned companies that have penetrated the American market. The volume of overseas-produced goods has intensified competition and, coupled with the unemployment and underemployment produced by declines in manufacturing jobs, have generated policy discussions and periodic political actions of a protectionist nature. Many states have begun to court foreign capital, and new industrial development has begun to occur out of the rubble of the rusting old industries. In fact, many traditional industries that had been facing demise just a few years ago have enjoyed a remarkable resurgence. Even more important than foreign capital has been the infusion of cheap immigrant labor. Although Hispanic immigrant workers have been the most visible and controversial, immigration from Asia has grown the most rapidly since 1965. Among Asian immigrants, those from the Philippines comprise the largest proportion.

In light of these trends, this paper will examine the garment industry in Hawai'i, that has traditionally employed mostly immigrant and women workers and has recently been undergoing substantial change. Immigrant women workers, most of whom are Filipina, play a vital part in the viability of the garment industry in Hawai'i (Aquino, 1980; Chinen, 1989). However, the workplace in which these women work is multiethnic. Thus, the situation of immigrant women workers will be examined vis-à-vis those of two other subgroups of workers found in the industry. A comparison of the working conditions and the domestic situations of these subgroups of workers may yield an understanding of the difficulties and the potential of coalition building for labor organizing within the local garment industry and, perhaps, for the building of a more inclusive feminist movement.

This analysis will examine what these garment workers have in common. For example, most of them share a common class and gender status; thus, as working women, what are their working conditions in both the workplace and at home? It will also examine areas in which they differ, such as in ethnic backgrounds, age, and generation. Finally, it will attempt to identify areas where the differences among women could be bridged. The objective is to illuminate how race, ethnicity, gender, and class conjointly operate for those workers to have both divergent and common experiences, assumptions, and interests.

After a brief review of the relevant literature on development, women and migration, and background on the garment industry in Hawai'i, procedures employed in gathering the data will be described. The situation of Filipina workers will be described and discussed vis-à-vis those of the other garment workers. After a discussion of the findings, some areas or points around which organizing could take place will be identified and discussed.

Background on Development, Women, and Migration

It is important to remember that international migration, as Portes has noted, is not a homogeneous process.

> It includes refugee movements forced by political repression and by dire economic conditions. It also includes colonizing movements bent on occupying territory in less-advanced countries and profiting from their land and labor. It comprises as well flows of skilled technicians and professionals moving in search of opportunities denied to them in their home countries. It includes, finally, massive displacements of manual labor moving, permanently or temporarily, to meet labor needs in the receiving economy. Many a contemporary

treatise on international migration has focused exclusively on one or another of these flows without explicitly recognizing its distinct character and its differences from other movements. (Portes 1987:53)

As a result, Portes claims we should concern ourselves with four major issues. These are the origin of migration, the stability of the workers' migration, how immigrant labor is used, and how immigrants adapt to their host countries.

While these issues may be useful for developing a better theoretical understanding of migration, they ignore a very important difference in the migrants, namely, the gender difference. This oversight is not totally unexpected; for many years the studies of national and economic development ignored women in much the same way (Boserup, 1970; Beneria and Sen, 1981). Development studies have since benefited from the explicit attention given to gender (Sen and Grown 1987; Ward 1990). A similar examination of women and migration would explore questions such as which women are more likely to migrate, from where, and in which historic periods? It would also ask how those forms of migration might be considered, especially within the development of the global political economy at specific historic moments. Finally, how the adjustments migrants make in their host countries will fit in with their relationships to their home countries.

Asian migration to the United States in the pre-World War II period is examined in a volume edited by Cheng and Bonacich (1984). The collection points out that the economic development of the western United States was built on the labor of Asian male immigrants. Within this socio-historic process, the migration of Asian women was mostly secondary; that is, Asian women who migrated to the United States were largely prostitutes and picture brides (Cheng and Bonacich, 1984; Glenn, 1984). Additionally, articles in the collection attempt to locate the impetus for the migration in the distortion of the economies of the migrants' home countries due to imperialism in this period. As Sharma points out, over half of the immigrant labor from the Philippines in the 1910-1946 period was from the Ilocos region (1984:337), which was tremendously affected by the reorientation of Philippines national policy on agriculture from subsistence to export.

The American and other host countries' immigration policies, as well as the nature of the relationships between home and host countries, were also important. The record of United States immigration policies clearly indicates an anti-Asian bias. It begins with the Chinese Exclusion Act of 1886, proceeds to the Gentleman's Agreement in 1907, and culminates with the Asian Exclusion Act of 1924. Asian immigration to the United States was slowed to a trickle until the Immigration Act of 1965, which changed the quotas and preference categories. That opened up the floodgates for Asian immigration to the United States (Pido, 1986; DeJong, Root, and Abad, 1986; Fawcett and Carino, 1987). DeJong et al. report that the Immigration Act of 1965's emphasis on family reunification meant that women and children from the Philippines were more likely than in the past to be migrants to the United States

Observers have also noted that the latest expansion of capital has produced readjustments within national economies, both in the industrialized and the industrializing areas. While some people may be becoming marginalized in rural areas of industrializing countries, their urban counterparts are being integrated into the export-oriented industrial and service industries in significant numbers. Both men and women are migrating from rural to urban areas in Newly Industrialized Countries and industrializing countries, such as the Philippines, in search of jobs. They are also migrating internationally to industrialized or affluent countries.

Still, women migrants are not a homogeneous group. Their destinations also differ depending upon their characteristics. Thus, it is mostly single women who seem to be migrating to Hong Kong to work as domestic servants (Kwitko, 1988), or to urban Japan to work as entertainers in the "hospitality industry." While they may have been recruited as singers and dancers, they often end up as barmaids, topless dancers, and prostitutes (*Honolulu Star-Bulletin,* 1989; Sturdevant, 1992). The income generated by these women tends to be remitted to their families in the home country and appears to play an essential part in the cash economy of the Philippines. On the other hand, those who migrate to the United States or rural Japan often do so to marry, to join other family members, or to work in professional or technical fields. While these women may continue their relationships with their families in the Philippines, send remittances, and are often the links for further chain migration, their adjustment and survival in the host country is more salient for this paper.

Consequently, examination of the international migration of women in general and of the immigrant women who come to work in Hawai'i's garment industry in particular, needs to be located within the context of global capitalist development. This development affects both industrializing and industrialized economies. It also affects the kinds of women who will migrate, their decisions about where to migrate and their varying strategies for adjusting to their host society (Sassen-Koob, 1986; Kwitko, 1988). It is also important to understand how other workers are affected by the adjustments in the larger global economy.

Specifically, how they adjust to the entry of immigrant women into their workplaces. In so doing, it becomes possible to view and to understand the basis for the diversity of strategies, employed by women migrants, the effects of those coping strategies, and, perhaps, to begin to find common a ground for broader collective and feminist action.

Background: The Garment Industry in Hawai'i[2]

The garment industry in Hawai'i is minuscule when compared with the garment manufacturing industry nationally. Yet they share a number of common characteristics. These include low capital requirements and intense competition over skilled workers, market shares, and access to fabric, materials, designs, and other resources (Lamphere, et al., 1980; Waldinger, 1986; Morgansky, 1988). Firms in this industry are notorious for springing up suddenly and then disappearing just as suddenly, only to reappear a few months later under another name.

In Hawai'i, the garment industry is the third leading manufacturing industry (after sugar and pineapple) and employs about 3,000 people. It comprises over a hundred firms that vary in size. The average shop employs about 30 workers. Some shops employ over 50, and others less than ten. Currently, about half of the shops are full manufacturing operations; the rest are designer-wholesalers or contractors[3]. As with the industry nationally, the workforce of the local garment industry is predominantly women, most of whom earn around $4.50 an hour. The garment industry workforce in Hawai'i is not unionized. To date, there have been only two shops that have organized workers. In one of the shops, the union was decertified a year after winning the right to represent workers in that shop because the owner virtually closed down and left the workers with no work. The second shop, which had a longer history, had been organized by the Amalgamated Clothing and Textile Workers Union. This shop was recently sold, and ultimately the union lost its right to represent workers. Thus, in direct contrast to the situation in other areas of the United States, where there has been a rich history of resistance and labor organization, the garment industry in Hawai'i remains largely untouched by labor organization (Jensen and Davidson, 1984; Fundaburk, 1965).

The garment industry in Hawai'i began in the early 1920s and, except for a disruptive four-year period of Martial Law during the Second World War, has grown steadily. From the 1950s until 1973, the Hawaiian garment industry burgeoned in terms of number of firms, employment, and sales, fueled largely by the growth of tourism in Hawai'i. But in 1974, the industry took a downturn and it was at this point that the state government, through its Department of Planning and Economic Development (DPED), became actively involved in the garment industry. DPED initiated a comprehensive study of the industry (Salmon, 1979) and, based on the study's conclusions and recommendations, embarked on a three-year program in the early 1980s to upgrade the industry.

This program of state assistance has been directed both at expanding the Hawaiian garment industry's markets and at upgrading its production processes; this paper is mainly concerned with the latter. The Garment Industry Training Program (GITP), was set up in a local community college. It reinforced a number of changes already going on in the industry. Demographic and other social changes had been transforming the nature of firms and workers within the industry. A new generation of entrepreneurs had been replacing many of the older firms, many of which had been folding due to the retirement of firm owners and the changing consumer market. Similarly, traditional workers approaching retirement were being replaced with newly-arriving immigrant workers, most from the Philippines (Aquino, 1980; Agbayani, et al., 1985), and with younger local workers trained by the publicly-supported community colleges.

The GITP offered free seminars to garment industry firm owners and managers on various production-related topics (e.g., on legal issues regarding contracting and fabric cutting techniques), and actually subsidized industrial engineering consultations for a small number of firms. GITP also ran power-machine classes (to train many immigrant and refugee women for work in the industry) and a series of workshops to upgrade the skills of production workers already employed in the industry. Thus, the state government's interest and involvement in the local garment industry were considerable.

Methodology

A three-tiered research design was used to carry out this study. Data came from three different sources: government documents, interviews with firm owners/managers (N = 36), and interviews with workers (N = 25). Pseudonyms are used when referring to firms and workers. The findings presented in this paper are based on data collected through intensive interviews conducted with 25 (23 women and 2 men) who worked in two garment manufacturing firms in Hawai'i. Workers in these two firms were selected because the firms represent contrasting conditions faced by garment industry firms in Hawai'i today: one firm, Tropical Sunsets, is on the decline while the other, Casually Chic, is expanding. More importantly, the firms represent the varying levels of direct and indirect assistance received from the state through its GITP and the Community College programs. The direct assistance that Casually Chic received consisted of a no-cost, in-factory assessment and set of recommendations provided by an industrial engineer whose services were paid for by GITP. The indirect assistance consists of referrals of graduates of the fashion technology program to the firm. By contrast, the only benefits Tropical Sunsets received were ideas from the production-oriented seminars, which are open to all firms in the industry.

The interviews with the workers of these two firms were conducted either at these women's homes or at a coffee shop near the factories where they worked. Most of the interviews took two hours, although they ranged from one and one-half to three and one-half hours in length. The interviews were not taped. Instead, detailed notes were taken. The topics covered in each interview ranged from the worker's family background, previous employment, current job responsibilities, and changes (if any) in the structure of production at their worksites. The interviews also sought their feelings and thoughts about their jobs and working conditions, as well as their personal values, family or household organization, domestic work, and future plans.

Results

In terms of demographic characteristics, the 25 workers interviewed clustered into three sub-groups, which will conceptually be called "Old Timers," "Recent Immigrants," and "Young Locals." All but one of the Old Timers (n=9) were *Nisei* (second generation Japanese) women. They ranged in age from 50 to 73 years, but most were in their 60s. Although individuals from other ethnic backgrounds may also be found among older workers in the local garment industry, Japanese seamstresses were the mainstay of the industry's labor force for some 40 years and, as was the case with domestic work (Lind, 1951), sewing work became, in effect, an *occupational ghetto*.[4] Despite their American citizenship, their families were financially strapped; consequently, most of these women terminated formal education early to take up employment to assist their families. Most had taken dressmaking courses for self-improvement (i.e., preparation for housewifery) or to pick up marketable skills, and spent most of their employed years in the industry.

The Young Locals (n=10) were generally younger than the other two groups. Additionally, they are more heterogeneous in their racial and ethnic backgrounds, are second- or third-generation descendants of immigrant workers, and of mixed and/or Part-Hawaiian backgrounds. Most of them are unmarried and living in family situations characterized by chronic problems of low income, illness and family violence. Another noteworthy feature of this group is their training backgrounds. Most of these workers received their training or education from vocational and technical programs offered by the state-supported community colleges.

As noted earlier, five of the six Recent Immigrants interviewed (n=6) were Filipino women, who immigrated to Hawai'i in the late 1960s and the 1970s. These women range in age from 25 to 45 years and are becoming the industry's primary workforce as the Old Timers retire. During the 1960s and 1970s the Philippines was undergoing industrialization, social dislocation and unrest, and martial law. Meanwhile, the United States was lifting restrictive quotas with the 1965 change in the immigration law. An interesting pattern found among the immigrants was a linkage to Hawai'i as a result of a relative or parent's earlier immigration to the Islands. For example, Maria's mother was born in Hawai'i, but taken back to the Philippines in her early childhood. She found out about her American citizenship while visiting with her cousins and decided to move her family to the United States.

All five of the Filipino immigrant women migrated from the Ilocos region of the Philippines, but are a varied group in terms of age, family composition, and educational attainment. The younger women in this group appear to be completing their education in the United States, whereas the older women in this group appear to have completed their education in their home countries. Whether educated locally or in the Philippines, the educational attainment levels of the Recent Immigrants are still higher than that of the Old Timers. Thus, employment in this industry is experienced differently. For both of the younger Filipina, it meant upward mobility; for two of the three older Filipina, it meant downward mobility, jobs they had to take because they were not able to use their past education and training in the United States. Financial necessity and employment leads provided by their friendship and family networks brought them into garment industry work. Another characteristic that all but one of the immigrant women share is their decision to settle permanently in this country (i.e., all of the Filipina have become naturalized United States citizens).

More than just three types of workers, these three subgroups reflect the historic evolution and recent changes in the garment industry in Hawai'i. Therefore, it is not wholly surprising that they are disproportionately represented in the two firms, and one might expect, in the garment industry as a whole.

Table 1.
Percentage Distribution of Types of Workers by Firm
(Number in Parentheses)

Type of Worker	Tropical Sunsets	Casually Chic
Old Timers	42.9% (3)	33.3% (6)
Recent Immigrants	28.6% (2)	22.2% (4)
Young Locals	28.6% (2)	44.4% (8)
Total	100.0% (7)	99.9% (18)

As can be seen in Table 1, Recent Immigrants make up the smallest, but most consistent, proportion of workers in both firms. Old Timers make up a slightly greater proportion in the older firm, Tropical Sunrises, whereas Young Locals are more likely to make up a larger proportion of the workforce in Casually Chic, the younger firm. Furthermore, the Young Locals are more likely to be found in the more technically demanding jobs such as pattern and marker making, grading, and cutting.

Workers were recruited into firms differently. Although personal networks were used in securing employment, the Young Locals were more likely to be referred to their jobs by their instructors, and that the newer firm, Casually Chic, was more likely to be the beneficiary of such trained workers. Additionally, it was found that at least two of the Recent Immigrants had participated in the Power Machine Operators Training Class through the Garment Industry Training Program and had been placed in other factories before securing their present jobs in these two firms. It, therefore, appears that between the training of machine operators and technicians, that the newer firm, Casually Chic, seems to enjoy more of the benefits from the state's interest in the industry.

What, then, are the consequences for workers in these two firms? In both firms most workers earned low incomes. Mean wages were $4.88 per hour in Tropical Sunsets and $5.04 per hour in Casually Chic, which is slightly above the $4.53 per hour average for the industry (Hawaii, 1986) and above the then minimum wage of $3.35 (Hawaii, 1988:346). In 1986, when these interviews were carried out, the estimated necessary weekly earnings for a low-budget household for a family of four was $414.12 (Hawaii, 1984:372). At the same time, weekly earnings in the garment industry were $169.37 or about 59.1% of what was needed to support that low-budget household (Hawaii, 1986:77-79E). In the area of paid benefits, however, there is some difference. The range of benefits offered at Casually Chic is much greater than that offered at Tropical Sunsets. Indeed, some of the benefits such as life insurance, which used to be offered, have been cut at Tropical Sunsets. Still, such benefits as paid sick leave are not provided at either firm, a cause of distress among many workers in both firms.

Problematic health and safety conditions existed in both firms, but potentially unsafe conditions because of overcrowding in the rapidly growing Casually Chic was a particular concern for its workers. Exposed wires, narrow aisles, and fabric debris on floors concerned several cutters at Casually Chic. Fabric dust and fumes from fabric dyes or synthetic fabrics were also a concern for the seamstresses.

Additionally, the women experience stress both in the workplace and in their households. At Tropical Sunsets, the decline in sales has meant that people often have to perform more than their assigned job in the workplace when other workers are laid off and not replaced, or face a reduced work week when production schedules are light, a particularly heavy burden when their wages and benefits are already low. As Angelina reports, "not enough sometimes, sometimes only three days—my pay is only $100 for two weeks—enough for only one time of grocery." On the other hand, Casually Chic is expanding, albeit unevenly. Thus, overtime work is often mandatory and, while the larger paycheck is appreciated, the workers often feel overworked.

Young Locals and the Recent Immigrants, who often contend with greater household responsibilities, are especially affected. While nearly all of the workers interviewed performed most of their household's tasks, Old Timers reported at least some help from their husbands. On the other hand, traditional family roles require the Recent Immigrant women to carry nearly all of the domestic workload. Rosita, who works at Casually Chic, reported that she does

> "...laundry—five loads—it takes about half a day on Saturday—I try to do it on Saturday—sometimes it piles up—vacuuming, same time as laundry—cooking takes about one hour, plus fast foods—[we] have dinner out about three times a week—about one hour a day for cleaning—I'm trying to train the boys, but they're copying their father—shopping, I do mostly after work—I hate to do it with the kids [it takes] about half an hour three times a week."

If immigrant husbands help at all with household work, it appears to be largely when there are very young children involved, not unlike the traditional American pattern. Maria reported, "it's kind of hard—he's from the Philippines—especially with the baby, but now he's helping." Indeed, most of the Recent Immigrants accept and interpret their husbands' nonparticipation in household work in cultural terms. As Rosita noted of her husband, "he's a typical Filipino man."

With such low wages and benefits, hazardous work conditions, and the bulk of household work, why do the women continue working in the garment industry? For many of the Old Timers, work is something useful to do. Many reported that they would not know what to do with themselves if they were to stay at home full-time. For the Recent Immigrants and the Young Locals, however, employment is critical for the economic survival of their family units, and it was among these women that dissatisfaction about the low wages was most pronounced. Although many workers expressed dissatisfaction, there was almost no evidence of collective resistance.

Most Recent Immigrants and Young Locals felt that they would continue to work at their present jobs because of the social relationships formed at the workplace. Most mentioned that they liked the people with whom and for whom they worked. The premium placed on good social relations is not unusual, and has often been interpreted as a gender-related characteristic. However, as Kanter (1982) points out, it is often a reasonable response to the lack of social opportunities for occupational advancement and men often respond in the same way under similar conditions.

How do the workers cope with the stress placed on them by the workplace and household? Most of the women, particularly the Recent Immigrants and the Young Locals, mentioned some religious affiliation, mostly with Catholic or fundamentalist sects, and generally attended church services regularly. Many of them also attend special events sponsored by their churches beyond the regular services such as Bible study and church cleanups. Additionally, some of the women were even involved in preaching as well. These activities supplement the social relationships formed at work and appear to provide important outlets for expression of their values and spirituality.

Strategies for Alliance Building and Change

The international migration of women was linked to the latest stage of capital expansion, which has produced social dislocations in Third World countries, and economic restructuring in First World countries. The Philippines is but one example of nations affected by this process. Filipino women are migrating from their homeland to seek employment in other countries, often ending up in low-wage occupational ghettos. The state of Hawai'i has been one of those destinations, and Filipina are increasingly being employed in the low-wage garment industry. Moreover, it appears that immigrant Filipino women are playing an increasingly important part in the survival and resurgence of the industry. In addition to immigrant Filipina, however, there are two other groups, Old Timers and Young Locals, who work in this low-wage, non-unionized industry.

While the three types of workers in the Hawaiian garment industry share a common status as low-wage workers in a gendered industry (i.e., one that is built on the conception that work is to be performed by women workers), this basic commonality has not proven to be a sufficient basis for building a women centered labor organizing drive in the Hawaiian garment industry. The historically-established unions (i.e., the International Ladies Garment Workers Union, the Amalgamated Clothing and Textile Workers Union, and the International Longshoremen and Warehousemen's Union) have made only feeble attempts or no attempt to organize workers in the local industry.

This study has shown that a major obstacle facing organization is that women workers are fractionalized by different age, generation, and ethnic characteristics tied to historically-related social forces. For example, the Old Timers are approaching retirement and do not have the same sort of investment in the improvement of working conditions, wages and benefits that the younger Recent Immigrants and Young Locals have. Even among the Young Locals and the Recent Immigrants, both of whom appear to be becoming the industry mainstays, language differences and their distribution in different firms appear to work against the two subgroups coming together.

What, then, are potential areas where bridging can begin? Alliance-building across ethnic boundaries can proceed in three possible areas. First, historic education is necessary for women workers to organize in their work settings. Women workers in the garment industry in Hawai'i are not likely to be able to do this for themselves at this point because of differences in their life situations and racial ethnic backgrounds. On the other hand, this is an area where labor organizers and feminist educators could play a critical role. Specifically, workers in the Hawaiian garment industry need to gain an understanding that both Japanese and Filipina garment workers have been and are being occupationally ghettoized, through a pattern of ethnic succession. Japanese women were ghettoized in the post-World War II growth era, and Filipina women appear to be becoming ghettoized in the contemporary period. In much the same way that the ILWU emphasized industrial unionism, and "an injury to one is an injury to all" in the 1930s through the 1950s, they need to educate women workers that they are all "sisters under the skin."

In addition to education on how and why occupational ghettoes are created, education needs to be provided on the contradictory and subversive nature of occupational ghettoes; that is, how occupational ghettoes can provide the bases for organizing. In this regard, an examination of the situation of racial minority women, especially Black women, who worked in domestic service can be useful. Dill (1980) and Palmer (1984) point out that once Black women realized that domestic service was virtually the only occupation in which they would be able to find employment, they began to organize, setting their own standards and own conditions for working in this area. This is a theme also found by Glenn (1986) in relationship to Japanese-American women in domestic service. Thus, the reorganization of domestic service from "live-in work," which constituted maximum exploitation, to "day work," which was considerably less exploitative, and the relative rise in job autonomy are but a few examples of the possibilities for empowerment coming from occupational ghettoization.

A second, but clearly more problematic, area wherein alliances may be built is on women's concern with the spiritual sides of their lives. Nearly all of the women interviewed were involved, to some extent, in various forms of religious activities. Religion is a two sided proposition. It has more often supported the status quo, rather than change. Furthermore, organized religion has traditionally been patriarchal, and women's participation has generally been in supportive, "behind the scenes" activities such as organizing receptions, coordinating flowers for the altar each week, and organizing visitations to church members who are hospitalized or homebound. However, through these activities, they can learn and utilize skills, receive some social recognition, and thus experience their abilities to "make things happen." Churches, or similar social service organizations, seem to provide a more comfortable setting for working-class women to organize themselves for action. Unless labor unions and political organizations, which have also been patriarchal, substantially change the way in which they involve their membership in issues or concerns, churches, at this point, will appear to be more effective in consuming the time and energies of women garment workers.

Finally, if there is to be alliance building among women beyond the confines of the workplace—indeed, beyond national boundaries—greater attention should be paid to the large-scale structural processes that are now taking place internationally. Leading the list is the restructuring of the global economy. An adequate understanding of the various facets of this process can reveal both problems and potentials for alliance building. However, given the sheer pace of global change and the mutability of patterns, this is a formidable endeavor, one in which limited expectations, if not downright pessimism, might well be in order. First, attending to the restructuring of the global economy highlights the gap being created between First World and Third World populations. In the Philippines, for example, capitalist industrial development has created severe economic and social inequality. Women are especially hard-hit by these social dislocations and are often forced to take very low paying jobs, to migrate, or to work as prostitutes. However, as Porio (1988) has pointed out, the growing impoverishment and decline of the position of the Philippines in the global economy has also created the conditions for the emergence of GABRIELA, a coalition of women's organizations that bridges class and ethnic lines within the Philippines. GABRIELA's agenda of social reforms to remedy social abuses against Filipino women directly indicts the political and economic imperialism of industrialized nations.

Another benefit of paying attention to the restructuring of the global economy is that it reveals international migration as both a consequence (or subprocess) of the uneven development created in Third World countries and a factor in the restructuring of industries and economies of First World countries. The movement of peoples, especially women of color, has created new pools of low-wage labor, increasing exploitation, and greater potential for racial and ethnic conflicts. Certainly, at a local level, the exploitation and the ethnic tensions could be seen in the lives of the three subgroups of women who work in Hawai'i's garment industry. At the national level, that exploitation and those tensions could be seen in the enactment of the Immigration Reform and Control Act of 1986, greater anti-immigrant sentiment; and the upsurge of incidences of violence against, as well as among, the various racial and ethnic groups in the United States.

Finally, the restructuring of the global economy has meant the simultaneous decline in higher-paying industrial jobs and increase of service-related jobs in First World nations. As higher-paying jobs disappear, so also does the possibility of the single-earner family. While these are pessimistic trends, they bring interesting contradictions that may ultimately contribute to progressive change.

Service jobs tend to be lower paying, and the employment of women in those jobs has also increased. Not only are work settings becoming increasingly feminized, but also women's expectations about the role of employment in their lives are beginning to change. As long-term employment becomes more of a fact in their lives, women's interest in labor organization and other areas for collective action may be increasing. Thus, attending to the restructuring of the global economy permits feminists to anticipate problem areas and potential areas in which alliances may be built.

If feminist alliance building is to succeed, it should direct attention and expend energies in at least three areas: (1) working with unions to provide historical education on occupational ghettoization, (2) working on recruiting women workers to more liberal religious organizations or similar organizational settings in which women seem more comfortable in participating, and (3) attending to the various consequences of the restructuring of the global economy. This list does not exhaust the strategies for alliance building among women; instead, it is merely a starting point based on listening to the stories of hard-working women in Hawai'i's garment industry.

Notes

1. An earlier version of this paper was presented at the National Women's Studies Association Annual Conference in 1988. This version has benefited from the questions, comments, and suggestions of Emma Porio, Ludmilla Kwitko, Lisa Albrecht, Rose Brewer, Teresa Bill, students in my UH-WO Social and Cultural Change class, and the anonymous reviewer of *Social Process in Hawai'i*. I gratefully acknowledge their assistance although I was not able to do justice to all their suggestions.

2. A more detailed account of the development of the garment industry in Hawai'i and of the process of state intervention in it can be found in my dissertation, (Chinen, 1989) and in Chinen (1986, 1987).

3. Garment firms are usually of three types: (a) Designer-Wholesaler, which designs and which wholesales the final product, (b) Contractors, who engage in the production or assembly of the garments, and (c) Manufacturers, which are engaged in all stages of the garment production process, from design, patternmaking, laying and cutting, assembly, and wholesaling to retailers.

4. Occupational ghettoes are occupations predominantly filled by persons who share certain characteristics (e.g., age, sex, race, etc.).

References

Acker, J. 1988 "Class, Gender and the Relations of Distribution." *Signs* 13, 3: 473-497.

Agbayani, A., Arnold, F., Caces, F., Carino, B., Fawcett, J., Gardner, R., Hecht, J., Rivas, R., Takeuchi, D. 1985 *Filipino Immigrants in Hawaii: A Profile of Recent Arrivals.* Honolulu: A Joint Publication of the East-West Population Institute, the East-West Center, and Operation Manong, the University of Hawai'i.

Alegado, D. 1991 "The Filipino Community in Hawaii: Development and Change." *Social Process in Hawaii*, 33.

Aquino, B. 1980 "Filipino Women Workers in Hawaii." Paper presented at the First International Conference on Philippine Studies, Western Michigan University, Kalamazoo, Michigan, 29-31 May 1980.

Beneria, L. and G. Sen, 1981 "Accumulation, Reproduction and Women's Role in Economic Development: Boserup Revisited." *Signs* 7, 2 (Winter): 279-298.

Boserup, E. 1970 *Women's Role in Economic Development.* New York: St. Martin's Press.

Cheng, L. and E. Bonacich (eds.) 1984 *Labor Immigration Under Capitalism: Asian Workers in the United States Before World War II.* Berkeley, CA: University of California Press.

Chinen, J. 1986 "The Historical Development of the Garment Industry in Hawaii." In Michigan State University, *Women in International Development Working Paper Series*, #113, May.

_____. 1987 "State-sponsored Economic Development: State-Firm Linkages and Labor in Two Firms." Paper prepared for presentation at the Annual Meeting of the Society for the Study of Social Problems, Chicago, Illinois.

_____. 1989 *New Patterns in the Garment Industry: State Intervention, Women and Work in Hawaii.* Ph.D. dissertation in Sociology, University of Hawaii.

Crouchett, L. 1982 *Filipinos in California: From the Days of Galleons to the Present.* California: Downey Press.

DeJong, G., B. Root and R. Abad 1986 "Family Reunification and Philippine Migration to the United States: The Immigrant Perspective." *International Migration Review* 20, 3:598-611.

Dill, B. T. 1980 "The Means to Put My Children Through: Childrearing Goals and Strategies among Black Female Domestic Servants." In L. Rodgers-Rose (ed.), *The Black Woman.* Beverly Hills, CA: Sage Publications.

Fawcett, J. and B. Carino (eds.) 1987 *Pacific Bridges: The New Immigration from Asia and the Pacific Islands.* Staten Island, NY: Center for Migration Studies.

Fundaburk, E. 1965 *The Garment Manufacturing Industry in Hawai'i.* Honolulu, HI: Economic Research Center, University of Hawai'i.

Glenn, E. N. 1986 *Issei, Nisei, War Bride: Three Generations of Japanese American Women in Domestic Service.* Philadelphia, PA: Temple University Press.

Hawaii. Department of Labor and Industrial Relations [DLIR]. 1986 *Labor Area News*, (July). Honolulu, HI.

Hawaii. Department of Planning and Economic Development [DPED]. 1984 *State of Hawai'i Data Book.* Honolulu, HI.

_____. 1985 *Lifetime and Recent Migration to and from Hawaii, 1980.* Statistical Report 178. Honolulu: DPED Research and Economic Analysis Division.

Honolulu Star-Bulletin. 1989. "Okinawan Activist Pushes Campaign to Get U.S. Bases Out of Her Country," May 14.

Jensen, J. and S. Davidson (eds.) 1984 *A Needle, A Bobbin, A Strike: Women Needleworkers in America.* Philadelphia: Temple University Press.

Kanter, R. M. 1982 "The Impact of Hierarchical Structures on the Work Behavior of Women and Men." In R. Kahn-Hut, A. K. Daniels, and R. Colvard (eds.), *Women and Work.* New York: Oxford University Press.

Kwitko, L. 1988 "Filipina Maids in Hong Kong: Servitude and Survival." Paper presented at the National Women's Studies Association Conference, June 22-26, Minneapolis, Minnesota.

Lamphere, L., Hauser, E., Rubin, D., Michel, S., and Simmons, C. 1980 *The Economic Struggles of Female Factory Workers: A Comparison of French, Polish and Portuguese Immigrants.* Conference on the Educational and Occupational Needs of White Ethnic Women, October 10-13, 1978. Washington D.C.: U.S. Government Printing Office.

Lind, A. 1951 "The Changing Position of Domestic Service in Hawaii." *Social Process in Hawaii*, 15.

Morgansky, M. 1988 "Organizational Size and the Perception of Problems and Opportunities in the Textile and Apparel Industries." *Journal of Small Business Management* Business Management (January):18-24.

Palmer, P. 1984 "Household Work and Domestic Labor: Racial and Technological Change." In K. B. Sacks and D. Remy (eds.), *My Troubles Are Going To Have Troubles With Me.* New Brunswick, NJ: Rutgers University Press.

Pido, A. 1986 *The Pilipinos in America: Macro-Micro Dimensions of Immigration and Integration.* Staten Island, NY: Center for Migration Studies.

Porio, E. 1988 "Women's Organizations in the Philippines: A Case Study of Alliance and Empowerment." Paper presented at the National Women's Studies Association Conference, June 22-26, Minneapolis, Minnesota.

Portes, A. 1987 "One Field, Many Views: Competing Theories of International Migration." In J. Fawcett and B. Carino, *Pacific Bridges: The New Immigration from Asia and the Pacific Islands.* Staten Island, NY: Center for Migration Studies.

Salmon, Kurt Associates 1979 *The Garment Industry in Hawaii.* Report prepared for the State of Hawaii, Department of Planning and Economic Development. Honolulu, HI: DPED.

Sassen-Koob, S. 1986 "Notes on the Incorporation of Third World Women into Wage-Labor Through Immigration and Off-Shore Production." *International Migration Review* 18(4).

Sen, G. and Grown, C. 1987 *Development, Crises, and Alternative Visions: Third World Women's Perspectives.* New York: Monthly Review Press.

Sharma, M. 1984 "The Philippines: A Case of Migration to Hawaii, 1906-1946." In L. Cheng and E. Bonacich, *Labor Immigration Under Capitalism.* Berkeley, CA: University of California Press.

Sturdevant, S. 1992 *Let the Good Times Roll: Prostitution and the United States Military.* New York: New Press.

Waldinger, R. 1986 *Through the Eye of the Needle: Immigrants and Enterprise in New York's Garment Trades.* New York: New York University Press.

Ward, K. (ed.) 1990 *Women Workers and Global Restructuring.* Ithaca, NY: ILR Press.

Kaua'i: Between Hurricanes

Jon K. Matsuoka
and
Davianna Pomaika'i McGregor

Introduction

The traditional Hawaiian epithet for the lush island of Kaua'i is "Nani Kaua'i/ Beautiful Kaua'i." The island's natural beauty was highly valued by the earliest Hawaiians and remains an integral aspect of the quality of life for Kaua'i residents. Kaua'i's cultural heritage is rooted in a distinctive Hawaiian tradition and was influenced by a plantation system and the mixing of indigenous and immigrant populations. Similar to other plantation-based economies in Hawai'i, however, the island of Kaua'i experienced a gradual decline in agribusiness and an increase in tourism. The same lush beauty that makes Kaua'i a special place to live also makes it an attractive visitor destination.

In 1982, 733,000 tourists visited Kaua'i. A year later, following the impact of Iwa, the visitor count dropped to 692,000. By 1990, after years of concentrated tourist-related development, the visitor count nearly doubled to 1,119,000. The major resort areas on Kaua'i were Poipu-Mahaulepu in the Koloa district; Wailua-Kapa'a in the Kawaihau district; Lihue in the Lihue district; and Princeville in the Hanalei district (Hawaii, 1991).

Hurricane Iwa devastated Kaua'i in November 1982. Beginning in 1983 through 1990, Kaua'i experienced a rapid period of population growth and land development associated with a tourism-based economy. The rate of growth and associated changes in country lifestyle and availability of natural resources concerned many Kaua'i residents. Between 1980 and 1990, the population of Kaua'i increased by 31% (38,856 to 50,947). The overall population of Hawai'i increased by only 15% during the same period. Some districts of Kaua'i grew at faster rates than others due to the migration of large numbers of people from the continental United States. For example, the district of Hanalei increased from 2,668 to 4,631 (74%), placing it third among the fastest growing districts in Hawai'i (Hawaii, 1990b). According to the Department of Business, Economic Development, and Tourism, four major ethnic groups comprised 95% of the Kaua'i County population (including Ni'ihau) in 1990. Caucasians (including Portuguese) were the largest group (35%), followed by Filipinos (25%), Japanese (20%), and Part-Hawaiians and Hawaiians (15%).

Economic development via tourism is primarily responsible for sustaining a local population through a transitional period (from agriculture to tourism) and incorporating newcomers into the economy. Kaua'i had a low unemployment rate of 2.8% in 1989. According to the 1991 *Kaua'i Data Book*, tourism, including related commercial trade, was the largest industry. The retail and wholesale trade industry employed the largest number of workers (6,400 or 24%), followed by hotels (4,250 or 16%), the state, federal, and county governments (3,200 or 12%), construction (1,300 or 5%), and sugar (950 or 3.5%). According to the Office of State Planning, other economic development possibilities include aquaculture, the film industry, the manufacturing of food products (e.g., ice cream, cookies, poi, etc.) as well as diversified agriculture (e.g., papayas, taro, and macadamia nuts) (Kaua'i Business and Realstate, 1991).

The 1984 Kaua'i County General Plan specified a set of goals that were intended to guide the future course of growth and development on the island. The goals were generally aimed at preserving Kaua'i's unique landscape and environmental character and maintaining its cultural and social structures. Growth was to be consistent with the overall ecology of the island and managed according to established population targets. As of January 1991, approximately 96% of Kaua'i's 353,900 acres were classified for either conservation or agricultural use while only 3.7% were classified for urban use (Kaua'i Business and Realstate, 1991).

Despite Kaua'i's existing rural character and efforts spelled out in the General Plan to preserve its environmental qualities, numerous efforts by local environmental and cultural groups reflected growing public concerns about urbanization and development impacts. Many of these concerns were expressed in recent years, after approximately 10 years of redevelopment following the destruction of Hurricane Iwa. Although the extent to which these concerns were held was unknown at the time, it had appeared as if Kaua'i was reaching a critical threshold of development. Opposition activities were related to resort and golf course development, tourism activities on the North Shore, militarization, the desecretion of Hawaiian cultural and historic sites, and access to subsistence and recreational areas.

This paper reflects public opinion on Kaua'i that had emerged prior to Hurricane Iniki and after the years following Hurricane Iwa. The areas explored in the research included economic satisfaction, environmental and cultural protection, and future planning. These findings have significant implications for future land use decisions and economic development.

Research Project

The figures on land classification, which reflect an island environment that remains generally undeveloped, often invite a variety of personal assessments on whether this situation is consistent with the "best interests" of Kauaʻi residents or serves to lower their standard of living by limiting their economic opportunities. The social tension that often arises out of competing viewpoints on appropriate development, places planners and government officials in a critical position to respond. In some cases, decision makers act according to the needs of special interests. In other cases, decisions are based on the actual or perceived interests of the larger population.

Research is an element that lends itself to conscientious decision-making by documenting community or group positions on issues. In cases where consensus is requisite to decision making, survey research provides a profile of community attitudes. Other research methods, including focus groups, lead to an in-depth, qualitative analysis of group concerns and sentiment.

In the fall of 1991, various community and government groups expressed an interest in conducting an island-wide study of Kauaʻi residents focusing on attitudes concerning environmental and sociocultural issues related to development. The timing of the research idea coincided with the offering of a research course taught through the Masters in Social Work (MSW) program at Kauaʻi Community College. The Kauaʻi MSW program is a part of a neighbor island extension program offered by the University of Hawaiʻi, Manoa, School of Social Work. Twenty-one graduate students from Kauaʻi were involved in developing the study design and data collection.[1]

The primary purpose of the study, which involved an island-wide survey and focus-group discussions, was to provide a profile of residential opinions regarding a multitude of environmental and sociocultural issues. It was also believed that the information derived from this study would be relevant to the island's planning process and that data reflecting community consensus and goals would have implications for planning and program development.

Survey

Method

Telephone interviews were conducted with adult representatives (18 years and older) from 280 randomly selected households. The response rate for households contacted by interviewers was 68%. The maximum error for a sample size of 280 is plus or minus 5%. In addition to the usual demographic questions, respondents were asked for their opinions on a wide range of issues including: (1) development activities and lifestyle issues, (2) an evaluation of government agencies (i.e., Mayor, County Council, County Planning Commission), (3) resort development in particular areas of the island (e.g., Westside, Mahaulepu), and (4) opinions regarding rates of growth and development over the next 20 years. The survey instrument was the product of a collaborative effort between University of Hawai'i professors, social work students, community leaders, and government officials.

Data Analysis

Basic data analyses conducted to provide a descriptive profile of residential attitudes (e.g., frequencies, percentages, means). In addition to these procedures, statistical analysis using Analysis of Variance (ANOVA) were used to investigate whether the means of the dependent variables related to attitudes differed according to values of the independent variables. More specifically, ANOVAs were used to examine differences in attitudes between various subgroups defined in relation to demographic characteristics (i.e., age, ethnic group, income level, area of residence).

Results

Demographics

Demographic data were collected to provide a profile of the survey respondents and serve as a basis for conducting subgroup comparisons. The age of respondents was relatively balanced across the age continuum and the median age of respondents was 40 years ($\underline{M}$ = 44 years). Gender representation was relatively balanced with 129 men (46%) and 140 women (50%). In terms of ethnicity, Caucasians were the largest group represented (45%), followed by Japanese (18%), Filipinos (12%), native Hawaiians (9%), and an other/mixed category (17%). Fifty-one percent of the respondents were born in Hawai'i (36% on Kaua'i), and the others were born on the mainland (39%) or in a foreign country (10%). The average amount of time respondents lived in Hawai'i was 27 years (23 on Kaua'i). The average amount of time respondents attended school was 13.7 years and 64% attended college. The median annual income of respondents was approximately $23,300. The sample was representative of all five Kaua'i districts (Waimea, Koloa, Lihue, Kawaihau, and Hanalei).

The racial composition of the sample raises mild concerns about the generalizability of the study results. There was an over-representation of Caucasians in the sample (45%), which is higher than their number reported in the U.S. Census report for 1990 (35% or 17,712 of the Kaua'i County population). It is also important to note, however, that local Portuguese were included in the Caucasian group. The discrepancy might be explained in terms of cultural factors that predispose some racial/ethnic groups to respond positively to interview requests. Language may also pose a barrier for those who are not proficient in English.

Social and Environmental Issues

The first set of questions was designed to measure respondent attitudes regarding a variety of social and environmental issues on Kaua'i. Respondents were presented a series of statements and asked to rate each one in accordance with their feelings or beliefs.

Table 1 indicates that a large majority of respondents (73%) were satisfied with their standard of living. Only 23% responded that they were not satisfied. Subgroup comparisons provided a more detailed analysis of the results. Contrasts between five age groups (18-29, 30-39, 40-49, 50-59, and 60 and older) found that younger people were less satisfied with their standard of living than older people ($F = 11,29$; $df = 4,26$; $p<.001$). Contrasts between four income-level groups (less than $10,000 annually, $10,000-29,999, $30,000-49,999, and over $50,000) found that the lowest income group was the least satisfied and level of satisfaction increased with income ($F = 2.64$; $df = 3,249$; $p<.05$). Comparisons between Kaua'i's five districts (Waimea, Koloa, Lihue, Kawaihau, and Hanalei) found the Kawaihau district to be significantly less satisfied than the Lihue district ($F = 2.58$; $df = 4, 217$; $p<.05$).

Table 1.

I am generally satisfied with my standard of living (e.g. income, buying power, material comforts).

	Frequency	%	
Strongly Agree (1)	59	21	N=277
Somewhat Agree (2)	145	52	Mean=2.14
Somewhat Disagree (3)	48	17	S.D.=0.85
Strongly Disagree (4)	25	9	

A large majority of respondents (92%) felt that protection of Kauaʻi's rural lifestyle should be a priority in land use planning (Table 2). Less than 10% believed it should not be a priority. No statistically significant results were found between demographic subgroups.

Table 2.

Protection of Kauaʻi's rural lifestyle should be a priority in land use planning.

	Frequency	%	
Strongly Agree (1)	161	59	N=275
Somewhat Agree (2)	90	33	Mean=1.53
Somewhat Disagree (3)	16	6	S.D.=0.74
Strongly Disagree (4)	8	3	

Seventy-five percent of respondents agreed that subsistence was an important food source for Kauaʻi residents (Table 3). Twenty-five percent did not feel that it was important. Subgroup comparisons yielded statistically significant results. The younger age placed a stronger value on subsistence than older age groups ($F = 3.66$; $df = 4,262$; $p<.05$). Contrasts between the four largest ethnic subgroups in the sample (Caucasian, Filipino, Japanese, and Hawaiian) found that Hawaiians placed the strongest value on subsistence compared to all other groups, and significantly more than the Japanese ($F = 2.98$; $df = 4,263$; $p<.01$). In comparing income levels, low-income groups felt more strongly about the importance of subsistence than higher income groups ($F = 4.11$; $df = 3,242$; $p<.01$).

Table 3.

Fishing, hunting, or gathering is an important source of food for residents of Kauaʻi.

	Frequency	%	
Strongly Agree (1)	117	42	N=276
Somewhat Agree (2)	91	33	Mean=1.87
Somewhat Disagree (3)	54	20	S.D.=0.89
Strongly Disagree (4)	14	5	

A majority of respondents (76%) believed that there was a growing rift between the rich and poor on Kaua'i (Table 4). Twenty-four percent did not agree with this statement. The younger-age groups (18-29 and 30-39) were in strongest agreement and the oldest group was in least agreement (F = 3.66; df = 4,253; p<.01). In terms of ethnicity, Caucasians and Hawaiians, compared to other groups, held stronger beliefs that there was a growing disparity in wealth (F = 2.16; df = 4,254; p<.05). Low-income groups were in higher agreement with this statement than high income groups (F = 4.11; df = 3,242; p<.01). Comparisons made by area of residence found the district of Lihue to have greater feelings of economic disparity than other districts, and significantly more than the district of Waimea (F = 2.40; df = 4, 209; p<.05).

Table 4.

Kaua'i is becoming an island of "haves" and "have nots" (rich versus poor).

	Frequency	%	
Strongly Agree (1)	100	37	N=267
Somewhat Agree (2)	104	39	Mean=1.90
Somewhat Disagree (3)	51	19	S.D.=0.85
Strongly Disagree (4)	12	5	

Government Agencies

Government agencies were rated according to how well they represented the interests of the respondent. The Mayor received the most favorable rating (Table 5). The County Council and the County Planning Commission received less favorable ratings. Subgroup comparisons yielded significant results. In terms of age, the younger age groups and the oldest group rated the mayor the highest (F = 2.84; df = 4,256; p<.05). The middle-age groups, especially the 30-39 group, held the most negative opinions of the County Council (F = 2.84; df = 4,250; p<.05).

Opinions varied significantly according to ethnicity. Caucasians and Hawaiians, compared to Filipinos, had lower ratings of the County Council (F = 8.25; df = 4,251; p<.01), and the County Planning Commission (F = 5.47; df = 4,245; p<.001).

Significant differences were also found in terms of income-level. Low-income groups held more favorable feelings for the Mayor (F = 3.54; df = 3,244; p<.01), and the County Council (F = 3.75; df = 3,240; p<.01) compared to high-income groups.

Table 5.

Rating of Government Agencies

	N	Mean	S.D.
Mayor	270	2.02	0.81
County Council	264	2.56	0.80
Planning Commission	258	2.57	0.82

Items were rated on a 4-point scale with 1 being very good

Resort Development

Respondents were asked to assess the appropriateness of resort development in areas where there has been some speculation of development. The results indicated that none of the four areas were considered appropriate for resort development (Table 6).

Interesting differences were found according to ethnic and district subgroups. Ethnic comparisons found that Filipinos favored resort development in each area, while Caucasians and Hawaiians opposed development. This pattern was evident in results concerning the Westside ($F = 3.20$; $df = 4,260$; $p<.01$), Mahaulepu ($F = 6.56$; $df = 4,252$; $p<.001$), Donkey Beach ($F = 2.96$; $df = 4, 253$; $p<.05$), and Kilauea ($F = 4.13$; $df = 4,260$; $p<.01$).

District comparisons revealed that Waimea residents were most opposed to development on the Westside ($F = 4.37$; $df = 4,209$; $p<.01$); Kawaihau residents were most opposed to development at Donkey Beach ($F = 4.37$; $df = 4,209$;

Table 6.

How appropriate is resort development in the following areas:

	N	Mean	S.D.
Westside	273	2.78	0.97
Kilauea	269	3.12	0.86
Mahaulepu	265	3.24	0.88
Donkey Beach (near Kealia)	266	3.26	0.82

Items were rated on a 4-point scale with 1 being very appropriate p<.01), and Hanalei residents were most opposed to development at Kilauea (F = 3.08; df = 4,211; p<.01).

Attitudes on Future Development

The next set of items was intended to measure residential attitudes towards future growth and development on Kaua'i. Most statements were designed to assess opinions on appropriate levels of development over the next 20 years.

A majority of respondents believed that tourist activity along the Napali Coast should remain the same (Table 7). A large percentage of respondents, however, believed that the current level of activity was too much and should be reduced. Subgroup comparisons found that Hawaiians were most inclined to support a decrease in tourist activity compared to other ethnic groups and significantly more than the Filipinos (F =2.93; df = 4,261; p<.05).

Table 7.

Tourist activities (e.g., boats, helicopters) along the Napali Coast should:

	Frequency	%	
Increase	13	5	N=274
Remain the same	161	59	Mean=2.32
Decrease	100	37	S.D.=0.55

Most respondents believed that the amount of hotels and vacation housing should remain the same over the next 20 years (Table 8. No significant differences of opinion were found between various subgroups on this variable.

Table 8.

Over the next 20 years, I would like to see the amount of hotels and vacation housing:

	Frequency	%	
Increase	40	14.5	N=276
Remain the same	189	68.5	Mean=2.03
Decrease	47	17	S.D.=0.56

A majority of respondents felt that the number of golf courses on Kauaʻi should remain the same over the next 20 years (Table 9). A relatively high percentage also expressed that there should be a reduction in the number of golf courses over this period. Subgroup comparisons found that the lowest-income group held the strongest desire for a decrease, especially when compared to the highest income group ($F = 4.25$; $df = 3,246$; $p<.01$).

Table 9.

Over the next 20 years, I would like to see the number of golf courses:

	Frequency	%	
Increase	40	14.6	N=274
Remain the same	170	62	Mean=2.09
Decrease	64	23.4	S.D.=0.61

Most respondents believed that Kauaʻi had an adequate number of shopping areas and the number should remain the same over the next 20 years (Table 10). A large number of respondents, however, felt that more shopping areas should be developed. Subgroup comparisons found Japanese, compared to Hawaiians, to be significantly more supportive of more shopping areas ($F = 2.67$; $df = 4,263$; $p<.05$).

Table 10.

Over the next 20 years, I would like to see the number of shopping areas:

	Frequency	%	
Increase	109	39.5	N=276
Remain the same	154	55.8	Mean=1.65
Decrease	13	4.7	S.D.=0.56

A large majority of respondents desired to see the number of farms on Kauaʻi increase over the next 20 years (Table 11). A large percentage also felt the number of farms should remain the same. Subgroup comparisons found the district of Kawaihau to be most supportive of more farms and significantly more so than the Koloa district ($F = 2.73$; $df = 4,216$; $p<.05$).

Table 11.

Over the next 20 years, I would like to see the number of farms:

	Frequency	%	
Increase	208	75.4	N=276
Remain the same	66	23.9	Mean=1.25
Decrease	2	0.7	S.D.=0.45

Over the next 20 years, most respondents wanted to see an increase in the amount of land zoned conservation and agriculture (Table 12). There was also a large percentage who wanted the current level to remain the same over this time period. Very few desired to see a decrease in the amount of land under this classification.

Subgroup differences were found according to age. Younger age cohorts had a stronger desire for more conservation and agricultural lands compared to older cohorts ($F = 3.14$; $df = 4,257$; $p<.05$).

Table 12.

Over the next 20 years, I would like to see the amount of land zoned conservation and agriculture:

	Frequency	%	
Increase	149	55	N=271
Remain the same	109	40.2	Mean=1.50
Decrease	13	4.8	S.D.=0.58

Most respondents believed that government agencies have done too little to protect historic Hawaiian cultural sites over the past 20 years (Table 13). A substantial percentage, however, believed that the amount of protection accorded historic sites has been about right.

Subgroup comparisons found significant differences according to age. Older people, compared to younger people, held the strongest views that not enough had been done to protect historic sites ($F = 2.97$; $df = 4,252$; $p<.05$).

Table 13.

Over the *past* 20 years, protection of historic Hawaiian cultural sites has been:

	Frequency	%	
Too much	7	2.6	N=266
About right	111	41.7	Mean=2.53
Too little	148	55.6	S.D.=0.55

Most respondents felt that growth on Kauaʻi over the past 5 years has occurred at too fast a rate (Table 14). A smaller percentage felt that the rate of growth has been about right.

Significant differences were found according to districts. The district of Kawaihau expressed the strongest concerns about the fast rate of growth, and significantly more than the district of Waimea (F = 2.81; df = 4,215; p<.05).

Table 14.

Over the *past* 5 years, the rate of growth on Kauaʻi has been:

	Frequency	%	
Too fast	176	64	N=275
About right	87	31.6	Mean=1.40
Too slow	12	4.4	S.D.=0.57

A majority of respondents felt that their quality of life would decline if growth on Kauaʻi continued at its present rate (Table 15). There was also a substantial number of respondents who believed that growth at its present rate would not affect their lives or it would lead to improvement.

Significant differences were found according to ethnicity. Filipinos expressed the most positive feelings about continuing the current rate of growth, and significantly more than Caucasians (F = 3.53; df = 4,257; p<.01).

Table 15.

If Kaua'i continues to grow at its present rate, your quality of life will:

	Frequency	%	
Improve	49	18.2	N=269
Stay the same	76	28.3	Mean=2.35
Worsen	144	53.5	S.D.=0.77

Respondents were posed with an open-ended question regarding the qualities of Kaua'i they liked best. The qualities that were mentioned most frequently were natural beauty and environment, friendly people and sense of community, and country lifestyle (Table 16). Family ties, recreation/subsistence, and open space were also commonly reported.

Table 16.

What 3 things do you like best about living on Kaua'i?

	Frequency	%
Natural beauty/environment	237	84.9
Friendly people/ Sense of community	189	67.8
Country lifestyle	154	55.3
Family/sense of place	58	20.8
Recreational/subsistence activities	48	17.2
Open space/no development	46	16.5
Economic opportunities	21	7.6
Local control over decisions	8	2.8
Other	39	14

Total number of responses exceeds 280 due to multiple responses

Summary of Survey Results

1. Respondents were generally satisfied with their standard of living. Standard of living is one indicator of quality of life. One could infer from this result and the results of other variables that residents were satisfied with their quality of life on Kaua'i.

2. The data generally reflect island-wide attitudes and values that support the preservation of Kaua'i's natural environment and rural lifestyle. There were also pronounced concerns regarding the future course and level of development (as evidenced through concerns regarding a growing divide between rich and poor and a potential decline in Kaua'i's quality of life).

3. Of the government bodies that were evaluated, the Mayor received the highest approval rating in terms of how she represented the interests of residents. The County Council and the County Planning Commission were viewed less favorably.

4. In general, there was a strong desire on the part of respondents to maintain Kaua'i's development status quo (as reflected in the high percentage of respondents reporting "about right" for most variables pertaining to growth over the next 20 years). Most people felt that growth was occurring at too fast a rate and believed their quality of life would decline if the current rate continued.

5. The qualities of Kaua'i that people valued most were its natural beauty/environment, friendly people and strong sense of community, and its country lifestyle.

6. Significant differences in attitudes were found according to age of the respondent—particularly when comparing young and older age cohorts. The age groups disagreed on satisfaction with their standard of living, the importance of subsistence, growing economic disparity, the Mayor, the County Council, zoning of conservation and agricultural lands, and the preservation of historic sites. In general, younger groups held stronger viewpoints on environmental and cultural preservation.

7. Significant differences were found according to ethnicity. Ethnic groups held differing opinions on the value of subsistence, Hanalei River boats, growing economic disparity, the County Council, the County Planning Commission, development on the Westside, Mahaulepu, Donkey Beach, and Kilauea; tourist activities at Napali, shopping areas, and the future quality of life. In general, Hawaiians and Caucasians held similar viewpoints favoring environmental and cultural preservation, while Filipinos and occasionally Japanese held departing viewpoints from the two aforementioned groups.

8. Subgroup comparisons found significant differences in opinion according to respondents' income-levels. Low-income and high-income groups differed in areas of standard of living, the value of subsistence, growing economic

disparity, the Mayor, the County Council, and the number of golf courses. The results generally reflected attitudinal differences based on life experiences related to economic status. For example, low-income groups were less satisfied with their standard of living and more concerned about growing divisions between rich and poor.

9. Attitudinal differences were also related to area of residence. Significant differences were found between districts in the areas of growing economic disparity, development on the Westside, Donkey Beach, and Kilauea; the number of farms, growth over the past 5 years, and government management of resources. These findings generally reflect the unique development experiences and the degree to which development has occurred within each district.

Discussion

Data from this study enable us to create an attitudinal profile of Kaua'i residents. There appears to be a shared appreciation for the natural environment and rural lifestyle and a willingness on the part of residents to subordinate future economic goals to shared values. Residents were opposed to development proposals that might disrupt their current way of life. These values emanate from a self-selected population that has grown up on Kaua'i and chosen to stay, and transplants who were attracted to the small-town, agrarian atmosphere. One could surmise that population growth on Kaua'i generally represents newcomers who possess interests and values that are congruent with agrarian lifestyles and environmental preservation.

Concerns regarding community dissolution reflect a perception that Kaua'i's social balance is vulnerable to an influx of newcomers exuding different values and lifeways. The extent to which changes and conflicts occur is related to rates of growth and the ability of host communities to absorb new people. Kaua'i's moderate growth rate over a protracted time period has generally allowed for the acculturation of newcomers towards local customs and lifeways.

Despite consensus in many areas, there are a diversity of opinions between demographic subgroups. Comparative analyses give us a broader understanding of differential perspectives and related rationales which often serve as a basis for political decision making.

The findings from this study suggest that younger people held viewpoints that were disparate from those of older people. A simple explanation for this disparity is based on generational differences related to life and work history and social conditioning. Older people on Kaua'i devoted their working lives to agricultural production and were often socialized according to a plantation mentality. Although they made major strides in gaining worker's rights through unionization, most major economic decisions were beyond their realm of control. Changing social and economic conditions have offered younger people greater participation and input into the governmental process. Younger people, who generally support the preservation of the status quo, may view outside generated growth initiatives as a threat to community self-determination and offer economic solutions that are considered antithetical to existing social values.

As a group, Hawaiians expressed the strongest sentiment for environmental and cultural preservation and against development propositions. A history of disenfranchisement and exploitation at the hands of outsiders had rendered many of them mistrustful of new development propositions. For many Hawaiians, future development would continue a cycle of change that detracts from traditional practices and is disruptive to ecosystems that serve as primary sources for subsistence.

One could surmise that the Caucasian group, who also espoused strong preservation viewpoints, was comprised of relatively young, new residents who were drawn to Kaua'i for reasons related to natural environment and rural lifestyle. The Filipino group which also represented a relatively new population came to Kaua'i seeking economic opportunities. This motive for settling on Kaua'i may serve to explain their consistent support for new economic development ideas.

Social class differences related to income level typically account for divergent attitudes and values. An irony about some of the data results pertaining to income-level is that low-income groups, who would benefit most from new employment opportunities generated by development, were rejecting some development proposals. Hawaiians were generally over-represented in low-income brackets, which partly explains these findings. To compensate for the lack of disposable income, however, many Hawaiians rely upon subsistence activities. High-income groups, on the other hand, were likely to support growth and development for economic reasons. Kaua'i businesses would benefit from increased contract work and overall cash flow resulting from population growth and large-scale economic development.

Regional differences in attitudes were reflective of island subcultures that have emerged from unique histories and settlement patterns. Community of residence was also correlated with age, ethnicity, and income level. For example, the district of Hanalei is comprised primarily of young Caucasians who have higher incomes relative to other districts. The demographic characteristics of residents living within each district accounts for some of the differences already explained. Other explanations can be based on the developmental histories of each district. For example, Kawaihau has witnessed relatively substantial growth over the past 5 years and Waimea has undergone minimal changes. Interestingly, people in each district (except for Koloa) were staunchly opposed to resort development within their own district of residence.

Development Trends and Issues

In the years following the destructive impact of Hurricane Iwa, decision makers and planners moved to rapidly rebuild Kaua'i in the same manner as before in order to reestablish its economy and tax base. Approximately 10 years later, the public sentiment towards growth and environmental preservation had changed to a point where many Kaua'i residents were questioning the feasibility of new development proposals. This was evinced by heated debates over controversial environmental issues (e.g., Hanalei River boating) and the election of a mayoral candidate advocating for slow-growth. Residents were generally concerned about quality of life issues and how further development and tourist-related and other activities that posed threats to Kaua'i's pristine natural environment would detract from existing lifestyles. An undercurrent of environmentalism and indigenous rights shed new light on sociocultural issues that were never considered during the era of Kaua'i's economic redevelopment.

Tourism development to diversify agriculturally-based economies has been viewed as a viable means for economic expansion in Hawai'i. Economic change in agrarian communities is based primarily on an inverse relationship between declining agriculture and increasing tourism development. The general decline in sugar production throughout Hawai'i has motivated major industries, land-owners, and the state government to convert agricultural lands into lucrative tourist-related ventures, which include resorts, golf courses, and housing for both the luxury and affordable markets. These shifts are also supported by organized labor (5,000 ILWU members on Kaua'i alone) that is concerned about finding replacement jobs for its members. In numerous situations, agricultural workers have been retrained to qualify as low-level service workers in hotels. A host of support industries (e.g., recreation, retail) have accompanied the growth in tourism. Despite the traditional arguments favoring tourism development, a shift in focus from agriculture to tourism had led to massive land transformations and demographic changes throughout the Hawaiian Islands (Matsuoka, 1988). Social and environmental changes that are both observable and empirically documented are the basis for the slow-growth or anti-tourism movement in Hawai'i.

Tourism and resort development tend to change the complexion of a community in numerous ways (Ap, 1990). The types of social changes that are typically associated with economic growth related to tourism development include: economic changes, for example, changes in employment, income, and cost of living (Minerbi, McGregor, and Matsuoka, 1993); changes in use of natural resources as a result of project development, for example, changes in residents' ability to exist by subsistence (Matsuoka and McGregor, in press); changes in community infrastructure requirements, such as the need for increased sewage capacity and more schools; and overall changes in the economic and social organization of communities (Gill and Shera, 1990; Wilkinson, 1984). Other less tangible, yet highly significant factors related to "quality of life" include community cohesion, psychological adjustment, values, and spirituality (Olsen, Canan, and Hennessy, 1985). These types of social change indicators, both objective and subjective, are more critically considered in the decision-making and planning process as environmental and cultural preservation advocates employ more sophisticated approaches in arguing their concerns.

Development impacts on native Hawaiians have included infringement on natural ecosystems used for subsistence, deprivation of vital natural resources (e.g., water), destruction or denial of access to sacred sites and places of worship, and the loss of ceded lands and Hawaiian Home Lands to non-Hawaiian and military users (Minerbi, McGregor, and Matsuoka, 1993). All of these effects cumulatively deprive many residents, both Hawaiians and non-Hawaiians, of the resources required to sustain a preferred lifestyle.

The momentum gained by environmental and native Hawaiian groups was sundered by the devastation caused by Hurricane Iniki in September, 1992. Although the devastation left by the hurricane provided Kaua'i with an opportunity to develop a new economy, based on a different ideology about human well-being, recovery efforts have thus far focused on quickly recouping a previous tourist-based economy. If Kaua'i continues to progress along these lines of redevelopment to a pre-hurricane level, public sentiment regarding environmental and cultural protection is bound to reoccur. Thus, the lessons learned from the political process, litigation, and conscientious planning will be lost.

The devastating impacts of Hurricane Iniki that caused an estimated $1.8 billion in damage in Hawai'i, mostly on Kaua'i, left the island in a position to consider alternatives to tourism development. Approximately one year after Iniki struck, the tourist industry was suffering from a major slump. Hotel room occupancy was operating at about 40%, 1,120 hotel jobs had been lost, and the retail and service sectors had lost about 2,100 jobs. For the first seven months of 1993, Kaua'i's tourism was down 55% at 294,000 visitors, compared to 658,000 the year before. The dramatic decline in Kaua'i's primary industry, which occurred virtually overnight, affirmed concerns about tourism's vulnerability and tenuousness. A more highly diversified economy whose health was not solely contingent upon external factors may have been more resilient to the impacts of Iniki and able to rebound faster.

In the aftermath of Iniki, many Kaua'i residents questioned the feasibility of tourism development—at least to the levels at which it had occurred previously. The destruction had created a new slate from which Kaua'i could redevelop in a more consciencious manner that would allow for diversification and community-based economic ventures. The promotion of a broader economic foundation, environmentally and culturally friendly businesses, and subsistence practices would serve to avert many of the problems and concerns cited in this study. These elements would also enable Kaua'i's economy to stem the tide of future natural disasters or unanticipated social events. A healthy, thriving economy is one that promotes mutuality, stability, affordability, environmental and cultural kinship and a sense of working together for collective gain. A collective sense of purpose and humanitarianism should not be limited to recovery efforts in the aftermath of a hurricane, but be an integral aspect of Hawai'i's economy.

Conclusion

The indicators are clear that if Kaua'i were to adopt the same strategy for economic growth that it did following Hurricane Iwa, the concerns and tensions evident in this survey would reemerge. The results of this study have significant implications for future social and land use planning. Data collection methods used in this study provide for a representative sample of residents' viewpoints and opinions that can be used by administrators and/or planners as a backdrop for planning and decision making on Kaua'i. Hawai'i is entering an era of locally-based, proactive planning that reflects a growing recognition of our unique cultural and environmental heritage. As regions and/or islands request greater control and participation in planning decisions that directly affect their jurisdictions, community or island-wide studies examining public sentiment towards development and preservation will serve as a critical beginning to this process. The lessons learned from the cycle of economic development and natural disasters on Kaua'i, along with trends in public sentiment towards socio-cultural and environmental impacts and, specifically, native Hawaiian rights, must become an integral part of planning decisions and future impact assessments.

Notes

1. The following students who were enrolled in the Social Work 640 research course during the Fall of 1991 made this project possible: Lisa Bauerle, Teveyeh Goldsman, Ray Ho, Gary Hoefle, Anne Hovland, Joyce Imaino, Barbara Johnson, Jill Kouchi, Mebine Manuel, Kimberly Mori, Raymond Mori, Susan Neil, Victoria Oana, Kelly Phillips, Honey Schimmelfennig, Layne Shigeta, Philippa Smith, Gail Stevens, Lisa Taniguchi, Joseph Uliana, and Jack Yatsko.

References

Ap, J. 1990. "Residents' Perceptions Research on the Social Impacts of Tourism." *Annals of Tourism Research* 17(4):610-616.

Hawaii. Department of Business, Economic Development, and Tourism (DBEDT). 1990a. *Resident Population in 1990.* Hawaii State Data Center, STF1A.

_____. 1990b. *Population of Hawai'i.* Statistical Report 219.

_____. 1991. *State of Hawai'i Data Book.*

Gill, A., and Shera, W. 1990. "Using Social Criteria to Guide the Design of a New Community: The Case of Tumbler Ridge." *Plan Canada* 30(1):33-42.

Kaua'i Business and Realstate. 1991. *Kaua'i Data Book.* Kapa'a, HI.: H & S Publishing.

Matsuoka, J. 1988. "Tourism in Hawai'i: An Examination of Some Critical Social Impacts." *Social Development Issues* 12(1):81-91.

_____. and McGregor, D. (in press). "Endangered culture: Hawaiians, Nature, and Economic Development." In M. Hoff and J. McNutt (eds.), *Social Work and the Environment.* London: Avebury/Gower House Publishers.

Minerbi, L., McGregor, D., and Matsuoka, J. 1993. "Native Hawaiian and Local Cultural Assessment Project: Phase I Problems/Assets identification." Hawai'i Environmental Risk Ranking Project, State of Hawai'i Department of Health, Honolulu, Hawai'i.

Olsen, M., Canan, P., and Hennessy, M. 1985. "A Value-Based Community Assessment Process: Integrating quality of Life and Social Impact Studies." *Sociological Methods & Research* 13(3):325-361.

Wilkinson, K. 1984. "Rurality and Patterns of Social Disruption." *Rural Sociology* 49(1): 23-36.

A Green Economy for Hawai'i

Ira Rohter

Postwar Economic Development: But at What Costs?

Before World War II, Hawai'i's territorial economy was based on sugar and pineapple exports, military spending, and a very small amount of tourism. In the mid-1950s, a political and economic revolution took place and a newly elected Democrat administration, allied with labor and business leaders, embraced a wholehearted strategy to develop mass tourism. Hotels and resort-golf course complexes, supporting airports and new roads spread throughout the Islands. In 1960 only 300,000 tourists arrived; by 1970 1,500,000 landed. In 1970 the visitor industry contributed only 38% of the money coming into the state, but by 1990, the $13 billion brought in by 6.5 million visitors comprised 67% of the income stream. Sugar and pineapple once the mainstay of the Isle economy- produce less than 4% of today's state income.[1]

Unfortunately Hawai'i's tourist-dependent economy has created a litany of problems. The environment has been ravaged by rampant overdevelopment, which has caused major losses of green space, beaches and marine life. Water aquifers on some islands are being overdrawn. Hawai'i's economy creates mostly low-paying jobs servicing tourism, while burdening many local residents with low wages, extraordinarily costly housing, and a cost-of-living 39% higher than on the Mainland U.S. More than 80% of mothers work, many husbands or wives hold second jobs, and most young people work too. One-third of our young adults are leaving Hawai'i for decent paying jobs and affordable homes elsewhere. We depend on imports for nearly all our needs, rather than on locally produced commodities. Most of our major productive resources-our larger businesses, our tourism facilities-are owned by off-shore corporations.

Many Native Hawaiians suffer from poverty and ill-health. *Kanaka maoli* (Native Hawaiians) have the highest rate in the nation of certain cancers, diabetes, heart disease, strokes, and hypertension. They not only die younger than other island ethnic groups, but suffer estrangement and alienation in high-growth, urbanized settings. Their unique culture and way of life has been seriously eroded. No wonder Kanaka maoli have the highest rate of high school dropouts and imprisonment, alcohol and narcotics use, and suicides.

An even darker future is foreshadowed if business continues as usual. Developers and State planners are busily promoting and preparing for nearly DOUBLING the number of tourists flooding the Islands, to 11,500,000, by the year 2005. Expanded airports, new resorts, hotels, convention centers, shopping malls, 105 new golf courses, all are designed to meet the needs of 200,000 more tourists per day, and 300,000 new residents who will migrate to the Isles to fill low-paying service jobs. The number of people present in Hawai'i on any single day will increase by 70%. Hawai'i's fragile bio-environment and social culture will be devastated by this massive growth.

Instead — A Sustainable Economy

Genuinely solving the many problems threatening Hawai'i requires that the economic philosophy guiding Hawai'i's development be fundamentally changed. We must reject the any-kind-of-growth-is-good strategies embraced by Hawai'i's economic and political leadership during the 1950s, and followed blindly ever since. We must design an economy more in harmony with nature and human fulfillment, that promotes the principles of sustainabilty, self-reliance, diversity, and democracy in both the economy and government (Ekins, 1986; Daly and Cobb, 1990).

"Sustainable development" includes several dimensions: it is *Ecologically Sound.* The well-being of future generations of humans and nonhumans must be primary. This new economy is *Multiple Need Oriented.* Both basic material needs and nonmaterial ones must be satisfied, including self-expression, creativity, artistic expression, equality, nurturing relationships, self-determination, and spirituality. It is *Indigenous.* Economic activities must be consistent with values that originate in the area's own culture, not imported from outside. It promotes *Self-Reliance.* Each region should rely on its own strengths and resources, as much as possible. And most importantly, it is *Based on Maximum Citizen Participation.* Institutions must be redesigned so as to alter the essential form of economic activities, social relations, and the distribution of power so that ordinary citizens are maximally involved in making decisions that affect them (Milbrath, 1989).

Green Tourism

Most tourists are attracted to Hawai'i because of its natural beauty and the Polynesian culture, yet increasingly many visitors are not coming, or not returning, because they feel the Islands have become too overdeveloped, commercialized, and lost their special "*aloha* spirit." Waikiki has turned into block after block of gigantic high-rises, its streets jammed with cars, its sidewalks filled with people, street hawkers, and tourist kitsch. Oʻahu's most popular beaches and other tourist attractions swarm with people. Maui, and parts of Kauaʻi and the Big Island have also become built-up. Cane fields have been transformed into golf courses, resorts, and subdivisions; once quaint small towns have turned into busy shopping centers. Shorelines are blocked off by miles of resorts, condominiums, and rows of expensive homes.

Attracting "New" Visitors: The Explorers and Learners

Hawaiʻi's tourism industry will only remedy its present decline by shifting its orientation away from mass tourism and more towards emphasizing its unique environment and multiple cultures. Around the world a whole new group of "alternative tourists" is seeking out unmatched natural settings and cultural experiences (Frommer, 1991). Such visitors are drawn to Hawaiʻi because of its magnificent natural attractions, such as Kauaʻi's Na Pali coast, the Big Island's volcanic eruptions and primal landscapes, the Hana highway's wondrous waterfalls and lush green vistas, Molokaʻi's remote valleys. Learning-oriented explorers also want to "incorporate within the travel experience . . . a sensitivity to the culture and values of the destination, a curiosity as to the genuine living conditions of the people" (Richter 1989:193).

Principles of Green Tourism

Environmental balance is one of the first principles of a sustainable tourism. Genuine eco-tourism must protect each island's unrivaled land and ocean ecologies, not destroy them. All facilities must conserve water and energy, and promote the recycling of waste and the use of renewable energy sources.

To minimize its impact on the natural and human ecology, genuine eco-tourism must be *decentralized and small*. It must fit into, but not dominate, the area's environment. It must be only one part of a truly diversified economy. Small hotels, lodges, inns, and Bed and Breakfasts, are preferred to massive resort complexes and huge high-rises.

In accord with the principles of *economic democracy*, Islanders must participate more in the direction and ownership of green tourist enterprises. The "localization" of tourism *decentralizes* decision making and spreads its economic benefits more widely. Minimally this calls for a partnership in management and sharing of profits of resorts and associated businesses, since local communities bear the brunt of ill effects of development, while receiving few of its benefits. At best, the community itself owns and manages the operation. Maximum community participation lies at the root of a fair economy.

Green tourism's *local emphasis* means island employees and products are used as much as possible. With supplies bought locally, more of the money that tourists spend would stay in the islands, not just "leak out" into offshore pockets.

Genuine eco-cultural tourism is based on each island's unique history and environment, not on the opulence and extravagance and architectural mishmash associated with "world class" resorts. Culturally, native ways are strengthened, not distorted or debased. A new class of visitors who travel, often with their families, for the opportunity to experience diverse cultures, natural beauty, and rich learning, will be attracted.

Some Examples of Green Tourism

Hawaiian Cultural Parks

Many visitors wish to explore Hawai'i's historical roots. Some residents on Hawai'i Island have taken the lead in restoring old Hawaiian villages and *heiau* (place of worship), where cultural festivals and ceremonies are regularly held. Efforts underway to restore *ahupua'a* (native diverse economic systems) can offer local and overseas visitors an opportunity to experience firsthand Hawai'i's ancient culture and lifestyle. Native instructors teaching in restored ancient fishponds and fishing villages will teach both residents and visitors alike an understanding and appreciation of the medicine, art, language, crafts, philosophy, history, and religion of Hawai'i's native people.

Plantation Villages

Hawai'i's past also includes the era of sugar and pineapple plantations, and the personal stories of Chinese, Japanese, Portuguese, Filipino, and Korean immigrants, who came to Hawai'i to earn their fortunes. *Plantation Villages* can combine a small working sugar or pine plantation with an interpretative plantation museum and tours, and rehabilitated rustic-style cottages for overnight guests. Tours of the working plantation's operations and mills can be offered. Interpretive museums containing plantation-era artifacts, staffed by historian-storytellers who know intimately the history of both the plantation itself and its surrounding district, can offer unique learning experiences.

Small-scale

Green tourism is best expressed at small guest facilities, with limited numbers of rooms, scattered around the islands. Small inns and Bed and Breakfasts provide a human-scale environment that humanizes the host and guest relationship. Their smallness allows them to blend into the environment, and easily employ solar energy sources, water conservation, and waste and refuse recycling methods. Being owned and managed by families or cooperatives allows island entrepreneurs and communities to share directly in the economic benefits of visitors. Local businesses construct the buildings, and provide food, furnishings, supplies, and services.

Rural Tourism

Rural Tourism can increase residents' incomes while providing cheaper accommodations for people enjoying active outdoor recreation. As in Europe and New Zealand, Bed and Breakfasts can be built for walkers, cyclists, and others who want to get away from urban settings and spend time experiencing the countryside. People staying at rural farm sites can participate in day-to-day farming activities, or visit nearby sugar or rice mills, sustainable farms, aquaculture ponds, and *kalo loʻi* (taro) and rice farms. This provides supplemental income for farmers and gives travelers a place to rejuvenate themselves in a tropical agricultural setting.

The Hawaiʻi Visitors Bureau can advertise small-scale facilities and offer information and centralized booking services. Co-ops and extension services can organize training sessions for rural small holders. Farm tourism has been successfully promoted in New Zealand, Canada, the Solomon Islands, England and France (Morris and Romeril, 1989).

Home-grown Tours

Small tour businesses owned by islanders can spring up. These tours would provide accurate and informative interpretation of the Polynesian culture, ancient sites, geology, history, oceanography, and the contemporary island lifestyle. Visitors learn about them through a reservation center (with mainland connections) that lists culturally-based events and sites. *Interpretive Centers* can be created to assist in researching indigenous culture and geology and disseminating this material to educate tour guides.

Old trails and historic sites can be reestablished, bringing in local communities and hiking clubs for management and upkeep. Cabins and campsites scattered in undeveloped areas can be owned and run by nearby residents. Knowledgeable islanders can lead small hiking, kayaking, and horseback tours into more pristine areas, providing a see-the-country and meet-the-people experience.

Hawaiian Handicrafts

Most tourists want to take home something distinctive from the place they visit. In Hawai'i this usually means a tee-shirt, aloha shirt, *mu'umu'u*, or some trinket which usually is manufactured overseas. These products can be made locally. Alternative tourism draws people more interested in native-made handicrafts. A substantial collectors' market exists for reproductions of ancient jewelry, clothing, musical instruments, wood products, and tools such as adzes, fish hooks, and weapons. Handicrafts of high quality and authenticity can be marketed to distinguish them from the cheap imitations normally sold at tourist stands. Craft cooperatives can be formed to manufacture and market these artifacts, as is done in some Pacific Island nations and in Alaska, Canada and Australia (Minerbi 1988:108). These cooperatives not only bring in a decent income, they keep alive and expand upon traditional arts, and train apprentices.

Enhancing Economic Self-Reliance

Hawai'i is almost completely dependent on offshore sources for food, energy, capital, construction materials, clothing, and other goods used in daily life. In 1989, 95% of our outside income came from two sources: tourism (79%) and military spending (16%). We exported only $1.4 billion in merchandise and commodities, yet brought in $7.7 billion worth of imported items to meet Islanders' and visitors' needs (Hawaii 1989:336, 338). Dominant sectors of Hawai'i's economy are owned by outsider corporations, with substantial sums of money taken out as profits by investors and corporations from the U.S. mainland, Europe, Japan, Southeast Asia, and the Middle East. Isle hotels are among the most profitable in the country, earning 55% more than average (*The Honolulu Advertiser* 4/21/91:B4). Since 1985, overseas investors, mostly Japanese, have plowed more than $17.5 billion into the Islands (Wiles, 1991). The $4.35 billion exported in fees and profits in 1990 represents 25% of the Gross State Product ("Hawai'i Gross State Product Accounts: 1958-1990"). Economists expect that during the next five years billions more of investment capital will flow into Hawai'i from Taiwan, Hong Kong, and Korea as well (Smyser, 1990a).

Economic self-reliance is the key to breaking Hawai'i's dependence on the offshore ownership of its major resources (Jacobs, 1984). This is done by: *(1) Plugging the unnecessary leaks from our Isles* by buying as much as possible from local enterprises; *(2) Strengthening existing business* via business assistance program and exporting more local products; *(3) Encouraging new local enterprises* through programs that get new businesses started and help them survive the first critical year; and *(4) Enhancing citizen participation* by assisting local citizens to gain control over the economy by fostering employee ownership of businesses (Lovins, 1986; Meeker-Lowry, 1988).

Sustainable Agriculture

Why should this chain of fertile islands have to import three-fourths of its food? Hawai'i's farmers had been losing ground to imported fruits and vegetables for years. Between 1963 and 1987 the *total* share of the market for locally grown fruits declined from 40% to 28%, while vegetables fell from a 47% share to 36%. Fishing repeats the same story; in recent years only 25% of the fish eaten here has come from Isle waters (*Statistics of Hawaii Agriculture 1963-1987*; Hawaii 1988:532). The situation gets worse each year because small, food-producing farmers cannot compete with builders of golf courses, resorts, and subdivisions to buy highl-priced land. And Hawai'i consumers now pay between 25-45% more for food than U.S. mainlanders (*The Honolulu Advertiser* 10/7/90: A13).

The "Hidden" Costs of Imported Food

Nor does the price we pay for shipped-in foods include the hidden costs of soil erosion, pollution, depletion, and contamination of the water supply, dependency on oil and toxic chemicals, and detrimental social impacts on human communities. Conventional accounting methods ignore these consequences. Taxpayers also subsidize the environmentally destructive agribusiness style of farming by tax write-offs, federally funded irrigation projects, credits, and commodity policies. Nearly half of the $30 billion in US farm subsidies paid out in 1986 was grabbed by only 10% of the producers-huge farm corporations (Ehrenfeld, 1987).

Large-scale farming also breaks down the agrarian lifestyle by wiping out rural communities (Berry, 1977). What are the prices we pay for the loss of knowledge about the land and methods of cultivation, the alienation experienced when people lose their sense of place and contact with nature? And what are the political consequences of being dependent on huge and powerful corporate farms and processors for most of our food?

The Solution: Regenerative Agriculture

Despite all the drum-beating to keep the plantations in business, growing sugar for export is far from the best use of Hawai'i's agricultural land. Production costs are lower on the mainland (for sugar beets and corn syrup sweeteners) and vastly lower in other countries. Diversified agriculture, on the other hand, brings in *ten* times more revenue, and employs nine times as many people, per acre (Hawaii 1988:333,514; Bank of Hawaii, 1987). Pineapple, while barely profitable, is also considerably less valuable per acre and employs fewer people.[2]

Hawai'i's farmers can join with others around the world who are cutting costs and chemical use in favor of more "natural" methods of farming and planting diversified food crops.[3] These methods include innovative cultivation and plowing methods that control weeds without herbicides; animal manures and nitrogen-releasing cover crops substituted for chemical fertilizers; and integrated pest control that lessen insecticide use. Straw and plant-waste mulches conserve soil moisture and enhance organic content, and crop rotation reduces pests and disease (Ehrenfeld 1987:54).

In contrast to conventional industrial farming methods, a sustainable agricultural system properly *internalizes* environmental costs, rather than *externalizes* or dumps them on others and future generations. Careful soil maintenance and integrated pest-and-disease control require a greater amount of hand-care and labor-intensive farming than simply dumping more chemicals on the soil. What appears as higher store prices for organic food is simply keeping a more complete and honest set of books; that is, paying for the true environmental costs of conventional farming.

New Incomes

Nevertheless, sustainable farming is profitable. Establishing sustainable agriculture in Hawai'i would produce enormous beneficial economic, social, political, and cultural-spiritual consequences. A sizable market exists for Hawaiian farmers and food processors to replace the $2.3 billion annually spent by Hawai'i's families and the $583 million spent by tourists for food (Engardio 1983:21; *Organic Gardening* 1987:14).

Hawai'i's food producers would receive nearly $500 million at "farm gate" prices for growing most of the food eaten in the Islands. (See Table 1). That would more than double what small Isle farmers, ranchers, and fishermen received in 1990. By setting up *cooperative plants* to process one-half of the crop, that amount would double again. Growing our own feedstock for the increased number of cattle and poultry we would raise would generate another $50-$70 million. So Isle farmers would end up with a net direct income of more than $1 billion. The multiplier effect would produce more than $2 billion in total economic activities streaming through Hawai'i's economy (Hawaii, 1988:54; Bank of Hawaii, 1987).

These dollar figures include only meeting our own food needs. Hawai'i's farmers could grow more crops for valuable export markets: flowers and nursery products ($56 million in 1988 dollars), macadamia nuts ($36 million), coffee ($4.8 million), ginger root ($4.5 million), and taro ($1.7 million). That would add another $100 million to the direct farm-income stream (Hawaii 1988:514, 516). Then, if the over a hundred million that could come from *new* export crops, such as vanilla, oranges, fish, forest products, and so forth were added on, the total value for agriculture and aquaculture would come close to $1.5 billion." This would be *five times greater* than the $305 million brought in by sugar and pineapple in 1989 (*Statistics Of Hawaiian Agriculture* 1989:5) . These profits would also stay at home.

Table 1.
Food Self-Reliance in Hawai'i
(in $ millions)

	Current Sales of Local Produce	% Local	Total Market	Potential New Sales of Local Produce
Beef/veal	$ 80-90	30%	$266-300	$210
Poultry	$ 14	17%	$ 82.3	$ 68
Fish	$ 20	25%	$ 80.0	$ 60
Vegetables	$ 30	36%	$ 83.3	$ 53
Fruits	$ 17.5	28%	$ 62.4	$ 45
Pork	$ 14	26%	$ 53.8	$ 40
Dairy	$ 30	80%	$ 37.5	$ 7.5
Rice	0	0%	$ 5.8	$ 6.0
Eggs	$ 13.5	84%	$ 16.0	$ 2.5
Totals	$229		$721	$492

Sources: *State Of Hawaii Data Book: 1988*, p.515; fish data from p.532 & estimates based on "Hawai'i Seafood Consumption," Department of Business and Economic Development, 1989. For rice see note 5.

New Jobs

Producing and processing our own food would create more than 30,000 new jobs for Hawai'i residents now filled by western and foreign farm workers, cross-country truckers, food packers, and warehouse laborers. These new jobs would come from growing our own produce, feed, and rice; raising beef, pork, and poultry; fishing and aquaculture; and in growing new crops. An equal number of people employed in processing locally grown food, and those working in ancillary businesses that supply farm equipment, seeds, insurance, and accounting, would also be added to Hawai'i's economy. And the move to producing our own food would create a group of economically and politically independent citizens.

Policies to Bring about Sustainable Agriculture

Sustainable agriculture can produce reasonably priced food for residents, provide a decent livelihood for Isle farmers, and protect the earth's resources for the needs of future generations (Cox and Atkins, 1979). Promoting sustainable agriculture on a large-scale basis requires enacting public programs that guide land-use decisions and technology by an ethic of land stewardship, favor small farmers instead of big agribusiness corporations, and encourage entry into farming. *Costs* can be reduced by establishing land banks and land trusts to make land for farming affordable; requiring strict adherence to existing agricultural zoning; diminishing input costs by using alternative energy sources, and reduced chemical and water use. *Marketing* is a second necessary ingredient, because a real commitment to local farming calls for enhancing existing markets and opening up new outlets for Hawai'i's agriculture. This can be best done by promoting "Buy Local" program and legislative mandates that require publicly supported facilities such as schools, hospitals, prisons, and cafeterias to purchase locally-grown and produced food. The Department of Agriculture could assist in setting up farmers' markets and consumers' co-ops, and other direct marketing mechanisms.

Income support is a third leg of a viable farming system. Conventional industrial-style farming passes on the many costs of its method of production—pollution, resource depletion, environmental destruction, chemical contamination—to the society at large. Sustainable farmers should be paid for their work as conservers of the land. They should be subsidized for maintaining the diversity and beauty of the countryside, and their efforts at reforestation, water conservation, and ending land erosion. The state should provide capital grants and low-cost loans for innovations that enhanced sustainability, such as buying equipment for composting, handling livestock waste, generating methane gas for running farm equipment, installing wind turbines and solar-powered heating and cooling systems, and water conservation. Marketing co-partnerships must be encouraged. Groups of consumers can directly contract with local farmers to share equally in the harvest. Low-cost loans, income subsidies, and training can be offered to interested homeless and unemployed people who want to have a new start, and for families who want to buy family-sized farms. Farmer co-op marketing and processing facilities must receive financial and administrative support.

Research, education and technical assistance must be redirected toward sustainable farming. Extension services must be expanded to assist farmers in converting to sustainable methods, and to instruct new farmers in regenerative methods as well as renewable energy, management techniques, co-ops organizations and marketing.

These Islands easily have enough fertile land and water to meet the demands of local consumers. Programs such as these are already being practiced on the mainland and around the world (Rohter, 1992, Ch. 12), and if implemented here, would make self-reliant, sustainable agriculture feasible in Hawai'i.

Greenbelts and Urban Economies

Just as agriculture can shift from export-oriented plantations and industrial farming methods to regenerative farming principles, so too can Hawai'i's urban communities be based on environmental and social sustainability (Register, 1986). These "eco-cities" can follow the "greenbelt" model, wherein suburban sprawl is contained within a system of agricultural and recreational lands that set limits to the growth of a city (Calthorpe, 1986).

All new (and redesigned) urban development projects in Hawai'i should be based on a mixed-use, urban eco-city model. Small businesses, cafes and restaurants, professional and government offices, arts and crafts, can be scattered about in a mixture of homes, low-rise apartments, parks, play and picnic areas, sidewalk cafes, and commercial activities. Adhering to energy-efficient building strategies would reduce expensive lighting and cooling needs. Recycling water and waste also preserve precious resources and save additional substantial sums of money for homeowners and renters (Van der Ryn and Calthorpe, 1986; Walter, Arkins, and Crenshaw, 1991).

Eco-cities provide a rich multiplicity of work opportunities. For example, consider the kind of jobs that could be created in Oʻahu's new "second city"-Kapolei-being built about 20 miles north of Waikiki. As Table 2 shows, if properly designed, a good mixture of occupations, ranging from solar technicians to accountants to craft workers, would be available for residents within a series of "eco-villages" and nearby Campbell Industrial Park.

Jobs in a Conserver Society

All forms of businesses that conserve energy and resources would be encouraged in a Green Hawaiʻi. Rising energy costs and environmental consciousness, especially the need to reduce carbon emissions, air pollution, acid rain, and toxic wastes, have already prompted a systematic recycling of metal, glass, paper, and other materials. In Europe and the United States, millions now work in environmental industries. Manufacturers have designed more durable and longer lasting goods; extending the life of products uses less energy and resources than fabricating new ones (Elkington, 1982, 1986; Renner, 1992).

In a conserver society many new jobs are created in the "4R" industries: repair, recondition, re-use, and recycle. The substitution of "reconditioning" for "production" offers real self-reliant wealth creation. The European Economic Community has found, for example, that extending the average life of cars from 10 to 20 years by means of reconditioning creates many more jobs than are lost. Recycling and reusing discarded materials provide a double savings for the community. Recycling reduces both resource depletion and pollution, and reduces the cost of waste disposal. Recycling enterprises create one new job for approximately every 250 tons of materials recycled (Meeker-Lowry 1988:168). Since the Islands generated about 10 times that much waste daily in 1990, nearly 2,000 jobs would be created just by recycling half of its waste. Using the collected materials to make new products would create even more jobs.

Most Isle communities now export recyclables. We should instead close the economic loop by converting our waste into re-manufactured products consumed locally. This would help us reduce imports of virgin resources, increase employment, and add value to products removed from the waste stream. For example, a ton of loose waste office paper can be sold for only $30; but pulped and converted into writing paper, its value climbs to $920 per ton *(Salvaging the Future*, 1990). Micro steel and aluminum mills can use melted-down worn-out automobiles, household appliances, and construction and industrial materials for locally needed metals. Hawaiʻi's non-biodegradable plastics can be recycled

Table 2.
Diverse Employment Opportunities in Kapolei
A Prototype Eco-City

- Farm supply centers for Ewa and Waiʻanae farmers, aquaculturists, and urban gardeners, selling seed, equipment, tools, composters, and doing repairs.
- Food processing (for local consumption, restaurants and tourism). Distribution services to nearby resorts and cities.
- Small-scale urban agriculture, mostly for Kapolei's own consumption.
- Farmers' markets.
- Sewage and garbage recycling for methane fuel and compost.
- Alternative energy projects: building solar panels, wind turbines, and methane generators in Kapolei and Campbell Industrial Park.
- Environmental Enhancement Centers. Research and consulting in regenerative agriculture and forestry, aquaculture, recycling systems, and solar energy.
- Recycling center, reprocessing and related manufacturing: rebuilding home appliances, cars, and trucks.
- Resource conservation: bicycle repair shops, home repairs and hardware stores.
- Solar installation.
- High tech industries, such as computer software design, ocean technology, bio-technology research and experimentation, telecommunications.
- Affordable housing: construction advisors/educators. Local products bought: lumber from Waiʻanae, recycled materials, furniture, reconditioned appliances.
- Habitat Design Centers: Professionals and consultants to integrate housing, parks, and work sites into livable communities. Offering services in legal, financial, construction, and consulting and management, to projects in Hawaiʻi and other Pacific nations.
- Teachers of gardening, home building, self-sufficiency household skills, co-op, and small-business expertise.
- Lumber yards and building supplies, with wood grown on isle reforested areas.
- Small businesses making things formerly imported: furniture, home furnishings, clothing, office supplies, books and art supplies.
- Cottage industries, handicrafts.
- Landscaping and maintenance people for Kapolei's many parks and streets.
- Bed and Breakfast, inns, and hostels for visitors who want to see life in a "greenbelt village"
- Business support services: management, banks and financing, insurance, accounting, duplicating centers, electronic communications centers.

into a host of valuable products: wall insulation, paint brushes, fiberfill for pillows, sleeping bags, jackets, detergent containers, strapping material, paint supplements, road construction materials, and rot-free and termite-proof plastic lumber, decking, and fencing materials perfect for Hawai'i's climate.[6]

The demand for recovered products can be enhanced by requiring government agencies to buy goods that contain a certain percentage of recycled materials. Reports, legislation, and tax forms can be printed on recycled paper; government vehicles can be lubricated with re-refined oil; and public roads can be paved with mixtures of recycled tires. Tax incentives and promotional campaigns likewise encourage businesses and citizens to buy recycled products.

Hawai'i can also become a world-famous source for research and consulting in environmental restoration and ecologically-appropriate businesses. Experts in regenerative agriculture and forestry, aquaculture, recycling systems, and solar energy can serve as advisors to Asian Rim and Pacific governments. Hawai'i's Pacific Ocean Science and Technology Center, Natural Energy Laboratory, and Pacific International Center For High Technology Research already attract millions of dollars from government and private corporations for ocean and solar-energy related research projects (Smyser, 1990b).

Economic Democracy

Political democratic ideals can only be fulfilled when economic democracy is encouraged (Dahl, 1985; Mason, 1982). Beginning in the 1830s, the Plantation Era spawned a small group of Isle Barons-the Big Five-who dominated all facets of the economy and politics (Kent, 1983). In the 1960s, major corporations from all over the world began to buy up large chunks of Hawai'i land and businesses. Since the mid-1980s almost all major economic decisions affecting the people of Hawai'i have been directed from distant corporate headquarters.

A community-oriented economy, in contrast, keeps business profits in Hawai'i, rather than being drained off by offshore corporate owners. Producers' co-ops and worker-owned businesses would more equitably distribute earnings among employees. Co-oppers would also manage their own enterprises either directly (in small enterprises) or through delegates, who decide on financial plans, determine salaries and bonuses, make investment and development decisions, and select administrators.

Cooperatives

Hawai'i's farmers, like millions of their peers around the world, can join together in cooperatives to sell crops and livestock, to buy production supplies, and to obtain services such as insurance, financing, health insurance, and telephones. Fishing co-ops aid boat owners in processing and marketing their fish and allow them to buy supplies, equipment, and services at reduced costs. Co-ops of Crafts-people help sustain quality handicraft production by furnishing necessary supplies and training programs, and provide marketing programs at both retail and wholesale sales. Small businesses can join together to buy insurance (fire, liability, health) and banking services. Consumer co-ops can run the spectrum from merchandise such as groceries, dry goods, books, furniture, bicycles, and drugs to services such as medical and dental care, housing, credit unions, mutual insurance, annuities and pensions, memorial societies, nursery schools, and housing (Abrahamsen, 1976).

Worker-Owned and Run Businesses

Workers own and manage many businesses, large and small, around the world (Zwerdling, 1978). In England the John Lewis Partnership employs 25,000 people; Baxi Heating is owned by its labor force of 900 workers (Ekins 1986: 285). In the San Francisco Bay area, more than 200 worker-owned and managed small enterprises run food stores, garages, bakeries, carpentry shops, schools, and law firms (Tokar 1987:109). The most dramatic success story of a democratically owned workplace is Spain's Mondragon Cooperative, which consists of 170 worker-owned-and-controlled businesses employing over 21,000 people, with more than $1.6 billion in sales. By the late 1960s Mondragon had become one of the most successful industrial groups in all of Spain, being the leading producer of industrial machine tools and consumer goods such as refrigerators, washing machines, and cookers. The cooperative's businesses include manufacturing, agriculture and food processing, a chain of over 200 co-op retail stores, and a co-op bank with assets of $2.9 billion and 400,000 accounts - all run as worker-owned-and-managed democratic cooperatives (Morrison, 1991; Oakeshott, 1978).

Humanistic Capitalism

While community-owned enterprises offer a countervailing force to economic dependency, private businesses owned by Hawai'i residents offer another source of economic independence. A new model of "Humanistic Capitalism" can be practiced based on small privately-owned businesses that involve employees in decision-making and profit sharing. New rules for successful businesses are emerging based not on ruthless competition but cooperation; openness, rather than secrecy; networking, rather than separateness (Hawkin, 1976). Welfare for the future, stewardship of the planet, and meeting human needs can be goals that co-exist with making profits. Many business people want to provide healthy foods, good tools, creative toys, honest services, and other useful products to their customers, and respect the environment and the Isles' social culture.

Financing the Community-based Economy

Creating a communitarian economy confronts the critical question of finances. Hawai'i especially needs to disengage itself economically from off-island investors who come mostly to build high-profit projects, such as resorts, hotels, golf courses, condominiums and shopping centers. Alternative sources for financing affordable housing, community-based enterprises, co-ops, worker-owned businesses, renewable energy and conservation, public marketplaces, credit unions and community banks, land trusts and urban neighborhood revitalization must be found.

It is a myth that Hawai'i must depend on off-island investors and speculators for capital to create jobs. In fact since 1975 Hawai'i has been a net exporter of capital (except for the recession years of 1980 and 1981). This outflow includes government surpluses invested abroad, corporate pension funds, insurance flows, lending by financial institutions and changes in their portfolio holdings, and an entire array of other individual, corporate, or public investment outside of the state (First Hawaiian Bank, 1991).

Many strategies are available to fund and organize community-centered and democratic-workplace projects in Hawai'i: federal and state funding and loans for lenders, cooperatives, and residents; public and privately funded foundations; joint ventures between public and private, profit and nonprofit agencies; sweat-equity and community-equity programs; social investment programs; and creative mixtures of these elements.[7] Sufficient financial resources can be tapped to make a Green economy work, if the leadership and citizens of the Islands want it.

The Politics of Change: Overcoming Political Dependency

For the last 200 years, Hawai'i has been under the sway of a capitalist value system that single-mindedly promotes the kind of "economic development" that creates major ecological and social problems. Once Sugar was King, and caused its share of problems. Hawai'i's economy today is largely dependent on the continuing growth of one industry-tourism-that rampantly destroys the environment and distorts the economy, producing a high cost of living and grossly inflated land and housing costs, yet pays below-average wages. Offshore corporations own most of Hawai'i's large facilities and businesses. In a setting where power is controlled by an elite, it is no wonder that the majority of Hawai'i's electorate do not even vote, let alone participate in decisionmaking, because they are distrustful, cynical, and disaffected. Changing Hawai'i's economic structure thus calls for the same kind of *perestroika*, that took place in Eastern Europe, today.

Genuine democracy requires a political transition from top-down decision making by a small elite, to face-to-face, citizen-based, local decision making. It also means dispersed economic power. Workplace democracy equalizes social power and schools people in responsible, participatory citizenship. Community and worker-owned cooperatives need to become a common form of economic enterprise. Institutions based on these "new" values are working well throughout the world. Whether a "Green Economy" will come about in Hawai'i is not a question of adequate theory or proven examples, but of political will and effort.

Bringing about change requires first the mobilization of existing Isle political activists, and facilitating a new consensus of common goals anchored in the values of the Green vision.[8] Already thousands of citizens around the Islands are involved in grassroots efforts to improve schools; oppose golf courses, resort, spaceport and geothermal developments; and work on environmental issues, such as water pollution, recycling and reforestation. Other activists labor for affordable housing, leasehold conversion, rent caps, and care for the homeless. Perhaps most important for change are the many kanaka maoli groups who are actively promoting Hawaiian rights and sovereignty. Redistributing land and water rights, which lie at the heart of Hawai'i's political, economy will have a profound effect on Hawai'i's governing elites (Cooper and Daws, 1985).

Growing citizen involvement needs to change the political process itself, so that it features initiative and referendum, term limits and strict limits on political contributions, multiple member districts, and granting real decision-making power to neighborhood boards and community associations (Barber, 1984). Community-based school management must be instituted and the Department of Education decentralized, so that parents, teachers, and students can directly run their own schools. Community and Island-wide taskforces must be established

A Green Economy for Hawai'i   141

to push through a host of changes in land planning, affordable housing, leasehold conversion and rental caps, environmental protection, the development of alternative energy and conservation, water usage, family farming and urban redevelopment (Berg, et al, 1989).

Social change is a multidimensional process (Korten, 1992). Ultimately the citizens of Hawai'i must engage in a process of ever-deepening questioning of the values and dominant assumptions of our culture. The very purpose of "economic growth"-that most cherished of modern goals-must be examined and redefined. The single-minded emphasis on material growth prevailing today must be replaced with the values of environmental sustainability and community-what Hawaiians call *malama 'aina* (to care for the earth) and 'ohana (family). Otherwise these islands once called Paradise will be completely overwhelmed and lost forever to the forces of modernity and the new World Order.

Notes

1. The substantial documentation for these statistics are cited in Rohter (1992), A Green Hawai'i: Sourcebook for Development, chapters 2 and 3.

2. Pineapple uses 14% of the land and brings in 11.5% of the State's agricultural revenue.

3. As many as 100,000 of the nation's 2.17 million farmers follow alternative agriculture methods. (Business Week, 11/6/89:76).

4. A detailed examination of these data is presented in Rohter, 1992.

5. Figures for 1987 rice production supplied by Hawai'i Department of Agriculture. Estimate of value based on assumption that Island rice growers would receive 6.93 ¢/lb. for 76,736,000 lbs. now shipped in.

6. See Young (1991) and citations in Rohter (1992, chapter 6).

7. These financial options are fully described in chapter 5, "Economic Democracy and Financing the Community-Based Economy" of Rohter (1992). See also Pierce and Steinbach (1987) and Meeker-Lowry (1988).

8. See Rohter (1992, chapters 8, 10-12).

References

Abrahamsen, Martin. 1976. *Cooperative Business Enterprise.* New York: McGraw-Hill.

Bank of Hawai'i. 1987 *Annual Economic Report.* Honolulu: BOH.

Barber, Benjamin. 1984. *Strong Democracy.* Berkeley: University of California Press.

Berg, Peter, B. Magilavi and S. Zuckerman. 1986. *A Green City Program.* San Francisco: Planet Drum.

Berry, Wendell. 1977. *The Unsettling of America.* New York: Avon Books.

Calthorpe, Peter. 1986. "A Short History of Twentieth Century New Towns." In Sim Van der Ryn and Peter Calthorpe, *Sustainable Communities: A New Design Synthesis for Cities, Suburbs, and Towns.* San Francisco: Sierra Club Books

Cooper, George and Gavan Daws. 1985. *Land and Power in Hawai'i: The Democratic Years.* Honolulu: Benchmark Press.

Cox, W. and M.D. Atkins. 1979. *Agricultural Ecology.* San Francisco: W.H. Freeman.

Dahl, Robert. 1985. *A Preface to Economic Democracy.* Berkeley: University of California Press.

Daly, Herman E. and John B. Cobb. 1990. *For the Common Good: Redirecting the Economy Towards Community, the Environment, and a Sustainable Future.* Boston: Beacon Press.

Ehrenfeld, David. 1987. "Sustainable Agriculture Takes Root In America's Countryside," *Technology Review* July:57.

Ekins, Paul (ed.). 1986. *The Living Economy: A New Economics in the Making.* London and New York: Routledge and Kegan Paul.

Elkington, John. 1982. *Seven Bridges to the Future: Industrial Growth Points for a Sustainable Economy.* London: World Conservation Strategy.

Elkington, John. 1986. "The Sunrise Seven." In Paul Ekins (ed.), *The Living Economy: A New Economics in the Making* (p. 258). London and New York: Routledge and Kegan Paul.

Engardio, Pete. 1983. "The Practice and Promise of Organic Farming," *Food Monitor* Jan./Feb.:21.

First Hawaiian Bank. 1991 "Is Hawai'i Short of Capital?" *Economic Indicators* (May/June): 3-4.

Frommer, Authur. 1991. *New World of Travel: A Guide to Alternative Vacations in America and Throughout the World.* New York: Prentice-Hall.

Hawaii. Department of Agriculture. 1990. *Statistics of Hawaiian Agriculture*, p.5.

Hawaii. Department of Business and Economic Development. 1991. "Hawai'i Gross State Product Accounts: 1958-1990."

Hawaii. Department of Business, Economic Development and Tourism. 1988. *State of Hawai'i Data Book.*

_____. 1989. *State of Hawai'i Data Book.*

Hawkin, Paul. 1976. "Principles of New Age Capitalism," *Briarpatch Review* (San Francisco) Fall.

Honolulu Advertiser. 1990, 10/7:A13.

_____. 1991, 4/21:B4.

Institute for Local Self-Reliance. 1990. *Salvaging the Future: Waste-Based Production.* Washington, D.C.

Jacobs, Jane. 1984. *Cities and the Wealth of Nations: Principles of Economic Life.* New York: Vintage Books.

Kent, Noel. 1983. *Hawaii: Islands Under the Influence.* New York: Monthly Review Press.

Korten, Francis. 1990. *Getting to the 21st Century: Voluntary Action and the Global Agenda.* West Hartford, CT: Kumarian Press.

Lovins, Hunter. 1986. "Four Steps to Self-Reliance." *Context* 14 (Autumn).

Mason, Ronald. 1982. *Participatory and Workplace Democracy: A Theoretical Development in Critique of Liberalism.* Carbondale: Southern Illinois University Press.

Meeker-Lowry, Susan. 1988. *Economics As If the Earth Really Mattered: A Catalyst Guide to Socially Conscious Investing.* Philadelphia: New Society Publishers.

Milbrath, Lester. 1989. *Envisioning a Sustainable Society.* Albany: State University of New York Press.

Minerbi, Luciano. 1988. *Alternative Forms of Tourism in the Coastal Zone: Searching for Responsible Tourism in Hawai'i.* Newport, OR: National Coastal Research and Development Institute.

Morris, Haydon and Michael Romeril. 1986. "Farm Tourism in England's Peak National Park." *The Environmentalist* 6(2):105-110

Morrison, Roy. 1991. *We Build the Road as We Travel: Mondragon, A Cooperative Social System.* Santa Cruz, CA: New Society Publishers.

Oakeshott, Robert. 1978. *The Case of Workers' Co-ops.* Boston: Routledge and Kegan Paul.

Organic Gardening. 1987. 34(7) (October).

Pierce, Neal and Steinbach, Carol. 1987. *Corrective Capitalism: The Rise of America's Community Development Corporations.* New York: Ford Foundation.

Register, Richard. 1986. *Ecocity Berkeley: Building Cities for a Healthy Future.* Berkeley, CA: North Atlantic Books.

Renner, Michael. 1992. "Creating Sustainable Jobs in Industrial Countries." In L. Brown, A. Durning, C. Flavin, H. French, J. Jacobson, M. Lowe, S. Postel, and M. Renner. 1992. *State of the World 1992* (pp. 127-187). New York: W.W. Norton.

Richter, Linda. 1989. *The Politics of Tourism in Asia.* Honolulu: University of Hawai'i Press.

Rohter, Ira. 1990. "Dwelling on the Land: Sustainable Agriculture in Hawai'i." Green Working Papers, Dept of Political Science, University of Hawai'i.

_____. 1992. *A Green Hawai'i: Sourcebook for Development Alternatives.* Honolulu: Nā Kāne O Ka Malo Press. (P.O. Box 970, Waipahu, HI 96797)

Smyser, A.A. 1990a. "Other Asian Investors May Follow Japanese Here." *Honolulu Star-Bulletin*, 8/9:A9.

_____. 1990b. *Hawai'i as an East-West Bridge: A Survey of the Economic Value of Non-Tourist International Activities in Hawai'i.* Honolulu: East-West Center.

Tokar, Brian. 1987. *The Green Alternative: Creating an Ecological Future.* San Pedro, CA: R. and E. Miles.

Van der Ryn, Sim and Peter Calthorpe. 1986. *Sustainable Communities: A New Design Synthesis for Cities, Suburbs, and Towns.* San Francisco: Sierra Club Books.

Walter, Bob, Lois Arkin, and Richard Crenshaw. 1991. *Sustainable Cities: Concepts and Strategies for Eco-city Development.* Los Angeles: Eco-Home Media.

Wiles, Greg. 1991. "Investment Totals Very Hard to Figure." *Honolulu Advertiser*, 11/24:A1.

Young, John. 1991. "Reducing Waste, Saving Materials." In L. Brown, A. Durning, C. Flavin, H. French, J. Jacobson, N. Lenssen, M. Lowe, S. Postel, M. Renner, J. Ryan, L. Starke, and J. Young. 1991. *State of the World 1991* (pp. 39-55). New York: W.W. Norton.

Zwerdling, Daniel. 1978. *Democracy at Work: A guide to Workplace Ownership, Participation and Self-Management Experiments in the United States and Europe.* Washington, D.C.: Association for Self-Management.

Sustainability Versus Growth in Hawai'i[1]

Luciano Minerbi

The development pattern in Hawai'i is determined by an export-led growth model based on real estate investment and speculation, which results in excessive population growth through immigration and the suburbanization of the Island of O'ahu. Past attempts to look at carrying capacity, cumulative project impacts, and alternative futures did not result in sustainable development.[2] Instead, a booming economy, developers' interests, and government policies have made suburbanization possible in the last 20 years. Massive redesignation from agriculture to urban use has taken place in Ewa and Central O'ahu.[3]

Economic growth in Hawai'i was prompted by several major factors: the availability of foreign and outside capital for investment, the development of large tracts of lands owned by major estates, redesignation and permit approval by government, and support for the notion that jobs and income are created by economic growth. The results are coastal resort developments, luxury housing subdivisions, exclusive golf courses and public infrastructure projects—a giant real estate operation—rather than a sound development plan. In the plantation era sugar and pineapple were the cash crops for exports. Today the cash crops are luxury houses, hotels, and resorts, the new plantations. But the undesirable impacts of mega-resorts can no longer be ignored (Minerbi, 1992).

The booming financial and real estate activity has left little time to reflect on the current growth-led model for Hawai'i, its appropriateness, present affordability, and long-term sustainability. An examination must be made to see whether basic needs are met and whether the island ecology is protected in the quest for suitable jobs and affordable housing for local people. Sustainable development and carrying capacity on the Island of O'ahu must be studied at various levels of analysis:

1. **Population Growth and Jobs**: What is the population projection basis for redesignation, resort, and subdivision development? Is the population growth projection predominantly based on growth by immigration? Is the population growth the result of jobs created beyond what the local labor force needs, wants, or is qualified for? Are there inequalities in the job market along ethnic lines? Or are jobs being created instead to meet the real needs of the local labor force and in tune with education and training programs to increase qualifications and competitiveness of local workers?

2. **Quality of Life**: Is the quality of life improving for local people? Is the cost of living being kept in check? Is the government subsidizing speculative private sector development? Is the ability to pay for basic needs keeping up with inflation? Are individual and families becoming more independent and self-reliant? Are special need residents, young, old, sick, and handicapped taken care of? Are production, distribution, and consumption patterns in line with ecological principles?

3. **Irreplaceable Cultural and Environmental Losses**: What is the extent and rate of irretrievable losses to the environment and to the ability of future generations to use land for open space, cultural pursuits, and agriculture, which is triggered by population growth and subdivision development? Is there a plan for the protection and perpetuation of Hawaiian culture and the Hawaiian people?

4. **Ecological Resilience**: To what extent is the ability of the environment impeded by development so that ecosystem integrity, genetic diversity, reproduction capacity of plants and wildlife are impaired? To what extent are suburbanization and land development interfering with the functioning of natural processes, thereby endangering the resilience of the natural processes on land, air, and water? Is there a planned vision of the island ecosystem?

Although some of the above questions have been addressed in Hawai'i, policy derivation toward sustainable development has not been adequately sustained.

The Recent Situation

Quality of Life and Economic Growth

The distribution of household income has deteriorated over the years with lower- and medium-income families increasing and upper-income families declining. The cost of living in Hawai'i grew six time faster in the 1980s than household income. The poverty status of persons has increased by 3% between 1980 and 1990, reaching a level of 121,000 people or 11% in 1990. There are also ethnic concerns: civilian unemployment among ethnic groups was greater than among the total resident population for Hawaiians and Filipinos; Hawaiians ranked the highest on O'ahu (Hawaii, 1988). One conclusion is that Hawai'i has experienced increasing relative poverty with unprecedented wealth: aggregate wealth has increased but distribution of that wealth has deteriorated (Pai, 1989).

The economy of the State of Hawai'i has been apparently growing. The gross state product (GSP) has increased 14 times between 1960 and 1990, but only 3.7 times in constant dollars. It reached a level of 29 billion dollars in 1992 corresponding to a GSP per capita of $25,288 in current dollars and of $16,458 in constant dollars.4 Annual visitor personal expenditures have increased 71 times and the annual number of visitors 24 times between 1960 and 1990. Visitor personal expenditures passed the 9 billion dollar mark and state tax receipts reached 4 billion in 1990. Total personal income had increased 15 times between 1960 and 1990, reaching $24 billion in 1992; per capita personal income increased 8.8 times to the 1990 level of $20,552 and median family cash income 6.7 times (Hawaii, 1992). But, while the GSP per capita measured in current dollars increased 91% between 1980 and 1990, the GSP per capita measured in constant dollars shows an increase of only 24%; meanwhile the consumer price index increased 66% and the state and county public bonded debt increased 138% in the same period, reaching more than 5 billion in 1991.5 The per capita income growth rate, adjusted for inflation, was only 1.7% for 1990. The per capita personal income between 1981 and 1991 increased 85% in current dollars, but only 14% in constant dollars, while the Honolulu Consumer price index increased 60% in the same years. The state's growing economy is associated with a deteriorating quality of life and entrenched inequalities among social classes. The labor force change from craft to services resulted in the long-term fall of the wage structure (Pai, 1989). In 1991 the hypothetical intermediate budget for a family of four reached $55,833, being 37.7% higher than the U.S. national average, 80.5% higher for personal income tax and 60% higher for shelter cost. The result is that: (a) Hawai'i has one of the highest rates of multi-wage earner families, with a high proportion of women in the labor force, particularly in service occupations; and (b) many residents leave the islands.[6]

Population Increase and Economic Growth

Population growth by immigration was the pattern in the plantation era and it is the pattern in the tourism economy. Net migration accounted for 55.6% of overall civilian growth in 1970-1980 and 48% or a net in-migration of 71,000 in 1980-1990 (Hawaii, 1987 and 1992). Migration is responsible for a large part of Hawaii's population growth, albeit less so than a decade or two ago. Annual arrivals have run between 18,000 and 25,000 in recent years with three-fourths of the civilian in-migrants coming from the mainland and one fourth from abroad (Hawaii, 1987).

Hawai'i needs a model of sustainable development, not the current one based on population growth through in-migration. Population and economic projections are periodically done by the State of Hawai'i (Hawaii, 1988). These population projections have been *de facto* used by the state and the county for planning purposes. Using population figures without substantial debate would confuse projection, prevision, and objectives. Thus, mixing up "what is extrapolated" and "what is probable" with "what is desirable" so that what is likely to occur will happen, and what will happen is what people should learn to expect—and accept—as inevitable. Using the population projections as policy objectives uncritically is unwarranted, as the authors of the state's projections clearly implied in their own introduction:

a. The population projections are based . . ."on their likelihood, not their level of desirability. . . ."

b. The population projections ". . . do not represent either a certain or unalterable future."

c. "Moreover, if the projections suggest future conditions which the community determines to be undesirable, policies can be formulated to help bring about a more desirable future; thus projections, regardless of their potential accuracy are not unalterable." (Hawaii, 1988)

These population projections were based on "powerful economic and demographic forces, which are not subject to either easy or rapid manipulation." But these projections are inappropriate because they are based on a model that mechanically responds to developers' proposals, instead of focusing attention on local employment needs and ecology. The result is population growth by immigration. As stated by DBED:

. . . the model is based on fairly straightforward concepts of regional growth . . . a region's exports are the driving force of regional economic activity. In Hawai'i, the principle exports are visitor services, national activity and agriculture . . . . Thus, if the natural increase in Hawaii's population, as projected by the demographic model, is inadequate to meet the economic projection of economic activity, increased net immigration will be projected until the gap in labor supply and demand is closed (Hawaii, 1988).

In other words, as long as outside capital sees investment opportunities in Hawai'i for speculative land ventures, luxury hotels, high-income housing, and exclusive golf courses; as long as landed estates provide the land; as long as government military operations grow in Hawai'i; as long as agribusiness expands its operation, a portion of the job and housing created will be filled by immigrants from outside the islands. This is hardly consistent with the concept of a steady-state sustainable development that postulates some closure in the economy.

Sustainability Versus Growth in Hawai'i 149

The state's model, based on growth trends for tourism, supporting industries and diversified agriculture, generated population estimates doubling the 1985 de facto population of Hawai'i, Kauai, and Maui Counties and increasing the de facto population of O'ahu by 27 % to 1,094,700 people in the year 2010 (Hawaii, 1988).

State law spells out objectives and policies for population growth management and for land and water resources in a coordinated manner. The Hawai'i Revised Statutes also charges government to:

> Encourage research activities and public awareness programs to foster an understanding of Hawaii's limited capacity to accommodate population needs and to address concerns resulting from an increase in Hawaii's population. (Hawaii. *Hawaii Revised Statutes*, 1993)

This language is weak: there is no real strategy to change from the self-fulfilling prophecy of excessive and continuous population growth to a more desirable model of development for Hawai'i. The state and county plans are designed to accommodate these population estimates as if they were desirable targets. This is evident by expansion and renovation of airports and ports, by amendments to redesignate to urban uses, and the building of more highways and infrastructure.

The County General Plan must conform to the State's Plan and State's Functional Plans, and this conformance is interpreted to include the State's population projections, although it is not "literally" required in the Hawai'i Revised Statutes. The City and County Charter mentions that the County General Plan shall spell out "the most desirable population densities within the several areas of the city," but it does not define the overall population level, which is simply lifted from the State's projections (Charter Commission, 1973). In fact, the City and County General Plan of 1988 had adopted, as its own population policy, the geographic distribution of residential population as a percentage of the State's island-wide population projection for the year 2005. The total population of O'ahu by the year 2005 ranges between 906,900 to 1,002,200 people (Honolulu. Dept. of General Planning, 1988). The acritical use of the State's population projections by the City and County is documented in the preamble to the General Plan:

> One of the key assumptions underlying many of the General Plan objectives and policies is anticipated future population growth for the Island of O'ahu as projected by the State Department of Planning and Economic Development (DPED). Consequently, whenever DPED revises its population projections for O'ahu, the objectives and policies of the Plan will be reevaluated in light of the

new projections, and amendments will be proposed as appropriate (Honolulu. DGP, 1988)

Is it possible to seek a sustainable development model for the island of Oʻahu when the county uses the state's population projections as unquestionable programmatic targets, subordinating its own general plan policies? The question "what is desirable growth?" is not raised.[7] Instead the prevailing view is that growth is inevitable. The developers ask: "Who will pay for growth?" (Davidson and Usugawa, 1988). They hope the Hawaiʻi taxpayers will.[8]

Population and Job Distribution

City actions have increased the planned population ceilings, rearranging the population distribution in the island in favor of suburbanization of both Ewa and Central Oʻahu. This increase in population, from the level of 830,700 people, was based on the population projection figures from the state. The city council relented to pressure from the developers and the city administration and approved additional housing projects in Central Oʻahu, leaving unresolved the issues of irreversible loss of agriculture land and open space, encroachment of water recharge areas and inadequate transportation, public services, and infrastructure (Kresnak, 1989). city and county documents shows that planned housing units would more than accommodate the state's population projections (Honolulu. DGP, September 1988). But the Development Plan capacity is in excess of 7,500 people in Central Oʻahu and of 19,500 in Ewa the maximum envisioned in the General Plan . The estimated additional jobs that will be dispersed throughout Oʻahu is a substantial 61,800. The need for services and facilities in the new developing areas will be increasing and the city and county does not have the budget to provide them, unless the state and developers help. All this is difficult to achieve with a tourism economy moving away from the boom of the 1980s.

Population and Affordable Housing

The gap between income and housing prices is widening, making affordability difficult. This is because average housing prices are increasing and average wages are decreasing due to the large and growing number of low-paying jobs in the service and tourism sector (Honolulu. DGP, 1988). With the most expensive housing in the country, the second highest rate of renters, and the highest number of people per room in the U.S., pressure for development is intense in Hawaiʻi, particularly on Oʻahu. Construction costs have doubled on Oʻahu since 1978, the median selling price of a single family home reached

$349,000 in 1992 and $193,000 for condominium units; the gross monthly rent reached $599 in 1990, more than doubling in ten years. Yet, by itself, suburbanization and housing development will not automatically improve the situation. Prices and purchasing powers remain unfavorable, even when interest rates are low. Too many people have limited financial abilities and cannot buy homes at current market prices. Rental units are not being built by the private sector, and too few are being provided with government assistance. For example, "Limited equity housing cooperative" (LEHC), an alternative between renting and home ownership, is not being promoted although it would provide a real opportunity to build multifamily housing units in and near Honolulu for the gap group. LEHC would be a way to meet the housing needs of the majority of the local population without suburbanizing the island and creating additional transportation, water, and open space encroachment problems; LEHC can be established by community groups with government help without building subdivisions with expensive homes for sale.

The lack of a housing policy for renters and for limited equity cooperatives is only one reason why a more sustainable land-use containment strategy has not been pursued. The primary reason is the role of large developers and large landowners in the housing industry, who have succeeded in their public opinion campaign by arguing that the affordable housing issue is simply a lack of sufficiently zoned land for housing and too much government regulation. Another reason is that the City and County lacks adequate fiscal resources and policies to tackle metropolitan redevelopment. Redevelopment entails policies and programs to: (a) deal with the minimization of displacement and relocation hardships to residents and businesses (Minerbi, 1980); (b) provide "land readjustment" to enable small property owners to engage in redevelopment without selling their land to bigger developers; and (c) provide an opportunity to establish local redevelopment authorities to engage in urban renewal on an areawide and project basis (Minerbi, Nakamura, Nitz, and Yanai,1986). The state has not helped the city and county to engage in metropolitan planning through revenue aid. Instead, the state has taken advantage of the city and county's limited resources to step into inner city redevelopment such as in Kakaako and on the waterfront, further eroding the autonomy of the local government. State-county jurisdiction remains at the core of planning issues for Oʻahu.

Searching for Sustainability

At times sustainability issues have been addressed in Hawaiʻi and Oʻahu: when population stabilization was investigated by the state, when the concept of carrying capacity was studied on Oʻahu; and when Hawaiʻi future scenarios were openly discussed in conferences and congresses. Unfortunately these studies and discussions have not moved Hawaiʻi away from the growth-led model and towards a sustainable development model.

Population Stabilization

In the 1970s there was an attempt to address population growth in Hawaiʻi with the establishment of the Temporary Commission on Population Stabilization. The report of the Commission recommended to achieve a viable economy within the limits of a sharply reduced population growth rate (Hawaii, 1972). It also encouraged federal action to control interstate migration. The report stressed that population forecasts are based largely on past trends and current expectations, with no allowances for deliberate efforts to modify population size, distribution and composition. It saw a possibility for the state to significantly influence the future demographic development of Hawaiʻi, and recognized that Hawaiʻi's economic policy is a major contributing factor in the growth of the State by encouraging in-migration from the mainland and foreign countries. It suggested that people will have to be satisfied with a given standard of living that all are guaranteed and foresaw the environmental crisis rooted in the modern life style and value system (Hawaii, 1972).

In a public opinion survey in January 1972 the Commission on Population and the Hawaiian Future probed the feelings and perceptions of Hawaiʻi's residents regarding the population (Hawaii, 1977). Results of the survey found that: population growth was a major concern and the state government in Hawaiʻi was seen as partly responsible for taking the initiative to address the population problem; the federal government should assist financially; migration into the state should be controlled, particularly foreign immigration; specific measures should be enacted to directly prohibit immigration or regulate it indirectly through the restriction of resources to persons who might move to Hawaiʻi; noncoercive methods of birth control education and services should be made available; a public campaign should be undertaken to discourage immigration; and some limitation should be enacted on the number of automobiles, roads and highways.

Respondents to the survey also had specific suggestions on how the population could be controlled by limiting migration, controlling welfare and unemployment benefits, job opportunities, residency requirements, land use, and taxes. Some responded that an amendment to the U.S. constitution should be introduced to deal with the population problems of a place as small as Hawaiʻi.

Redistribution to other islands could be achieved by limiting educational institutions on Oʻahu, and moving state jobs to the outer islands.

Food self-sufficiency was another priority. There was disagreement with the statement that "nothing can be done about population growth in Hawaiʻi." Measures that received more than 50% approval dealt with direct immigration control, regulation of social services, family planning, and regulation of transportation by limiting importation of cars and building of additional roads. To address the survey results would require embarking upon a sustainable development path for Hawaiʻi.

Another courageous study was Babbie's (1972) *The Maximillion Report*. Babbie felt that the quality of life had already declined by 1972 due to population growth and that the optimum population for Hawaiʻi had already been reached. Thus the report explored ways to stabilize the population of the state around one million people, a level bypassed by 101,000 people in 1990. The report proposed: (a) different ways to stabilize the population; (b) family planning to reduce natural increase; (c) discouraging economic activities not fit for the local labor force; and (d) the avoidance of housing and real estate advertisement on the mainland and abroad.

Carrying Capacity

In the mid-1970s it was recognized that carrying capacity would help the growth management task of the state and would establish overload conditions of the environmental and resource systems. Case studies of carrying capacity were conducted for the island of Oʻahu.[9] But aside from water related studies by the Board of Water Supply, and the work carried out on land use and infrastructure by the city and county Dept. of General Planning, little happened in spite of the intent to include carrying capacity as part of government's routine work.

Regional carrying capacity studies included the Kanehoe Bay study (Hawaiʻi Environmental Simulation Laboratory, 1975) and the land suitability study conducted on central Oʻahu (Hawaii, 1973). Because of the rapid growth and change on Oʻahu, carrying capacity approaches are needed to study the demand of facilities and infrastructure and to deal with the wave of multiple impacts and overload on people and nature for years to come. In fact, the 1989 legislature mandated the Office of State Planning to develop and test, on a limited site, a carrying capacity methodology focusing on land and infrastructure capabilities (Act 357, SLH 1989; Hawaii. Office of State Planning, January 1990). In 1990 S.B. No. 3229 required the Office of State Planning to conduct carrying capacity studies every five years to assess the impact of population and visitor growth on: physical infrastructure demand; land use and zoning; and social, economic, cultural, environmental, and safety, issues. Another bill (H.B. no. 2296 H.D. 1, 1990) included the consideration of "community-well being" with a study of the "social" carrying capacity of housing, community services, employment, outdoor recreation and visitor population." Eventually, Act 160 (amending Sect. 225 M-2 HRS) [Sect. 9. A, Sect 9. B. and Sect 9. C.] called for: (a) the determination of the capability of regions to support projected increases in resident population and visitors; (b) determine the impact of such projected increase; and (c) determine the maximum annual capacity by each region, county, and island. The report responding to Act 160 (Hawaii. Office of State Planning, 1991) looked at the carrying capacity of infrastructures, data needs, and implementing measures for planning areas, without altering the state's projections of 1988.

In the end a concept of carrying capacity, useful for policy making, must integrate: land capability analysis, infrastructure service system (supply-side), present and future resource (supply side), a range of population projections (demand side), resource demands combining population and level of service, strategies to meet demand with resources and with infrastructures, and investment schedules. Additional considerations include: biodiversity, scenic views and areas, social equity, cultural preservation, Hawaiian lands, and public input (Ibanez, 1991).

Future Scenarios

Efforts were made to look at alternative futures for Hawai'i at the 1969 Governor's Conference on the year 2000. *Hawai'i 2000*, which resulted from the conference, outlined "alternative Hawai'is" (Chaplin and Page, 1973). These "alternative Hawai'is" were a first attempt to envision the future. The scenarios are very important for the recognition of political choices toward a sustainable future or toward disaster for Hawai'i.

These scenarios are:

- "Pacific Coconut Republic," the playground for those who can pay for it.
- "Battlefield of Protracted Struggle," where the poor and those cast aside confront the entrenched power interests;
- "Ideal American State," where traditional American dreams come true;

- "Hawaiian Restoration," a participatory monarchy with preferential treatment to persons of Hawaiian ancestry and search for both traditional Hawaiian lifestyles and progressive and modern societal quests in many fields.
- "Ecological Commonwealth," focusing on man's (a) back to nature and (b) post-industrial technology with the state petitioning for federal aid to become a "national park" and even a "world park" and headquarters of the United Nations.
- "Experimental Hawai'i," for continuous, pluralistic, small-scale experiments supported by people and government alike.

All the scenarios (except the first two) show some of the dimensions to be considered for future planning and sustainability in Hawai'i: the political constituency (U.S., Native Hawaiians, and the international community); the operating scale (people, small businesses); the environmental philosophy (ecological practices); the futuristic orientation (participatory, experimental society); the international role (Hawai'i, where certain international services and experimentation may take place).

In 1982 Farrell described a desirable scenario where education at all levels would be a top priority and where the State of Hawai'i would lobby in Washington for a Constitutional amendment to regulate in-migration and immigration to Hawai'i. Speculative investment on open space and agricultural land would not be allowed. Environmental quality was kept and economic diversification pursued. A compromise was to be reached with the Native Hawaiian community to redress its claims. Farrell felt that this desirable scenario was unattainable because of the players involved. But he predicted that Hawai'i would chart an erratic course until it eventually veered towards his desirable scenario (Farrell, 1982).

This wide array of scenarios was narrowed down by Smyser (1988) with the assumption that Hawai'i would remain a State within the Union with immigration and external investment less controllable, than if Hawai'i were to become an independent country. Smyser envisioned Hawai'i as an international center with resorts, convention centers, international meetings, military bases, advanced and appropriate technology, travel research, and international sport events. But the quest for this future state has the same dangers as the disaster scenario: immigration and overcrowding; exacerbation of rich-poor differences; and the disregard of Hawaiian rights and of local residents' lifestyles.

The 1988 Governor's Congress on Hawai'i's International Role, focused on quality of life, economic goals, community and government infrastructure, and Hawai'i's image. The thrust was for a strong economy with limited population growth, economic diversification, middle-class jobs, cultural/recreation opportunities, education, ethnic pride and participation, and a stop to the brain drain. The concern was on how to find an international role for Hawai'i that would allow it to become competitive, to find an international niche, and continue to prosper. But this vision is still based on an export-led policy for growth.

What the congress and these authors may have not fully anticipated is the speed and the dynamics of change in the scenarios: from economic boom to bust and the Hawaiian sovereignty movement. In this context the alternative future of "Green Hawai'i" (Rohter, 1992) has a role to play.

Conclusion

This paper has described the contradictions of a booming economy in Hawai'i and of land development on O'ahu that result in increased relative poverty with unprecedented wealth. It has discussed the problems arising from adoption of the state's population projections prompted by externally induced real estate and tourism investment schemes, instead of through developing desirable policy objectives and targets for local residents.

It has shown that the City and County of Honolulu accommodates the projected population growth by redesignating for suburbanization, which is essentially a real estate bonanza for the large estates that control the land on Central O'ahu and Ewa in the path of development. Affordable housing provisions remain incidental to this real estate activity dictated by profit motives and speculation. The interest of large land estates, the lack of a strong urban renewal policy and municipal capability have precluded the choice of developing Honolulu as a city instead of a series of subdivisions.

This paper has reviewed the search for sustainability and the efforts to explore ways to achieve population stabilization, the use of carrying capacity to determine overloads, and attempts to chart a more desirable alternative future for Hawai'i. These objectives are more elusive in the 1990s than in the 1970s because there is more outside control of wealth, power, land, and economic activities now and because the wave of foreign investment has impacted Hawai'i by increasing the cost of practically everything.

Government and the community must rediscover sustainable and desirable development and plan to minimize the adverse cumulative impact of projects on the people and on the environment of the Hawaiian islands, particularly O'ahu. This entails finding ways to: (a) limit population growth from in-migration by linking job creation to local labor force needs; (b) curb speculative development by decentralizing certain planning and zoning decision at the community level to discourage undesirable projects; (c) devise more equitable employment and income opportunities for local people by investing in education and research and development (R&D); (d) keep the costs of living in check by changing wasteful and anti-ecological lifestyles; (e) develop policies to foster urban reinvestment by creating land readjustment legislation with appropriate displacement and mitigation measures, and (f) aggressively protect open space by avoiding highrises and low-density subdivisions and opting for "high density-low rise," a more human scaled urban form. Economic austerity, the Hawaiian movement, and the Green movement are new factors that give some hope to the idea of sustainable development for Hawai'i. But the quest for an environmentally sustainable, economically affordable, and just development will succeed only by redefining the planning principles of public health, safety, and welfare using quality of life and sustainable economic development indicators, island by island, and community by community. This means revising the Hawai'i Statutes by redesigning the policy of economic development using an environmentally-based, bottom-up approach and decentralizing more planning decision making at the local level.

Notes

1. This paper is a shorter, updated version of the introduction to the report: Sustainable Development or Suburbanization? Cumulative Project Impacts in Ewa and Central O'ahu. (Dept. of Urban and Regional Planning, 1989)

2. Sustainable development deals with intergenerational equity, self-reliance and affordability for local residents, particularly the needy, minorities and indigenous people, and the integrity of biological and natural processes of the island ecosystem. Carrying capacity refers to the load or the population the island can sustain without irreversible damage to the resident population, the land and the natural environment and to the ability of infrastructure and facilities to perform their function at acceptable levels of service. Cumulative project impacts are of two types: (a) the sum effect of diverse projects (people, housing, cars) on given localities, their residents and environment; and (b) the growth, exponential or otherwise, of a particular item, such as cars or water pollution, which impacts a locale.

3. In 1989 new planned residential development alone accounted to more than 5,500 acres in Ewa and to more than 3,000 acres in Central O'ahu (Jones, 1989).

4. The 1992 implicit price deflator for expenditures on GSP increased almost 60% since 1982.

5. There is a clear need to trace government subsidies project by project and aggregate that data sector by sector to assess statewide how much the Hawai'i taxpayer is contributing to corporate tourism, agriculture, etc.

6. The interstate movement of workers shows a two-to-one increase proportion of island workers looking for job on the Mainland over Mainland workers seeking a job in Hawai'i in 1991 (Hawaii, 1992).

7. Only in 1992 the Office of State Planning recognized that the state's own population projections, calling for 11 million tourist, 56,300 additional hotel rooms, and a 1.5 million population for the year 2,010, was excessive and should be revised downward. (Yamaguchi, 1992).

8. The operating budget of Honolulu City and County grew by 143% and property tax collection climbed 109% in 10 years. While the nominal per capita income in Hawai'i grew 9.1% in 1990, when adjusted for inflation, the per capita growth is a low 1.7% (Waite, 1991).

9. See References for the carrying capacity reports.

References

Babbie, E. 1972. *The Maximillion Report.* Honolulu: Citizens for Hawai'i.

Chaplin, G. and G. Page, (eds.). 1973. "Toward the Futures: Alternative Hawaiis." *Hawai'i 2000.* Honolulu: University Press of Hawai'i.

Davidson, D. and Ann Usugawa. 1988. *Paying for Growth in Hawai'i: An Analysis of Impact Fees and Housing Exactions Programs.* Honolulu: Land Use Research Foundation of Hawai'i.

Department of Urban and Regional Planning. Spring 1989. *Sustainable Development or Suburbanization? Cumulative Project Impacts in Ewa and Central Oahu.* Honolulu: University of Hawai'i.

Farrell, B. 1982. "Where Now?", in *Hawai'i, the Legend that Sells.* Honolulu: University Press of Hawai'i.

Hawaii. Department of Business, Economic Development and Tourism (DBEDT). October 5, 1987. *Hawai'i's Migrants, 1986. Statistical Report No. 203.* Honolulu: State of Hawai'i.

_____. 1988. *Population and Economic Projections for the State of Hawai'i to 2010 (Series M-K).* (November). Honolulu: State of Hawai'i.

_____. 1992. *Hawai'i Data Book. Honolulu: State of Hawai'i.*

Hawaii. Department of Labor and Industrial Relations (DLIR). April 1988. *Labor Force Information for Affirmative Action Programs.* Honolulu: State of Hawai'i.

Hawaii. Department of Planning and Economic Development (DPED). January 1973. *Central Oahu Planning Study.* Honolulu: State of Hawai'i.

Hawaii. *Hawai'i Revised Statutes.* 1993. "Act 213, A Bill for an Act Relating to State Planning." Honolulu: Seventeenth State Legislature Regular Session P. 365.

Hawaii. House of Representatives Fifteenth Legislature. 1990, H.B. *No. 2296 H.D. 1 Relating to Tourism.* Honolulu: State of Hawai'i.

Hawaii. Office of the Governor January 1972. Report of the Temporary Commission on Population Stabilization. Honolulu: State of Hawai'i.

_____. July 1977. Population Growth Policies and Strategies: A Public Opinion Survey.

Hawaii. Office of State Planning. January 1990. Carrying Capacity: A Pilot Study - Report to the Legislature on Act 375, SLH 1989.

_____. May 1991. *Carrying Capacity: Program Proposals - Report to the Legislature on Act 160, SHL 1990.* Honolulu: State of Hawai'i.

Hawaii. Environmental Simulation Laboratory. 1975. *Carrying Capacity Analysis in Context —Application to Growth Management in Hawai'i.* (January) Honolulu: University of Hawai'i.

Hawaii. Governor's Steering Committee for Carrying Capacity Studies. 1975. *An Approach for Developing, Assessing and Utilizing Carrying Capacity Concepts and Criteria for Growth Management.* (January) Honolulu: State of Hawai'i.

_____. 1976. *Carrying Capacity Prototype Investigations in the State of Hawai'i-Summary Report.* (February). Honolulu: State of Hawai'i.

Honolulu. Charter Commission. 1973. *Revised Charter of the City and County of Honolulu.* Honolulu: City and County of Honolulu.

Honolulu. Department of General Planning (DGP). 1988. *General Plan Objectives and Policies.* Honolulu: City and County of Honolulu.

_____. September 1988. Development Plan Sta*tus Review, Vols I, II, and III*. Honolulu: City and County of Honolulu.

Ibanez, Carol, Ann. December 5, 1991. "Hawai'i's Experience with Carrying Capacity Studies." Honolulu: University of Hawai'i, Department of Urban and Regional Planning, Unpublished Paper for Plan 645.

Jones, Susan. 1989. "The Development Process and the Residential Development in Ewa and Central O'ahu." In Department of Urban and Regional Planning. Spring 1989. Su*stainable Development or Suburbanization? Cumulative Project Impacts in Ewa and Central O'ahu.* Honolulu: University of Hawai'i.

Kresnak, W. January 29, 1989. "General Plan Reflects New Thinking on Growth: Critics Say Developers' Pressure Prompted Shift." The Sunday Sta*r-Bulletin & Advertiser*, January 29. Honolulu.

Minerbi, Luciano. 1980. "Redevelopment Impact on Small Businesses: Studying it Before it Happens: (The Kakaako District in Honolulu)." *Socio-Economic Planning Science*, 14:257-266.

_____. 1991. *Alternative Forms of Tourism in the Coastal Zone: Searching for Responsible Tourism in Hawai'i - A Summary*. Newport: National Coastal Resource Research and Development Institute.

_____. 1992. "Impacts of Tourism Development in Pacific Islands." Monograph, Greenpeace Pacific Campaign. Honolulu: Greenpeace.

_____. Peter Nakamura, Kiyoko Nitz, and Yane Yanai (eds.) 1986. *Land Readjustment The Japanese System: A Reconnaissance and a Digest*. Cambridge: Lincoln Institute of Land Policy and Oelgeschlander, Gunn and Hain.

Pai, Greg. March 19, 1989. *Long Term Changes in the Structure of the Hawaiian Economy and Their Impact on Social and Economic Welfare in Hawai'i*. Honolulu: Church of the Crossroads.

Rohter, Ira. 1992. *A Green Hawai'i: Source Book for Development Alternatives*. Honolulu: Na Kane O Ka Malo Press.

Smith, Kit. August 7, 1992. "Isle's Rich Getting Richer, Poor Poorer." *The Honolulu Advertiser*.

Smyser, A. A. 1988. *Hawaii's Future in the Pacific: Disaster, Backwater or Future State?* Honolulu: East-West Center.

State of Hawai'i Legislature. 1989. *Act 357, SLH*. Honolulu.

_____. 1990. Act 160, SLH. Honolulu

The Senate Fifteenth Legislature. 1990. *S.B. No. 3229 S.D. 1 and Standing Committee Report no. 2294. Relating to Planning*. Honolulu: State

U.S. Department of Planning and Economic Development. 1978. *Carrying Capacity Action Research: A Case Study in Selective Growth Management, Oahu, Hawai'i*. Washington, D.C.: U.S. Department of Housing and Urban Development.

Waite, David. August 28, 1991. "City's Budget Outgrows Inflation." *The Sunday Star-Bulletin & Advertiser*.

Yamaguchi, Andy. March 1, 1992. "Isle Planning Experts Dispute Projected Tourism Growth." *The Sunday Star-Bulletin & Advertiser*.

_____. December 1988. *Report of the Governor's Congress on Hawaii's International Role*, Honolulu: University of Hawai'i and The East-West Center.

Why There Are No Asian Americans in Hawai'i: The Continuing Significance of Local Identity

Jonathan Y. Okamura

The term "Asian American" is not commonly used in Hawai'i except by academics and the media. In everyday discourse, the much more frequently used related term is "Oriental," although it tends to be applied primarily to Chinese, Japanese, and Koreans and less so to Filipinos, Southeast Asians, and South Asians. In other contexts, individual Asian American groups will be specified, since there are only four major groups (the first four noted above), rather than a collective term being employed. At the individual level, people in Hawai'i claim to be Chinese, Filipino, Japanese or Korean, as the case may be, rather than Asian American.

Beyond the use of the term, the concept, Asian American is even less recognized and advanced in Hawai'i. There is essentially an unfamiliarity with the political significance of the concept rather than a conscious disavowal of it. There are very few specifically Asian American organizations or social movements in Hawai'i. Communities, cultural activities, and other social processes also tend not to be referred to or identified as Asian American. The newer terms, "Asian and Pacific American" or "Asian and Pacific Islander American," are even less commonly used in Hawai'i despite the presence of several Pacific Islander groups including Native Hawaiians, Samoans, Tongans, and Guamanians.

One of the factors that contributes to the marginality of Asian American identity in Hawai'i is the significance of another panethnic identity that Asian American groups and individuals can affirm, i.e., local identity. This paper reviews various economic and political developments and changes in and beyond Hawai'i during the past decade and assesses their impact on the significance and meaning of local identity. These developments include: substantially increased investment from Japan during the latter half of the 1980s, the tremendous expansion of the tourist industry in the economy of Hawai'i, the continued development of the movement for Hawaiian sovereignty and for recognition of their rights and claims as the indigenous people of Hawai'i, and the widening social cleavage between Japanese Americans and other ethnic groups, particularly Filipino Americans, Native Hawaiians, and haole or white Americans. In very different ways, all of these economic and political developments have contributed to the continuing significance of local identity in Hawai'i. However, it is argued that tourism development and Japanese investment have had the greatest impact on the maintenance of local identity through their increasing marginalization of Hawai'i's people to external sources of power and control. Continued affirmation of local identity over the past decade represents an expression of opposition to outside control and change of Hawai'i and its land, peoples, and cultures.

Local Versus Asian American Identity

Over ten years ago, an article on local identity and culture in Hawai'i discussed their historical and contemporary sources and accounted for the increasing salience of local identity since the 1960s (Okamura, 1980). In particular, various external social and economic forces of change perceived as detrimental to the quality of life that local people had come to value with living in Hawai'i were specified. These factors included substantial inmigration of Whites from the U.S. mainland, increased immigration from Asia and the Pacific, and the tremendous growth in the tourist industry. As a result, it was argued that the notion of "local" had come to represent the common identity of people of Hawai'i and their shared appreciation of the land, peoples and cultures of the islands. Given this commitment to Hawai'i, *local* also had evolved to represent the collective efforts of local people to maintain control of the economic and political future of Hawai'i from the external forces noted above.

On the U.S. mainland during the 1960s, Asian Americans were engaged in a similar movement to develop a panethnic identity and consciousness for themselves (Wei, 1993). However, the concept of Asian American identity has never taken hold in Hawai'i even though there are several Asian American groups that represent significant proportions of the population including Japanese (22.3%), Filipino (15.2%), Chinese (6.2%), Korean (2.2%), Vietnamese (0.5%) and other Southeast Asian (e.g., Laotian and Kampuchean) (Hawaii, 1993:44). Asian Americans collectively comprise a little less than one-half of the state population of 1.1 million. Because of the considerable populations of Japanese, Filipino, and Chinese Americans and the overall structure of ethnic relations in Hawai'i, these groups have not found it necessary to establish and affirm collectively a specifically pan-Asian American identity or movement. Instead, there are separate organizations to represent the interests and regulate the affairs of those groups such as chambers of commerce and statewide ethnic community associations.

The political and economic necessity to develop such a panethnic organization and consciousness prevailed during the pre-World War II period of plantation labor recruitment to Hawai'i. Local identity has its historic origins in this period based on the common working class background of Native Hawaiians and the immigrant plantation groups including Chinese, Filipinos, Japanese, Koreans, Okinawans, Portuguese and Puerto Ricans. Together these groups shared a collective subordinate social status in opposition to the dominant *haole* (white) planter and merchant oligarchy. Over the years, local identity gained greater importance through the social movements to unionize plantation workers by the International Longshoremen's and Warehousemen's Union (ILWU) in 1946 and to gain legislative control by the Democratic Party in 1954.

The emergence and significance of local identity can be viewed as ultimately contributing to the nonsalience of Asian American identity in Hawai'i, especially since both movements developed in roughly the same time period, i.e., the mid-1960s to early 1970s. Japanese, Chinese, Filipinos, etc. may lack an appreciation of Asian American identity since they already share another panethnic identity with one another that also includes several non-Asian groups such as Native Hawaiians, Portuguese, and Puerto Ricans. Furthermore, the notion of local is essentially specific to Hawai'i, emerging as a result of its particular social history, whereas Asian American is a much broader category with relevance in communities throughout the United States.

The larger political and economic structure of ethnic relations in Hawai'i is the primary factor in the nonemergence of Asian American identity. While the socioeconomic status of Asian Americans in Hawai'i and on the continental United States is generally similar, the former, particularly Japanese and Chinese Americans, wield much greater political power at the state level than do their mainland counterparts. The lesser political power of mainland Asian Americans is indicated by their relative representation in the population. In California, the 2.7 million Asian Americans—including Filipinos (732,000), Chinese (705,000), Japanese (313,000), Vietnamese (280,000), Koreans (260,000), and Asian Indians (160,000)—far outnumber their counterparts in Hawai'i but represent only 9.1 % of the California population of 29.9 million (Los Angeles Times, 1990). In the context of much larger White (17 million) and Hispanic (7.7 million) groups and a substantial African American (2.1 million) population, Asian Americans face a much greater need for coalescing their numbers in pursuit of their common political and economic interests than they do in Hawai'i.

Similarly, at the national level the 6.9 million Asian Americans, who together represent a minimal 2.8 % of the U.S. population, need to view themselves as a collectivity with shared problems and concerns in relation to the larger dominant society. But in Hawai'i, certain Asian American groups, such as Chinese, Japanese and locally born Koreans, can be considered part of the dominant society, thus lessening the political and economic relevance of Asian American identity for them.

Local Culture and the Ethnic Rainbow in Hawai'i

It is widely believed by both academic researchers and laypersons that ethnic relations in Hawai'i are qualitatively "better" than on the U.S. mainland and in other parts of the world. The multiethnic riot in Los Angeles and violent outbreaks in other cities in April 1992, following the verdict in the Rodney King case, will certainly not go unnoticed by the proponents of this argument. The latter also maintain that "Hawai'i's ethnic rainbow of shining colors, side by side" has valuable lessons to offer to the rest of the nation: "If America's mushrooming minority populations are to live together in harmony, perhaps they should take a close look at our multicultural test tube" (Yim 1992:B1). One reason advanced for the more tolerant ethnic relations in Hawai'i is the "unique" local culture of the islands, which is a "prime example of the ability of diverse peoples to live harmoniously together" (Ogawa 1981:7). Even Hawai'i's governor, John Waihee, has argued that, "we've tried to call that culture which allows everybody to kind of exchange, go in and out of, enjoy various things ... in its best sense, local culture. What glues it all together is the native Hawaiian culture" (quoted in Yim 1992: B1).

This view of local culture as the result of "blending, sharing and mixing" processes is not especially insightful (Okamura 1980:122-123). These are highly imprecise and misleading terms that ignore the far more complex political and economic processes that were involved in the development of local culture and identity, in particular the historical oppression of Native Hawaiians and the immigrant plantation groups prior to World War II. Nonetheless, Ogawa (1981:7) has stated that "Hawaii's peoples have created a culture in which everyone feels they can make a contribution, be a part of. It is a culture which provides a sense of shared experiences or 'points of commonality' where people come together and create a mutually beneficial and enriching experience." These points of commonality would include eating certain foods (e.g., plate lunches), the practice of particular customs and habits (e.g., "low keyed" and considerate interactions), modes of entertainment (e.g., ethnic jokes) and shared folklore (e.g., supernatural beliefs). With the exception of social interactions, all of the above common areas are trivial and can hardly serve as the collective basis for a shared culture that is supposed to underlie social relations in Hawai'i.

With regard to ethnic interactions in Hawai'i, an argument could be made that they do involve a certain degree of tolerance and acceptance, at least compared to the mainland (Kirkpatrick 1987:310). This cultural emphasis, popularized as the "aloha spirit," is very much part of the public code of ethnic relationships in Hawai'i, which maintains that ideally such interpersonal relationships should proceed without reference to ethnic stereotypes or prejudice. However, as noted by Odo, the danger of idealizing ethnic interactions is that it tends to deny the reality of ethnic conflicts. Odo states, "It's kind of a mythology that allows us to cover up bad interethnic, interracial relations" (quoted in Yim 1992:B1). The tradition of tolerance allows for Hawai'i's people to avoid acknowledging and confronting the institutionalized inequality among ethnic groups and the resultant tensions and hostilities that are generated. This, perhaps, is the primary reason for the continued emphasis on the tradition of harmonious ethnic relationships despite evidence and knowledge to the contrary. In fact, it has been argued that the cultural emphasis on tolerance and the presence of ethnic antagonisms are "complementary" rather than contradictory insofar as interethnic ties become even more valued in the context of harsh ethnic stereotypes (Kirkpatrick 1987:310).

Without recourse to the notion of a shared or mixed culture, local identity can be seen to derive its significance primarily from structural rather than cultural factors. This structural dimension of local identity is based on the categorical opposition between groups considered local and those considered nonlocal, including haole, immigrants, the military, tourists, and foreign investors. Local is essentially a relative category; groups and individuals are viewed or view themselves as local in relation to others who are not so perceived. From this perspective, local identity is very exclusive rather than all inclusive and serves to create and maintain social boundaries between groups. The political and economic changes described below have heightened the boundaries between local and nonlocal groups and thereby enhanced the salience of local identity.

Japanese Investment in Hawai'i

Clearly, the most dominant economic force in Hawai'i during the 1980s, especially the latter half, was dramatically increased Japanese investment in tourism, resort development, and real estate. Local economists have maintained that virtually all of the economic growth in Hawai'i in the late 1980s was due to Japanese investment and, as a result, the state had experienced its "greatest period of prosperity since the boom years of the 1970s" (Ho*nolulu Star-Bulletin (HSB)* 1990a:A8). Between 1986 and 1990, Japanese investment in Hawai'i, including purchases of real estate and businesses, totaled more than $11 billion, with well over one-half of this amount in 1989 ($2.8 billion) and 1990 ($3.8

billion) alone (*Sunday Star-Bulletin & Advertiser (SSBA)* 1991a:A1). In 1990, Japanese expenditures were divided among hotels and resorts ($1.52 billion), land ($919 million), office buildings and other commercial property ($885 million), residential property ($413 million), and businesses ($44 million) (*SSBA* 1991b:A8). Japanese corporations presently own 65 % of the hotel rooms in Hawai'i, more than 50 % of the office space in downtown Honolulu, and over one-half of the private golf courses. In addition, Japanese investors purchased about 5,900 higher-priced homes and condominiums valued at $3.2 billion between 1986 and 1990 and thus own 11 % of the total value of real estate in Hawai'i (*SSBA* 1991a:A9).

The cumulative economic impact of Japanese investment in Hawai'i is evident from estimates of the multiplier effect their expenditures have on the state economy. In 1989 direct and indirect economic activity resulting from Japanese investment and tourist expenditures generated $9.5 billion, which, by one way of calculation, was equivalent to 45 % of the $21.3 billion gross state product for that year, although not all of the former amount represented original expenditures from Japan (*HSB* 1990a:A1). (Private sector economists laud Japanese investment in overly positive terms. They maintain, for example, that such investment has reduced unemployment and underemployment in the state. It is evident however that the economy of Hawai'i and thousands of jobs are now dependent on a single foreign country). Japanese corporations accounted for the great bulk (86%) of foreign investment in Hawai'i between 1986 and 1989 (*HSB*, 1990d:A1). Of necessity then, economic developments in Japan, especially their economic, business, and financial problems, have to be of major concern to the local economy and population.

The substantially increased Japanese investment in Hawai'i and throughout the world in the late 1980s was due to the specific convergence of several factors in the Japanese financial sector. These factors included the doubling in value of the yen in relation to the U.S. dollar, the tripling of stock-market values, very low interest rates along with an aggressive lending drive by banks, and runaway urban land prices. However, for various reasons including a crash of the Japanese stock market, these factors are no longer present. As a result, Japanese investment in Hawai'i has declined tremendously from the boom period of the late 1980s; for example, Japanese real estate purchases dropped from $2.9 billion in 1990 to $328 million in 1992 (*HSB* 1993a:A1). Since 1991, Japan-financed construction projects, particularly resort compexes and hotels, have been stalled or canceled resulting in a downturn in the Hawai'i economy, especially in the construction and tourist industries. These are clear indications of the fundamental vulnerability of the economy and the local people to unpredictable and uncontrollable forces from outside the Islands.

During the past decade, Hawai'i's people have become increasingly aware of their expanding economic subordination to Japan and Japanese investors. In a statewide survey of Hawai'i's registered voters (n=408) conducted in 1990, 46 % of the respondents agreed with the statement that "Hawai'i is on the verge of becoming a colony of Japan," although 52 % expressed disagreement (HSB 1990b:A8). Two-thirds (67%) of the respondents believe that Japanese nationals "don't care about Hawai'i except as a place to play or make money," and 60 % do not "trust the political motives" of Japanese investors. These responses are consistent with the view that Hawai'i already is an economic colony of Japan, especially as a result of tourism investment (Kim 1993:239).

Tourism Overdevelopment

Tourism continues to be the mainstay of the Hawai'i economy representing a whopping 38.3 % of the gross state product (GSP) of $28.6 billion in 1991, far exceeding military expenditures (10.9%) as the second largest contributor to the GSP (Hawaii 1993:343). The annual number of visitors currently totals 6.5 million or almost six times the state population of 1.1 million (Hawaii 1993:185). On any given day, there are more than 150,000 tourists in the islands who would represent about 14 % of the resident population. On the neighbor islands with their much smaller population, the average daily number of tourists comprises substantial percentages of the resident population, e.g., Maui (41%) and Kaua'i (37%) (Hawaii 1993:187). However, after years of consistent growth the annual number of tourists to Hawai'i began to decline from its high of seven million in 1990 as a result of the mainland recession and the Persian Gulf War. Visitors from the mainland and Canada have decreased from 4.7 million in 1990 to less than 4 million just two years later, with a consequent decline of $1.1 billion in visitor expenditures in 1992 (*HSB* 1993b:A1). These are clear indications that the Hawai'i tourist industry has entered the maturation, if not saturation, phase of its development in which such decreases are inevitable (Mak and Sakai, 1992:188).

The overall social and economic impact of tourism in Hawai'i extends far beyond the physical presence of tourists. Direct visitor-related expenditures totaled $11 billion in 1991, which represented nearly a doubling since 1985 (Hawaii 1993:203). Tourism generated $6.5 billion in household income and another $1.2 billion in state and county tax revenues in 1991 which was about

40 % of total tax revenues collected (Hawaii 1993:203). Most significantly for working people, 140,000 jobs are generated directly and 250,000 jobs are created directly and indirectly by tourism, which represents about 40 % of the employment positions in Hawai'i (Hawaii 1993:204). These generally low pay, low mobility, and low security jobs in the tourist industry are primarily in service and sales work: hotel services (28%), "eating and drinking places" (24%), other retail trade (19%) and other services (13%) (Hawaii 1992:200).

Overdependence on tourism has essentially resulted in a "locked-in economy" in Hawai'i in which economic diversification becomes increasingly more difficult to develop (Aoudé, 1993). The state economy was recently rated the worst in the nation by U.S. News and World Report, particularly in terms of decline in unemployment, business bankruptcies, and income growth rate (*HSB* 1992b). A tourism-dependent economy, with its generally low wage and insecure jobs, provides limited opportunities for socioeconomic mobility or even for maintaining a certain standard of living (Okamura, 1992). It is not surprising then that a recent statewide survey (n=419) reported that 81 % of the respondents believe that Hawai'i is "too dependent" on tourism (*HSB* 1993d:E5).

The restricted economic opportunities that result from tourism dependence are compounded by the extremely high cost of living in Hawai'i, with Honolulu having the dubious distinction as the second most expensive metropolitan area in the nation (*HSB* 1992a:A1). Housing costs in Hawai'i also are among the highest in the country and prevent an estimated 80 to 90 % of renters from becoming homeowners. It is estimated that it costs 38 % more to live in Hawai'i, the so-called paradise tax, than on the mainland (H*onolulu Advertiser (HA)* 1992), a price that local residents have been forced into paying.

Because of the overdependence on tourism, the overall quality of life for Hawai'i's people is especially vulnerable to worldwide fluctuations in economic activity and to uncontrollable international political events. Recent state budget reductions for government services and programs have been necessitated by a substantial decline in government tax revenues, which have resulted from a slowing down of the economy beginning in 1991, especially in tourism. As a consequence of the economic downturn, unemployment has reached its highest level (5%) in over five years, particularly in the neighbor island tourist industry.

With regard to Japanese investment in tourism, particularly in hotel and resort development, the economy of Hawai'i has never been as dependent on foreign investment and control. Because Japanese corporations have so heavily invested in hotels, resort complexes, golf courses, and other sectors of the tourist industry, there is concern for their trend toward "enclave investment." Enclave investment establishes a closed system for the ultimate benefit of investors in which profits flow out from an investment site back to the investors' base. Japanese purchases and development of hotels, resorts, golf courses, restaurants, and shopping centers in Hawai'i—in collaboration with travel agencies, airlines and tour companies in Japan—comprise all the necessary elements for enclave investment. The result is that profits from Japanese tourism activity return to Japan rather than benefit the local community, aside from the creation of low paying sales and service jobs.

Japanese represent about 25 % of the annual number of tourists to Hawai'i (*HSB* 1993c:A1). However, in contrast to the substantial decline in visitors from the U.S. mainland, and Canada in recent years, Japanese tourists have more than doubled in number since 1986 to over 1.6 million in 1992. Like Japanese investment in Hawai'i in the latter half of the 1980s, this considerable increase also can be attributed to the enhanced value of the yen. While there are considerably fewer visitors from Japan than from the United States, and their average stay of six days is shorter than that of mainland visitors, Japanese tourists spend $344 a day as opposed to $141 for their mainland counterparts (Hawaii 1993:197). Japanese tourists contributed $2.8 billion directly into the Hawai'i economy in 1991 (compared to $5.8 billion by American tourists), which represented almost a tripling since 1985 (Hawaii 1993:201). Thus, Japanese tourists have a disproportionate impact on the state economy in relation to their absolute numbers due to their greater purchasing power and also their supposedly greater potential for market growth compared to mainland visitors. Hawai'i has recently dropped to third place behind Australia and Europe as the destination choice among the ten million Japanese who annually travel abroad. This is another indication of the fickleness of the tourist market that can have disastrous consequences for local working people and their quality of life.

Hawaiian Sovereignty and Identity

One of the most significant changes in ethnic relations in Hawai'i during the past decade has been the further development of the Hawaiian sovereignty movement. Its more recent origins can be traced to the 1970s with the emergence of various politically-oriented Native Hawaiian organizations concerned with protesting land abuses and advocating their rights and claims to a land base (Trask 1984:122). Since then, the movement has developed to include occupations of restricted areas and finally to declarations of sovereignty based on indigenous rights to the land (Trask 1984-85:119).

Trask (1984-85:121) distinguishes the "Hawaiian Movement" from other protest struggles in Hawai'i by its demand for a land base, which follows from the native rights of Hawaiians as the original inhabitants of the islands. Other community struggles, such as those against the eviction of residents of Waiahole and Waikane valleys and Ota Camp, advocated the rights of local people to maintain their cultural lifestyle in their established communities (Okamura 1980:134). However, Trask (1984-85:121) notes that as the 1970s proceeded, the indigenous rights of Native Hawaiians as "historically unique" from the rights of local groups began to be asserted in other community struggles.

During the 1980s several organizations were established to advocate either sovereignty or independence for Native Hawaiians. Perhaps the largest and best organized of these groups is *Ka Lahui Hawai'i* (The Hawaiian Nation), which was formed at an islands-wide constitutional convention in 1987. Ka Lahui Hawai'i has over 16,000 members, a formal constitution, elected officials and representatives from each island, and executive and legislative government branches. Its approach to establishing a sovereign nation is to have Native Hawaiians recognized under the U.S. government policy that gives all Native American peoples the right to self-governance (*Ka Lahui Hawai'i* 1991:4). The land base for the Hawaiian nation would include half of the 1.4 million acres of ceded lands presently under state control, the 190,000 acres of land administered by the State Department of Hawaiian Home Lands, and additional lands provided in compensation for the overthrow of the Hawaiian monarchy in 1893 (Trask 1992:255).

In addition to the sovereignty movement, the past decade also has been distinguished by continued expression and affirmation of Native Hawaiian identity, particularly through its cultural revitalization of values, beliefs, and customs. Hawaiian traditional dance, arts and crafts, and music have continued to flourish. Interest has been renewed in traditional health and healing practices and in religious rituals and beliefs. Most importantly, the Hawaiian language, at one time prohibited to be used in the public schools, continues its revival with the establishment of the Punana Leo language immersion schools in which Native Hawaiian children are taught in their own language. These and other similar manifestations represent continued revitalization and articulation of Hawaiian culture and identity, a process that began in the early 1970s as the Hawaiian *renaissance* (Kanahele 1982:25).

The development of the sovereignty movement and the general affirmation of Native Hawaiian identity have implications for local identity insofar as they have undoubtedly influenced many Native Hawaiians to view themselves as Na

Kanaka Maoli, the indigenous people of Hawai'i. As the indigenous people, Hawaiians have native rights to own and control land, to worship, to fish, hunt, and gather natural resources, and other ancestral rights that distinguish them from other local groups. It is not clear what proportion of the Native Hawaiian population considers themselves more as indigenous than as local, but they can claim both identities without contradiction.

Asserting their collective identity as the native people of Hawai'i may create divisions between Native Hawaiians and other local groups, but these divisions are not necessarily absolute cleavages. Many non-Hawaiians have kinship ties with Native Hawaiians through marital relationships. The attitudes toward and the extent of support for Hawaiian sovereignty among non-Hawaiians are presently unknown, but some local groups have expressed support. The Hawai'i chapter of the Japanese American Citizens League (JACL) introduced and adopted a resolution at their 1992 national convention that called for JACL support for Hawaiian sovereignty.

Cleavage Among Ethnic Groups

Since the 1970s there has been a widening social cleavage between Japanese Americans and other ethnic groups in Hawai'i including Filipinos, haole, and Native Hawaiians. Native Hawaiians have expressed resentment against Japanese American "racial exclusiveness in social relations and their patronage system" (McGregor 1985:2 cited in Kent 1989:114). Filipino Americans along with haole have been quite vocal in accusing Japanese Americans of discriminating against them in employment, particularly for state government positions. Filipino Americans (12.9%) and haole (22.8%) were underrepresented among permanent state employees (excluding Department of Education teachers and University of Hawai'i faculty) hired in fiscal year 1989. Japanese Americans (31.9%) were hired at a much higher rate, proportional, however, to their representation in the Hawai'i labor force (HSB 1991: A4). These hiring imbalances contribute to the widespread perception that Japanese Americans "control" state government employment through favoring their own applicants, thereby discriminating against non-Japanese.

Hostility against Japanese is not a new phenomenon; it has been present in various forms throughout much of their historical presence in Hawai'i. As a result of their participation in the sugar plantation strikes of 1909 and 1920 and their growing American-born population, Japanese encountered tremendous racism and discrimination from the larger society during the 1920s. However,

 the more recent antagonism against them differs from previous such expressions insofar as it has been described as an "anti-Japanese backlash" (Kotani 1985: 174; Boylan 1986: 1). The use of this term indicates that the more recent hostility against Japanese Americans is a response to their perceived higher political and economic status and thus to a perceived division between them and other ethnic groups in Hawai'i.

The anti-Japanese backlash resulted from a prevalent negative stereotype of Japanese Americans that they "dominate" Hawai'i both politically and economically. As noted by Odo (1984), this stereotype is based more on a "mythology of AJA power and arrogance" that is partially attributable to various types of mid-level administrative, professional, and clerical occupations they hold, particularly in the public sector. Japanese Americans are especially well-represented in the state Department of Education as school administrators (52%), elementary (63%), and secondary (50%) schoolteachers, and clerical staff (50%) (*HSB* 1990c:A3). In those positions, they come into direct contact with a considerable segment of Hawai'i residents and their children, and oftentimes are made to bear the burden of blame for the failures of the long underfunded public educational system.

In the larger economic sphere, contrary to popular misconception, Japanese Americans do not have the highest occupational status in Hawai'i. Chinese Americans and haole have such status, based on their substantial overrepresentation in professional, management and executive positions (Okamura 1990:5). Japanese American men continue to be well-represented in blue-collar work in Hawai'i where they comprise 36 % of construction workers, 40 % of mechanics, and 41 % of precision production workers. (Kotani 1985:154). Japanese American women constitute 41 % of secretaries and 26 % of sales cashiers. Given their older median age, Japanese Americans are the largest group in the Hawai'i labor force (although a rapidly declining one with the ongoing retirement of the Nisei second generation), which also contributes to a perception of economic power and employment discrimination against non-Japanese.

The supposed economic dominance of Japanese Americans in Hawai'i is especially absent in terms of corporate power. Of the 50 largest corporations in Hawai'i (based on sales in 1992), only four, i.e., Servco Pacific (no. 12), Tony Management Group (no. 44), Kuakini Health System (no. 45), and Star Markets (no. 46) are owned and controlled by local Japanese Americans (*Hawaii Business*, 1993). The largest corporations in Hawai'i still include a few of the former "Big Five" companies, i.e., Castle & Cooke (now known as Dole Food, no. 1) and Alexander & Baldwin (no. 6), along with other multinational corporations. Japanese Americans also tend to be considerably underrepresented among the leading business executives who wield corporate power in Hawai'i through holding multiple directorships in locally-based corporations (Kotani 1985: 172). In essence, as argued by Kent (1989:114),

> the AJA elite has never *constituted a legitimate ruling class in Hawai'i.* Instead, they have skilfully performed a multitude of roles—front men, middle men, mediators, agents, and power brokers—in the service of the authentic ruling class, much of which does not reside in the islands and which prefers invisibility as one element of its power. (emphasis in original)

The real sources of power over the Hawai'i economy are multinational corporations based on the U.S. mainland or abroad, including United Airlines, Torray Clark, Prudential Life Insurance Co., Jardine Pacific in Hong Kong, and Kyo-Ya Co., Azabu Group, Seibu Group and Kumagai Gumi Co. in Japan.

Despite the fallacious nature of the "dominating" stereotype, the backlash and cleavage against Japanese Americans are very real in their consequences. In many ways, Japanese Americans have replaced haoles as the scapegoat group in Hawai'i toward which the hostilities of other ethnic groups, including haoles, are directed. As scapegoats, they may perceive their collective identity and acceptance as local being threatened, especially since the negative stereotypes applied to them, such as "dominating," "arrogant," and "clannish," are clearly nonlocal characteristics.

Japanese Americans, particularly those of the third and fourth generations, have responded to the backlash against them not by reorganizing themselves to maintain their social status or to advance their collective concerns but by downplaying their Japanese American identity. They can be seen as emphasizing the local dimension of their ethnic identity in their appreciation of Hawai'i and its peoples and cultures. In doing so, they reaffirm their social ties with other local groups and to Hawai'i as a special place for them to live, work, and maintain family and friendship bonds. Twenty years ago, Yamamoto (1974:101) argued that the increasing identification of third-generation Sansei Japanese with being local served as a compromise resolution of a developing cultural identity crisis between being Japanese and being committed to Hawai'i and its people. This identity dilemma is still with local Japanese but has been made more problematic by the widening cleavage with other ethnic groups.

In the 1970s, in response to the influx of Philippine immigrants who appeared to pose a threat to their collective identity, local Hawai'i-born Filipinos engaged in a similar process of asserting the local component of their ethnic identity. Filipino immigrants were perceived by their local-born counterparts as reinforcing derogatory stereotypes that had originated with the predominantly uneducated and lowly employed plantation labor recruits. To emphasize their local identity and to dissociate themselves from immigrant Filipino stereotypes, Hawai'i-born Filipinos engaged in violent conflict with the immigrants and avoided them (Okamura, 1983).

Conclusion

The continuing salience of local identity can be attributed to various external and internal forces of development and change, discussed above, that gained considerably in their scope and intensity during the past decade. In particular, substantially increased Japanese investment, especially in tourism, and the continued overdevelopment of tourism, have had the greatest impact on the meaning and significance of local identity. In the 1970s, Yamamoto (1979:114) argued that "Being local assumes that while social, cultural, and economic changes are going to move the overall social structure of Hawai'i further away from traditional community, the changes need not entail the total Americanization of Hawaii's people." However, the decade of the 1980s has resulted not so much in the Americanization of people in Hawai'i but in the ongoing internationalization of the islands through their further incorporation into the global capitalist economy.

Globalization of Hawai'i's economy and other political and economic processes are contributing to the increasing marginalization of Hawai'i's people to external sources of power and control. As a result, local identity has been maintained as an expression of resistance and opposition, albeit unorganized, to such outside domination and intrusion. The designation *Local* continues to represent the shared identity of people in Hawai'i who have an appreciation of and a commitment to the islands and their peoples, cultures, and ways of life, which are perceived as being threatened by external forces of development and change, e.g., tourism and foreign investment. However, while there has been increasing recognition among local people of their peripheral status in Hawai'i, there has not been a resulting collective effort to regain control of political and economic forces in the islands from external sources.

In the late 1970s, such an effort was described as *Palaka* Power, named for the durable cloth used to make the work clothes of plantation laborers, stevedores, and other working-class people in Hawai'i. Palaka Power, or what might be termed local advocacy, sought especially to promote and protect the interests and values of local people during the 1978 State Constitutional Convention;

however, it never developed into an organized social movement. State Representative David Hagino, the principal theorist of the Palaka Power initiative, attributed its failure to the yuppie generation of political leaders currently in power who are more concerned with "grandiose projects, ostentatious spending and conspicuous consumption" than with social justice and equality (*HA* 1993: B1).

In his 1989 address at the 18th annual meeting of the Japan-Hawai'i Economic Council in Nagoya, even Hawai'i's governor acknowledged the ongoing process of marginalization of Hawai'i's people.

> while there is no doubt that Hawaii's residents have benefited from an economy that is fueled by dollars from Tokyo, Vancouver, Sydney and Chicago, there is also no doubt that Hawaii's residents are experiencing a sense of loss—loss of their land to others and, more important, loss of control. (*Hawaii Business* 1990:29)

While the governor may speak about loss of land and control to outside investors, his and previous state government administrations have not done very much to limit those losses and, in fact, have facilitated them through their subsidizing of the tourist industry with taxpayer monies. In typical response to the ongoing slump in the tourist industry, the Hawai'i Visitors Bureau received an additional $8.5 million from the State Legislature in 1993 so that it could lure tourists from Germany, Taiwan, Hong Kong, and other far flung places to Hawai'i even though its supplementary promotional funding the previous year had not resulted in an increased number of tourists. The lack of political leadership and long-term vision on the part of elected government officials towards the development of an alternative economic future for Hawai'i, at least one not so heavily constrained by tourism and foreign investment, only contributes to the growing feeling of loss of control to outside forces among local people.

The perception of powerlessness among local people to change the economic and political future of Hawai'i is evident in the increasing migration of tens of thousands of island residents to the U.S. mainland each year. This movement of "voting with one's feet" indicates the growing level of dissatisfaction with life in Hawai'i, particularly in terms of the high cost of living, the relative lack of financially rewarding jobs, and the high cost of housing. The mainland migration (excluding military personnel and their dependents) to only four western states (California, Washington, Oregon, and Nevada) has been estimated at almost 11,000 annually (*SSBA* 1992: B1), while the total civilian movement to the mainland is estimated at 21,740, nearly 2 % of the state population (Miklius 1992:242) which is a considerable percentage considering the cost of moving to the mainland.

Local identity, while not organized into a viable social movement, will continue in its significance for Hawai'i's people if only because of their further marginalization through the ongoing internationalization of the economy and overdependence on tourism. Because of this overdependence, it may well be too late for the necessary changes to be initiated that can give power and control to the people of Hawai'i.

References

Aoudé, I.G. 1993. "Tourist Attraction: Hawaii's Locked-in Economy." In P. Manicas (ed.), *Social Process in Hawai'i: A Reader.* Pp. 218-235. New York: McGraw Hill, Inc.

Boylan, D. 1986. Interview in *Hawaii Herald.* "Japanese Americans and Elections '86." September, pp. 1, 5, 12.

Hawaii Business 1990. "The Japaning of Hawaii." January.

———. 1993. "The *Hawaii Business* Top 250." August.

Hawaii. Department of Business, Economic Development and Tourism (DBEDT). 1992. *The State of Hawaii Data Book 1991.* Honolulu: DBEDT.

———. 1993. *The State of Hawaii Data Book 1992.* Honolulu: DBEDT.

Honolulu Advertiser 1992. "Paradise Tax Highest Ever, But May Start Falling." September 25.

———. 1993. "Another View: Much Endures." April 4, pp. B1, B4.

Honolulu Star-Bulletin 1990a. "Japanese Money Fired Isle Growth." April 11, pp. A1, A8.

———. 1990b. "Half Believe State Nearly a Japan Colony." April 25, pp. A1, A8.

———. 1990c. "Most Education Jobs Held by 1 Racial Group." August 16, pp. A3.

———. 1990d. "Investors Fear Backlash in Islands." November 20, pp. A1, A8.

———. 1991. "Judiciary Tallies its Ethnic Hires." August 2, pp. A4.

———. 1992a. "Mastering Isles High Living Cost Takes Scrimping." August 11, pp. A1.

———. 1992b. "Isle Economy is Rated Worst." September 16, pp. D1.

———. 1993a. "Japanese Investing Falls 80%." March 18, pp. A1.

———. 1993b. "Spending by Tourists Shows Sharp Decline." May 8, pp. A1, A8.

_____. 1993c. "HVB Report Full of Facts on Tourists." May 15, pp. A1.

_____. 1993d. "Isle Residents Don't Want to Foot the Bill on Tourist Promotion." June 16, pp. E1, E5.

Ka Lahui Hawai'i 1991. "Ka Lahui Hawai'i, The Sovereign Nation of Hawai'i." A Compilation of Legal Materials for Workshops on the Hawaiian Nation.

Kanahele, G.S. 1982. "The New Hawaiians." *Social Process in Hawaii*, 29:21-31.

Kent, N.J. 1989. "Myth of the Golden Men: Ethnic Elites and Dependent Development in the 50th State." In *Ethnicity and Nation-building in the Pacific*. Pp. 98-117. Tokyo: The United Nations University.

Kim, K. 1993. The Political Economy of Foreign Investment in Hawai'i. In P. Manicas (ed.), *Social Process in Hawai'i: A Reader,* Pp. 236-245. New York: McGraw Hill, Inc.

Kirkpatrick, J. 1987. "Ethnic Antagonism and Innovation in Hawaii." In J. Boucher and D. Landis (eds.), *Ethnic Conflict: International Perspectives,* Pp. 298-316. Beverly Hills: Sage Publications.

Kotani, R.M. 1985. T*he Japanese in Hawaii: A Century of Struggle.* Honolulu: The Hawaii Hochi, Ltd.

Los Angeles Times 1990. May 11, pp. 5.

Mak, J. and M. Sakai 1992. "Tourism in Hawai'i: Economic Issues for the 1990s and Beyond." In Z.A. Smith and R.C. Pratt (eds.), *Politics and Public Policy in Hawai'i.* Albany: State University of New York Press.

McGregor, D. 1985. The Hawaiian Perspective on Japanese in Politics and Business. Unpublished paper.

Miklius, W. 1992. "Outmigration." In R.W. Roth (ed.), *The Price of Paradise: Lucky We Live Hawai'i?* Honolulu: Mutual Publishing.

Odo, F. 1984. "The Rise and Fall of the Nisei." *Hawaii Herald*, August-November (six part series).

Ogawa, D.M. 1981. "Dialogue: What is Local?" *Humanities News* 2(1):1, 7.

Okamura, J.Y. 1980. "Local Culture and Society in Hawai'i." *Amerasia* 7(2):119-137.

_____. 1983. "Immigrant and Local Filipino Perceptions of Ethnic Conflict." In W.C. McCready (ed.), *Culture, Ethnicity and Identity,* Pp. 241-263. New York: Academic Press.

_____. 1990. "Ethnicity and Stratification in Hawaii." *Operation Manong Resource Papers*, No. 1. Operation Manong Program, University of Hawai'i.

_____. 1992. "People of Color in Hawaii's Ethnic Rainbow." Paper presented at Annual Conference of the Hawai'i Sociological Association, Honolulu, Hawai'i, March 21.

Sunday Star-Bulletin & Advertiser 1991a. "Japan Investors Pull Back After Record Haul in 1990." November 24, pp. A1, A9.

_____. 1991b. "Japanese Investment in Hawaii During 1990." November 24, pp. A8.

_____. 1992. "Moving to Mainland: Trail of Plastic Hints at Growing Migration." April 19, pp. B1.

Trask, H.K. 1984-85. "Hawaiians, American Colonization and the Quest for Independence." *Social Process in Hawaii*, 31:101-136.

_____. 1992. "Kupa'a 'Aina: Native Hawaiian Nationalism in Hawai'i." In Z. A. Smith and R. C. Pratt (eds.), *Politics and Public Policy in Hawai'i*. Albany: State University of New York Press.

Wei, W. 1993. *The Asian American Movement: A Social History*. Philadelphia: Temple University Press.

Yamamoto, E. 1974. "From 'Japanee' to Local: Community Change and the Redefinition of Sansei Identity in Hawaii." Senior thesis, Department of Sociology, University of Hawaii.

_____. 1979. "The Significance of Local." *Social Process in Hawaii*, 27:101-115.

Yim, S. 1992. "Hawaii's Ethnic Rainbow: Shining Colors, Side by Side." *Sunday Star-Bulletin & Advertiser*, January 5, pp. B1, B3.

The End of the American Age of Abundance: Whither Hawai'i?

Noel Jacob Kent

The Hawai'i economic model evolved during the 1950s and 1960s. Its core strategy was to utilize the Islands' mid-Pacific location and status within the United States to develop into a center of high technology, education, research, finance, and tourism in the Pacific Rim. A thriving, dynamic and diversified local economy would then surely evolve. To achieve this meant attaching Hawai'i to U. S. (and other centers of global) capital.

For many reasons the hi-tech-finance-research-education area of this scenario did not occur. Tourism-land development, however, not only fulfilled the expectations for it, but much more besides, and by 1970 had emerged as the dominant centerpiece of the new economy (Kent, 1993).

Timing was absolutely critical here: Hawai'i's tourism industry developed during the postwar heyday of stable, high economic growth in the United States, low unemployment, upward consumption and unchallenged world economic leadership. It was assumed by tourism's promoters that the Age of Abundance would continue to provide the capital and constituency, the stablility and long-term expansion the industry needed; inevitably, the affluence of the mainland U. S., in particular, would spill over to envelop the Islands.

This notion was fairly valid for the first quarter-century or so after statehood. The revenues generated by tourism (and to a much lesser extent, military and agriculture) contributed to a rapidly expanding state sector. A substantial local middle class emerged tIed to public employment and small business activities. Shortfalls were seldom a dilemma. Where difficulties arose, these were in the form of excess and uneven development. Overinvestment was rife in the tourism-land development sector, particularly in touristic spaces like Waikiki, Kihei, Lahaina, Kona, as was overbuilding in downtown/central Honolulu. Meanwhile, there was noticeable underdevelopment of affordable housing, public services and viable alternative industries to complement tourism. Asians and Caucasians prospered more than the other ethnic groups.

The strength and attractions of Hawai'i tourism were such that even during the years since 1973—a period when the U.S. economic growth has been slowed—the industry continued to enjoy generally high levels of growth in tourist arrivals and revenues.

But the "contained depression" of the early nineties marks a watershed. The stagnation and decline in the U.S. economy has been directly mirrored in the decline of Hawai'i's tourism. More to the point, the American Age of Abundance is being succeeded by the Age of Downsizing and Insecurity. The deep-seated structural transformations in labor markets and income possibilities now in evidence throughout the mainland are undermining Hawai'i's tourism base. The real incomes of many in the tourism constituency are falling; so is the confidence they have in their careers, job security, possibilities of home ownership, and future mobility. Thus, our recent experience in Hawai'i, the 1970s and 1980s, cannot be relied upon as a guide to the years to come. What happens, then, to an industry built on mass abundance when the foundations of abundance wither?

The Great Hawai'i Boom

Since statehood in 1959, Hawai'i has experienced a number of periods of unabashed economic euphoria. None was more powerful than that of the late 1980s. Its locomotives were logically enough, those twin dynamos of Island growth, the United States mainland and Japan. The long (if relatively modest) wave of Reaganist economic growth that began in 1983 lasted into the first year of George Bush's office. Hawai'i's tourism profited from the aura of optimism generated during these years and the increased affluence and hedonism of the upper/upper middle class. Driven by favorable federal tax laws and heady prospects for profits in the Island economy, construction of hotels and office buildings soared. The booming California economy (which supplied one-half of Hawai'i's mainland tourists) had a key role here (Markrich, 1993). There was, to take a notable example, the Los Angeles corporate raider, David Murdock, whose control over Castle and Cooke gave him the leverage to build a hi-tech park on O'ahu and transform the pineapple island of Lanai into an "upscale" tourism complex (Wood, 1988; Griffen, 1994).

Certainly, Japan-based capital was not new to Hawai'i. Firms like Kokusai Kogyuo and Kyo-ya had substantial tourism sector investments dating back to the 1960s. Later, Dai'ei had purchased the massive Ala Moana Shopping complex. If the Japanese, by the mid-eighties, were by far the largest foreign investor (and the cause of some local resentment and anxiety), their position was not perceived as threatening dominance. Towards the late eighties however, sparked by the unprecedented strength of the yen to the dollar, the huge cash resources of Japanese banks, and a rapid (and government sanctioned) increase of Japanese tourists to Hawai'i, this changed dramatically (Kent, 1993).

Companies such as Seibu, Azabu, Nansay Hawaii, and Otaku bought up a slew of venerable hotels and developed new ones. A substantial share of prime downtown Honolulu commercial space fell into Japanese hands. The launching of Ko-Olina, a hotel/condominium project of mini-Waikiki dimensions on Oʻahu's Ewa coast, evoked more than usual hype. While the vast majority of Japanese investment was concentrated in the "commanding heights" of land and tourism, some did filter into supermarkets, department stores, fast food franchises, locally patronized restaurants (Wood, 1990).

The $1.8 billion of new Japanese capital, in 1988, became $4.4 billion the following year, catapulting total investment to over $8 billion (Yoneyama and Hooper, 1990). In combination with a strong rise in U.S. and Japanese visitors, this launched a startling economic boom, especially in areas like South Kohala, North Kona, and Wailea-Kihei, favored by hotel builders and an "upscale" tourism clientele. Hawaiʻi gross product grew by one-third from 1986-89; state government revenue surpluses reached $500,000,000 in that last year (Yoneyama and Hooper, 1990). Construction, boasting a hugely swollen workforce of thirty thousand people, emerged as Hawaiʻi's second largest industry (Martin, 1991).

Economic growth since statehood has proven grossly uneven in terms of its benefits to various classes and ethnic groups. This pattern can be laid to the alliance of outside investors with landed estates, financial institutions and local political insiders, and the absence of countervailing working class-lower middle-class political power (Kent, 1993)

The late 1980s boom and the huge scale of the projects it created, and the need by overseas investors for political access and island allies, simply accentuated this economic growth. Politically connected "local boy" lawyers had a field day powerbrokering for foreign corporations seeking entree. Local estates and banks made lucrative deals. And homeowners (especially on beachfront property) waxed wealthier as the median price of the single family Oahu home nearly doubled in price between 1987 and 1990 (Roth 1992:18-21).

The downside of boomtime was considerable. Rapidly rising rents and the sheer absence of affordable housing units pushed marginal working-class people to work extreme hours, or out of the housing market altogether. The homeless became noticeable around beach areas and parks. The outmigration of young graduates (a veritable "brain drain") became more pronounced. Nasty problems of growth run wild exacted a price: the overwhelming of transportation, housing and sewage infrastructure by tourism growth on Maui and West Hawaiʻi's "Gold Coast" (Wood, 1990). Right through 1990, popular wisdom had it that the

Japanese and California connections had made Hawai'i "recession proof." Indeed, the state's $12 billion a year tourism industry and $3.7 billion construction industry remained remarkably unaffected by the U.S. mainland's nosedive into recession. Unemployment rates were miniscule. Japanese investment stayed high and the growing number of visitors from Japan seemed to provide a cushion for any downturn in North American visitors (Yoneyama and Hooper, 1990; Hooper, 1991).

The Waihe'e administration and the politically monopolistic Democratic Party remained loyal to the existing economic model. Tied through multiple networks to the local financial establishment, the Bishop Estate, hotel interests, developers, and construction unions, it could do no other. And the huge budget surpluses and miniscule unemployment seemed to point to a successful policy.

There was, moreover, an utter bankruptcy of alternative visions of the future. Not only was Governor John Waihe'e, himself, a leader of limited abilities, but he took the "politics of cronyism" so prevalent in Hawai'i's politics to new heights of cynicism. The award of non-bid state contracts to leading donors to the governor's political war chest became routine. After altering a document to protect a Bank of Hawaii lobbyist, a politically-connected judge remained unindicted. The monumental stink of insider corruption and bribery hung over the deal with developer Sukarman Sukamto to secure a convention center site. Occasionally, Waihe'e overstepped the bounds: His appointment of a daughter of a leading Democratic Party fixer to the Hawai'i Supreme Court was rejected by the state senate amidst a torrent of public criticism (Lind, 1992; Roth 1993:195).

The irrepressible fantasy that Hawai'i could capture a niche as a hi-tech center continued. Against the wishes of local residents, the administration promoted a Big Island space launching project. A Manoa Valley "Innovation Center" was built to house some extremely dubious hi-tech companies. Meanwhile, the much ballyhooed Mililani hi-tech park, designed in the 1980s to accommodate a mass infusion of new enterprises employing 12,000 workers, had attracted only a handful with 350 employees. In view of high operating and living costs, remoteness from major markets, educational infrastructure, etc., this latest thrust toward hi-tech status remained as doomed as earlier ones (Ishikawa, 1992).

Meanwhile, a so-called major priority, reform of a scandalously inept public educational system, stagnated. The state's reliance on a policy of requiring developers to devote a percentage of new developments to "affordable homes" did not begin to stem the mushrooming housing crises. Honolulu remained the least affordable metropolitan housing market in the United States (*Honolulu Star-Bulletin and Advertiser [HSBA]*, 1992).

Hawai'i's Ungay Nineties

The Gulf War exploded the myth of Hawai'i's economic invulnerability. Tourist arrivals plunged a sharp 13.5% during early 1991, and hotel occupancies dived below profitable minimums (Hooper, 1991). Suddenly, the Tokyo stock-market bust, starkly falling real estate values, and a rash of bankruptcies revealed the fragility of Japan's prosperity. Growth and profits fell to unprecedented levels, and companies began restructuring their organizations. Official policy mandated a general tightening of speculative activity and lending abroad. By 1992, new Japanese investment in Hawai'i dwindled to $328 million (Ma and Markrich, 1993). Large investors in Hawai'i such as Azabu, Asahi Jyuken, and TSA International found their financial structures overextended. They proceded to freeze or cut back on planned developments such as Ko Olina, Kawela Bay, and the Ke'eaumoku superblock in Honolulu. So-called "trophy" investments were put on the market for a fraction of their cost (Taketa, 1992).

In a portent of the future, the higher end, luxury hotels bore the brunt of the downturn. The 1992 and 1993 occupancy rates in Maui, whose tourism plant was geared to the affluent trade, were in the low (and money-losing) 60 percentile (Tagawa, 1993). Tourists were more price-conscious now and more of them were repeat Hawai'i visitors; they stayed in cheaper accommodations. Functioning at half occupancy, the "upscale" resorts unsuccessfully offered free nights and cars to attract clientele (Taketa, 1992a). The year 1992 saw a 5% drop in tourist arrivals from a dismal 1991; the 7 million of 1990 became the 6.4 of 1992 (Parris, 1993). A further decline of over 6% came in 1993. Hotel layoffs were widespread. The vacuum of Japanese money spelled finis for the hotel and commercial building boom and rapid "downsizing" occurred in the workforce of architects, ironworkers, carpenters, laborers, and real estate agents.

The fragility of Hawai'i's labor market was rendered more acute by the death throes of commercial agriculture. The first months of 1993 witnessed the closing of the Big Island's Hamakua sugar plantation throwing 600 out of work, and the abrupt end of Dole's Lanai pineapple operations affecting 160 more (Tagawa, 1993; *Honolulu Star-Bulletin [HSB]*, 1992).

For a tourism-dependent economy, the impacts of negative growth were felt along a broad spectrum. State and county revenues had large shortfalls; $115 million was cut from the $4 billion 1992 state budget (Tagawa 1993:46-52). Essential social welfare programs lost funding; several thousand individuals and families were cut from the welfare rolls in 1993 (personal interview, State Department of Human Services). Mental health services were pared down. The Department of Education, in need of new funds to implement an innovative decentralization program, was, instead, cut back. An already inadequately-financed University of Hawai'i system took a series of budget hits to instructional programs, support and maintenance services, libraries, faculty positions, and salaries (*HSB*, 1993b).

True to form, the response of the state was to prop up tourism and attempt to lure new investors from Southeast Asia and China to replace the Japanese (Ma and Markrich, 1993; Taketa, 1993). The Hawai'i Visitors Bureau received an emergency $6 million in 1991 to run a blitz of advertisements and a record $22 million allocation for 1992-93, followed by another significant increase the next year (Ishikawa, 1994). A special legislative session was convened to sanction the building of a mammoth convention center and $136 million expended for a site. The state started pumping almost $3 billion into a multi-year airport enlargement program. A number of new luxury hotels were coming on line in Maui and the Big Island. The Kauai hotel plant was being reconstructed after Hurricane Iniki.

This "Build it and they shall come" approach had been successful in sparking renewed growth in the aftermath of previous recessions. But there was a dramatic new wild card about; the crisis of m*ass abundance itself in the United States*. The underlying structures had changed dramatically and thus the prospects for Hawai'i's economic recovery.

The New American Order

The current decade has been the proverbial "morning after" for the United States. How remote the eighties suddenly seem, with its the sky's-the-limit euphoria of the Reagan years, with an artificial prosperity induced by monstrous military budgets and mountainous corporate and consumer debt, the hype of junk bond kings and real estate moguls.

Since the 1990s began, the Great American Growth Machine has remained stuck. At a mediocre 1.5% or so, not the 4% or so it needs to generate new jobs and real growth. A key index, productivity growth, is in actual decline. Recessionary levels of high unemployment and underemployment mock the notion of "recovery." Even record low interest rates cannot generate a business boom.

Premonitions of this descent began a quarter-century ago. The white-hot years spanning 1967 and 1974 furnished the crucible; incapable of managing its domestic or foreign affairs, the nation slid into a deep, multifaceted crisis from which it has never truly emerged. Confidence in major institutions like the presidency, congress, and large corporations eroded as they proved unable to respond to the interlocking structural crises at hand.

The closing of the Age of Abundance was, at once, a symptom, cause and casualty of the decline of the nation. Although Americans like to believe their personal fortunes transcend their country's, these are, as Joel Kurtzman suggests, intertwined: "For more than a decade and a half-America has been getting poorer as a nation, while Americans have been getting poorer as individuals" (Kurtzman 1988:19).

"In some ways," Frank Levy and Richard Michel say, "1973 was the last good year" (Levy and Michel 1986:34). Since then, the average worker's earnings have dropped a startling (inflation adjusted) 17% (Mishel and Simon 1988:Table 23). Household income forms the axis around which the drama plays itself out. The inflation indexed median family income for 1986 or 1993 was ominously close to what it had been in 1973. The most favorable studies show nothing better than growth of slightly more than 1% in real after-tax earnings for typical middle-income families during the 1980s. Even before the early 1990s recession ravaged incomes, consumption power was barely at late 1970s levels (Mattera, 1989; Pollin, 1989; Updegrave, 1990). Personal savings have also fallen steeply from 7.9% in the 1970s to around 4%.

What makes all this so extraordinary is that Americans have pulled out virtually every stop to stem the tide and it has not worked. Between 1973 and 1986 the number of work hours increased by 20% and leisure correspondingly diminished. Family survival strategies mean a greater percentage of citizens working two and three jobs than at any time in the last 30 years. The massive mobilization of female labor power has, of course, been central here. Back in 1973 less than one-half of all married women worked outside the home; 13 years later, it was two-thirds.

Women workers have propped up the crumbling foundations of the American Dream; had they not been available, family fortunes in the U.S. would have really nosedived (Rose and Fasenfast, 1988; *HSB*, 1993a). Yet the transformation of American women into paid employees has not led to higher living standards. The average family must simply work one more day a week to maintain itself at 1970s' levels. Reasonable hopes that more hard work would yield returns have been foiled by a gargantuan presence looming over individuals and families; the restructuring of the U.S. economy (Sweeney and Nussbaum, 1989).

Ultimately, the fortunes of working and middle-class Americans have been hostage to what Philip Mattera cogently calls, "an unprecedented alliance of business, the federal government and the Right, all dedicated to a radical restructuring of the United States political economy" (Mattera, 1990; Faux, 1989; Kolko, 1988).

Big Business has been the main player. Faced by sharpened competition and plummeting profit levels, corporate CEOs jettisoned the 1950s-1960s "social contract" and began to attack high labor costs. Hence, conscious corporate policies of wage reductions, elimination of high-wage jobs, anti-union campaigns and the outsourcing of jobs to cheaper labor areas. To reduce the role of skilled workers in the production process, automation systems aimed at de-skilling were pushed on line. Leadership here was taken by such bellweather manufacturers as General Motors, U.S. Steel, and General Electric, which closed down large amounts of capacity, only to reinvent themselves as conglomerates sporting large acquisitions in the more lucrative financial services and energy areas. This trend was accentuated by the great corporate financing revolution of the eighties that left monster companies burdened with enormous debts and strong incentives for going lean and mean.

Restructuring was aimed at creating a docile, vulnerable, dependent American labor force. Its initial victims were the so-called "aristocrats of labor," metalworkers, autoworkers, shipworkers, meatpackers, long-haul truckers (Freedman, 1988; Shaiken, 1984). Huge numbers were permanently laid off. The term "giveback" entered union parlance and concessions became a way of life; by the mid-1980s, one-third of all workers under new contracts took wage cuts. Here, the pro-business, free-market agendas of the Reagan administration dovetailed with corporate restructuring of wages and the job market.

In an age of transformation, the labor market opportunities for Americans have been wholly transformed. This is really what the end of abundance is all about. The solid primary sector jobs, the ones with middle class incomes, career ladders, and job security are being driven out by what Chris Tilly calls "firms that have adopted a low-wage, low skill, high turnover employment policy;" thus secondary sector drudge jobs become the growth poll of the economy (Tilly, 1990).

The labor market is pried apart. Certain professional-technical-managerial occupations are expanding, but so are nonprofessional, nontechnical ones (janitors, fast food, hotel, and retail clerks). Middle-strata jobs are being permanently lost, at the same time low wage jobs are increasing in absolute and relative numbers, and the high salaried by a smaller percentage. What is paramount is that the old "family wage" blue-collar jobs—which a generation ago allowed high school graduates and dropouts to build families, own homes, and be self-respecting citizens—are being rapidly automated out of existence or relocated to the global factory enclaves of Mexico or East Asia.

And for the first time modest white-collar jobs are for export: The revolution in telecommunications means a wide assortment of American companies are beginning to process insurance forms, airline reservations, credit card payments, and so forth in cheap labor areas like the Caribbean, Ireland, and the Philippines (*International Herald Tribune*, 1991).

This leaves noncollegiate workers the myriad number of jobs offering paltry wages and interchangable skills in the service industries, the area that produced some 80% of private sector jobs like retail, trade, health, and business services employment during the 1980s. Here, the boundary between low-skill entry level jobs, and those with large possibilites for mobility, is increasingly severe (*New York Times*, 1990).

The split has been intensified by corporate policies of maintaining a core of stable, relatively privileged personnel surrounded by a periphery of low paid, casual, contract workers lacking rights or benefits. The appearance of such contingent employees (35.6 million in 1988) as the new work force growth pole marks a decisive step in the abandonment of the American worker by business. One-half of all new jobs in the 1980s were filled by temporaries (increasing 117%) and part-timers (40%); leased workers now number a million. A contract labor force of huge dimensions has emerged lacking job security, company pensions or medical care and receiving 60% of average full-time wages. By 1991, nearly 6 million people were involuntary part-timers. More Americans are working than ever before, and at more jobs, but at lower wages and for fewer benefits (Sweeney and Nussbaum, 1989; *U. S. News and World Report*, 1991).

It should be noted that their comparative powerlessness (and long history of inequality in the labor market) make females natural fodder for the contingent work force. It is they who furnish the homeworkers for the newly popular "electronic cottage," which flourishes from Silicon Valley to Boston's hi-tech corridors, the "temps" sent out by agencies, the part-time department store clerks. Eileen Applebaum's emphasis on "the pivotal role of the gendered nature of employment relations" is well taken (Applebaum and Schettkat, 1990). That women are among the primary victims of restructuring goes a far piece in explaining why their masive surge into outside work has done so little to resuscitate the fading American Dream. So the mobilization of women to counter the harsh realities of life in the New American Order must be recognized for what it is; a failed holding action. This is most apparent during years of special hardship such as 1990-1992, when the real net worth of households declined (*Business Week*, 1991).

The "female option" has failed. So has the strategy of working more jobs. The upshot is that many American households in the lower three- quarters of the income hierarchy, those with stagnating or downward real incomes have two stark choices; they can go into debt to maintain their lifestyle or change their consumption patterns. Throughout the mid-late 1980s, the first was dominant, as run-of-the-mill families borrowed to finance rising mortgage costs, basic transportation, and daily necessities. Household debt ran wild. This had exhausted itself even before the downturn of 1990. Since then, the imperative has been to reduce spending and cut back nonessentials (which, in turn, extended the recession). *Business Week*, analyzing why the recession would not quit, spoke of the "many untraditional drags on demand" such as "heavy debts, low savings and meager growth in incomes" (*Business Week*, November 1990 and July 1991).

Certainly, the New American Order has its robust beneficiaries; those heavily skilled professionals Robert Reich calls "symbolic analysts" and those who employ them (Reich, 1991). The Age of Abundance is still alive and well in upper-middle-class/upper-class enclaves from Orange County to Suffolk County (Justen, 1988). But anywhere from 75 to 85% of the population are losing ground absolutely and relatively. This is absolutely critical for the future of Hawaiian tourism. The stable American working class and lower middle class (the second and third fifths of the class structure) are experiencing income loss and stagnation. Even during the 1980s, the lower middle had no economic gains; the middle fifth gained an anemic 2.3%. The downturn beginning in 1990 has affected them severely in terms of jobs, incomes, and homeownership possibilities. (Updegrave, 1990; Fallows, 1990; Economic Committee of Congress, 1990).

We should pay particular attention to the next income level (the upper-middle fifth), a prime constituency for Hawaiian tourism. This group achieved modest income growth in the 1980s. But the nineties have savaged them in an unprecedented manner. *White-collar middle managers and professionals are now subject to downmobility in the same manner as blue-collars.* Between mid-1989 and 1991, corporations shed half a million white-collar jobs, including many in the executive-professional class. A large number of these jobs are permanently gone and, as a consequence, many of those laid off are working at lower paying jobs or are underemployed. During these years, Inflation-adjusted, white-collar incomes have actually fallen (*Wall Street Journal*, 1991). The curtailing of corporate and public recruitment has meant the job market for newly-minted college graduates has dwindled ominously in recent years (*Across the Board*, 1992; McFadden, 1991).

Indeed, Americans have not been so insecure since the Great Depression. The recent "recession" has amply illustrated the striking vulnerability of ordinary household economies in this country. One group of middle-income families interviewed by *Fortune* "all know they are just a pink slip away and a medical mishap away from ruin" (1992:48). Downmobility has become such a routine experience for the middle class that some analysts argue the class itself is a declining proportion vis-à-vis the rich and the lower classes (Newman, 1989; Justen, 1988, *Wall Street Journal*, 1986; Bradbury, 1986). No one, except the super rich, really feels safe. "People feel terrified since nobody knows who is next," remarked one Digital Computer employee, after a major downsizing. (*International Herald Tribune*, 1992). In an ever harsher world where corporate and governmental responsibility are obsolete, and jobs, cherished skills, career ladders, and company pensions vanish overnight, people will dream more of escape fantasies, but lack the resources and confidence to indulge them.

Future trajectories point to an intensification of the process. Pushed by various forces, U.S. corporations are adopting minimalist and globalist strategies. Minimalism focuses upon reducing costs of labor, inventory, and production/distribution to the rock bottom. It slashes staff mercilessly, erases whole divisions, purchases vital services from independent contractors (Heenan, 1991) The coming on line of revolutionary robotics technology, the so-called intelligent machines, will mean that this technology can continue to create more output with less workers. New technologies and corporate reorganizations will continue to force managers into other lines of work. The eminent management authority Peter Drucker comments: "The typical business 20 years hence will have fewer than half the levels of management as its counterpart today, and no more than a third of managers" (*The Economist*, 1989). Increasingly the career will be a preserve of top management. At leading companies like Motorola, Hughes, Bank of America, and Hewlett Packard, long-established career lines have been discarded.

A second critical strategy is globalism or Internationalization of production. The imperative will be to maximize worldwide profits without regard to source of production or national boundaries" (*Business Week*, 1978). Within this framework, the Mexican *maquiladores* subcontrating economy becomes the prototype of how future U.S. assembly line work will be performed (*Business Week*, 1990).

But this is only the proverbial tip of the iceberg. During the nineties and beyond, American manufacturers and service producers will have the capacity to relocate a startling variety of production sites to cheap labor areas, especially since productivity in developing countries is rising faster than in the United States. Fluid capital, in combination with new production and communications technologies, will see a vast assortment of goods and services from fiber optics to electrical equipment and chemicals to airline reservations and software fabricated abroad. U.S.-owned plants overseas will increasingly outsource to local suppliers. In the 1990s and beyond, the U.S. service sector will be profoundly affected Services of varying sophistication will be routinely outsourced to the multitude of cheap labor English-speaking places. Witness the burgeoning software industry in India, busily developing software programs, chip design, and computer specification for leading U.S. firms (*International Herald Tribune*, 1991; Mead, 1990).

The acceleration of minimalism and globalism and the trend towards treating American workers of all collars as a disposable commodity trivializes the much-heralded "human capital" strategy for national recovery.

In the teeth of different corporate agendas, President Bill Clinton's notions of using retraining, upgrading, and higher productivity to re-create the abundance and security of the past must remain a fantasy. The increasing inequalities and sheer precariousness of life in the United States (and perhaps, Canada, Japan, and western Europe, also) may not effectively doom Hawai'i's tourism, but it does mean the glory days of stability and growth are now over.

Conclusion

The tourism-based Hawai'i economic model was founded on the assumption that the postwar American Age of Abundance would provide the economic resources necessary for an ever-expanding tourism clientele. This condition (despite uneven development and sharp inequalities) did transpire for nearly half-a-century. Now, the Age of Abundance is being replaced by one of increasing austerity, insecurity, and inequality. The tumultuous restructuring of U.S. corporations and labor markets is both cause and signpost here. Meanwhile, the bill for the reckless extravagance and mismanagement of the American political-economy over the last 40 years has come due in the form of a $4 trillion debt, extremely costly toxic waste cleanups and dismantling of an inflated military sector.

What the New American Order does is make it harder for Americans to be genuinely middle class. And being in the middle is no longer a guarantee of middle-class status. The middle Americans who form the indispensable clientele for island tourism will experience eroding incomes and higher taxes, and feel less economically secure. Debt is no longer the option it was in the 1980s. California, a major source of visitors, confronts particularly difficult structural problems (defense cutbacks, hi-tech shakeouts, state deficits, declining educational systems) in moving towards economic recovery.

Given this context, mass tourism stagnates and contracts. The industry moves from late maturity into decline. Visitors will, of course, continue to arrive in the millions, but at diminishing rates, and they will spend more modestly when they do come. Ironically, the American people may have more leisure in the future, but less discretionary income to spend on trans-oceanic vacations.

Naturally, the implications for Hawai'i are profound. The years ahead will be more crisis-ridden. Economic decline can only magnify the developing crisis of political legitimacy. A shrinking pie deprives the Island power structures of the resources they require to coopt the rising Hawaiian sovereignty movement, the increasingly vocal demand for affordable housing, and the growing confrontation between the land rich and land poor. This raises the spectre of societal disintegration in the form of ethnic/class polarization, *or* the possibilities of a dynamic, innovative new politics based upon local integrity, respect for indigenous rights, community development, and incorporation of the marginalized.

References

Across the Board. April 1, 1992:5.

Applebaum, Eileen and Schettkat, Ronald. 1990. *Labor Market Adjustments to Structural Change and Technical Progress.* New York: Praeger.

Bradbury, Katharine. 1986. "The Shrinking Middle Class." *New England Economic Review.* Sept-Oct.

Business Week. 1978. "Made in U.S.A. Means Little to the Multinationals." April 10:60.

_____. 1990. "Mexico: A New Economic Era." November 12.

_____. 1991. July 29:21.

Dawson, Donne. 1990. "A Roof Over Maui's Head." *Hawaii Investor.* November.

Economic Committee of Congress. 1990. *The Concentration of Wealth in the U.S., Trends in the Distribution of Wealth Among American Families.* Washington, D.C.

The Economist. 1989. Oct. 21:20.

Fallows, James. 1990. "Wake Up America." *New York Review of Books.* March 1.

Faux, Jeff. 1989. *Sending the Bill to Those Who Went to the Party.* Washington: Economic Policy Institute.

Fortune. 1992. Feb. 24:48.

Freedman, Audrey. 1988. *Social and Labor Bulletin.* March 4:37.

Griffen, John. 1994. Lanai: Private Island?" *Honolulu Advertiser.* 1/13:A17.

Heenan, David. 1991. *The New Corporate Frontier: The Big Move to Small Towns.* New York: McGraw-Hill. 1991.

Honolulu Advertiser. 1993. 2/23:1-2.

Honolulu Star-Bulletin. 1992. "Paty Marks End of Pineapple Era." 11/14.

_____. 1993a. "US Family Incomes Keep Slipping." 3/5.

_____. 1993a. "Hawaii Tourism No Rebound Yet." 1/22.

Honolulu Star-Bulletin and Advertiser. 1992. "Housing Takes its Biggest Pay Bite Here in Honolulu." 2/2:A 32.

Hooper, Susan. 1991. "Waiting Out the Slump." *Hawaii Business.* June:18.

International Herald Tribune. 1991. "White Collar Jobs Go Offshore." 10/7.

_____. 1992. "Digital to Cut 6,000 By Year's End." 11/28-29.

Ishikawa, Lisa. 1992. "High Tech Wanna Be." *Hawaii Business.* February:48-51.

_____. 1994. "Redo for Paradise." *Hawaii Investor.* January:19.

The Joint Economic Committee of Congress. 1990. *Report.* Washington, D.C., December.

Jokiel, Lucy. 1993. "Reinventing Maui." *Hawaii Investor*:10

Justen, Thomas. 1988. "The Distribution of Wealth in the United States Economy." part 2, *Economic Outlook.* 14(4) (Spring).

Kent, Noel. 1983. *Hawaii Islands Under the Influence.* New York: Monthly Review Press.

Kolko, Joyce. 1988. *Restructuring the World Economy.* Pantheon, New York.

Kopkind, Andrew. 1992. "A Manufactured Candidate." *Nation.* February 3.

Kurtzman, Joel. 1988. *The Decline and Crash of the American Economy.* New York: Norton.

Levy, Frank and Michel, Robert. 1986. "The Economic Bust for the Baby Boom." *Challenge*:34.

Lind, Ian. 1992. "Architects and Engineers Provide Bulk of Democratic Funds." *Monitor*. 3(1) (December).

Louis Harris and Associates. 1987. *Inside America*. New York.

Ma, Cynthia and Mike Markrich. 1993. "A Tailwind for Tourism." *Hawaii Business*. May:19.

Mak, James and Sakai, Marcia Y. 1992. "Foreign Investment." In Randall Roth, *The Price of Paradise*, pp. 33-37. Honolulu: Mutual.

Markrich, Mike. 1993. "The Morning After." *Hawaii Business*. June:17.

_____. 1993. "Economic Force, The Lonely State." *Hawaii Business*:21.

Martin, Daniel. 1991. "Construction's New Frontier." *Hawaii Business*. March.

Mattera, Philip. 1990. *Prosperity Lost*. New York: Addison-Wesley.

McClain, David. 1992. "Hawaii's Competitiveness." In Randall Roth, *The Price of Paradise*, pp. 23-25. Honolulu: Mutual Publishers.

McFadden, Robert. 1991. "For Class of '91, Bleakest Prospects in a Decade For That Foot-In-The-Door-Job." *International Herald Tribune*. 4/23.

Mead, Walter Russell. 1990. *The Low Wage Challenge to Global Growth*. Washington, D.C.: Economic Planning Institute.

Mishel, Robert and Simon, Jacqueline. 1988. *The State of Working America*. Washington, D.C.: Economic Policy Institute, Table 23.

New York Times. 1990. "'K Mart Economy' and 'Dreams of Young Wither as Economy Dries Up.'" 11/7:A 14.

Newman, Katherine. 1989. *Falling From Grace: The Experience of Downward Mobility in the American Middle Class*. New York: Free Press

Parris, Ellen. 1992. "Hawaii Calls." *Hawaii Investor*. October.

_____. 1993. "Surviving Tough Times." *Hawaii Investor*. January:50.

Pollin, Robert. 1990. *Deeper in Debt: The Changing Conditions of U.S. Households*. Washington, D.C.: Economic Policy Institute.

Reich, Robert. 1991. *The Work of Nations: Preparing Ourselves for the 21st Century*. New York: Knopf.

Rose, Stephen and David Fasenfast. 1988. *Economic Policy Institute Working Paper No. 103*. Washington, D.C.: Economic Policy Institute.

Roth, Randall W. 1992. *The Price of Paradise, Lucky We Live Hawaii*. Honolulu: Mutual Publishing.

_____. 1993. *The Price of Paradise*. vol. 2. Honolulu: Mutual Publishing.

Schor, Juliet. 1991. *The Overworked American: The Unexpected Decline of Leisure*. New York: Basic Books.

Shaiken, Harley. 1984. *Work Transformed, Automation and Labor in the Computer Age*. New York: Rhinehart and Winston.

Sweeney, John J. and Nussbaum, Karen. 1989. *Solutions for the New Workforce*. Washington, D.C.: Seven Locks Press.

Tagawa, Glen. H. 1993. "What's in store for 93?" *Hawaii Investor*. January:45-52.

Taketa, Mari. 1992. "Sweating Out the Slump." *Hawaii Business*. March:26-27.

_____. 1992. "New Moves For Tourism." *Hawaii Business*. May:26-28.

_____. 1992. "Taming of the Yen." *Hawaii Business*. June.

_____. 1993. Editor's column. *Hawaii Business*. June.

Tilly, Chris. 1990. *Short Hours, Short Shrift: Causes and Consequences of Part-Time Work*. Washington, D.C.. Economic Policy Institute.

United States Dept. of Labor. 1988. *BLS*, Washington. August 2.

Updegrave, Walter. 1990. "How Are We Doing?" *Money*, Money Extra Issue:26.

U. S .News and World Report. 6/17/91:50.

Wall Street Journal. 1986. "The Middle Class at Risk: Growing Gap: US Rich and Poor Increase in Numbers: Middle Loses Ground." 9/21.

_____. 1991. "Going Broke." 6/26:1.

Wood, Bill. 1988.. "Pied Piper in Pin Stripes." *Hawaii Investor*. March 1988:17.

_____. 1990. Bill Wood. "We Will Now Do a Slowdown," *Hawaii Investor*. November:1

Yoneyama, Tom and Susan Hooper. 1990. "The Japaning of Hawaii." *Hawaii Business*. January:14-16

Missionaries, Polynesians, and Tourists: Mormonism and Tourism in La'ie, Hawai'i

T. D. Webb

Introduction

In September 1993, when he was named president of the Hawai'i Visitor's Bureau, Thomas S. Sakata announced that the Bureau's campaign to revitalize tourism in Hawai'i will emphasize Hawaiian culture and values (Wiles 1992:E3). The strategy to capitalize on local color, ethnicity, and the mystique of Island lifestyles, however, is not new to Hawai'i. It was introduced on a large scale when the Mormon church opened the Polynesian Cultural Center 30 years ago, shrewdly combining religion and commerce in a way that is characteristic of Mormonism. And the Center is only the most recent phase of the Mormons' long experience attracting tourists to La'ie.[1]

The Center, or PCC, pioneered in Hawai'i a brand of tourist attraction that is now called "cultural" or "ethnic" tourism. This type of tourist industry draws on travelers' interest in native dwellings, ceremonies, foods, and the like. It also provides the travelers with a sense of having witnessed alternate lifestyles, thus broadening their awareness of the larger world (Smith 1989: 4-5). Of course, the cultural portrayals at such expositions are often artificial and shallow.[2] Nevertheless, cultural tourism has become immensely popular in the last two decades.

The success of the PCC has inspired a number of other establishments to venture into Hawai'i's cultural tourism market. But unlike these other commercial ventures, the creation and success of the PCC can be attributed to a set of religious precepts and historical precedents that made La'ie a most fertile ground for such an endeavor. In fact, Mormonism, commerce, and tourism are so intertwined in La'ie and its world-famous cultural center that the PCC could only have been realized by the Mormons.

The PCC occupies a 42-acre site in the predominantly Mormon town of La'ie. Since its opening in November 1963, it has become one of Hawai'i's most popular paid tourist attractions, entertaining about one million customers annually. Its annual revenues now total 40 million dollars (Hooper 1992:111).

The Center was created to provide financial support to the Church College of Hawai'i, which opened in 1955 and later became the Hawai'i campus of Brigham Young University (Britsch 1986:88). Located adjacent to the Center, the university is also a Mormon property.

The PCC provides outright gifts to the school as well as wages for approximately 700 students who work part-time in the Center's seven "villages" of more or less accurate replicas of traditional dwellings, in its famed night show, and in other park capacities. The Center also employs another 300 or so persons from the community. The majority of the full-time and part-time employees are Mormon Polynesians. Yet the Center's directors and top administrators, appointed by church officials in Salt Lake City, have predominantly been white ecclesiastical leaders from the mainland United States. Some have been apostles of the church, men revered as prophets.

The PCC is an unusual tourism enterprise because it has assumed the stature of a quasi-religious experience for its employees. This phenomenon is not simply because the Center's revenues go to the church-run university or that its leaders are high church officials. Though unacknowledged, a complex combination of historical events and theological precepts have raised the PCC to its near-sacred importance. The Center expresses a number of fundamental Mormon beliefs including elevation of materialism to a religious importance, reverence for ancestors, and a fascination with Polynesian origins. These and other religious precedents give the Center's employees the extra commitment that has made it so financially successful.

This study will discuss the religious foundation that made the PCC a resounding and unique financial success. The study includes findings taken from extensive interviews with PCC employees, personal observations of the Center over a nine-year period, and a lifelong familiarity with the Mormon people, their history, rituals, beliefs, doctrine, and scriptures.

La'ie's Early Tourism Ventures

The church purchased La'ie in 1865 as a gathering place for Hawaiian converts, and produced sugar there for several decades. Even during these early times, La'ie entertained notable guests. King Kalakaua and Queen Kapiolani visited Laie repeatedly. The king was intrigued by the high fertility of the Hawaiian converts (Chase 1981:95, 99). The queen was impressed by the church's organization for women, and used it as a model for a women's organization among her own followers (Spurrier 1978:20).

After La'ie's imposing temple was completed in 1919, tourists made it a regular stop on coastal tours. Guidebooks of that period listed the temple as a main attraction on the north shore, comparing the visual effect of its striking whiteness with that of the Taj Mahal (Pierce 1956:15; Forester 1986:63;

Cummings 1965). Temple planners were expecting visitors, and built an information bureau on the grounds where attendants still answer tourists' questions, distribute Mormon literature, and lead tours of the grounds.

Later, as La'ie's sugar industry declined, Hawai'i's tourism industry was growing. With thoughts of profiting from the large numbers of tourists coming to Hawai'i, La'ie residents introduced the well-known *hukilau* (lit. pull ropes) on the shore of La'ie Bay. The La'ie hukilau began in 1937 to raise funds to build the Beretania Street Tabernacle in Honolulu, and continued for several years (Kawahigashi 1968:1-2). The Hukilau reappeared in 1948 and brought considerable revenues into La'ie until the PCC opened (Britsch 1986:161).

Each monthly hukilau attracted hundreds tourists from Honolulu. They joined La'ie residents in setting the net in the bay and pulling it in, net making and patching, singing, and ukulele playing. After a noon *luau* (Hawaiian feast), tourists were entertained with songs and dances performed by the La'ie residents, who showed a true entrepreneurialism by operating a sustained program to market the multicultural talents of their village (Kawahigashi, 1968).

Unlike the PCC, which is directed by church appointees from the mainland, the hukilau was devised and produced by La'ie's residents. Because they could see that the major obstacle to success was the distance of La'ie from the tourist centers in Honolulu, they became adept at marketing, and even made promotional deals with hotels, tourist bureaus, and military bases (Kawahigashi, 1968).

With the hukilau, tourism in La'ie was on the verge of becoming an industry to replace the defunct church-run sugar plantation that had earlier sustained the community. By 1959, church and college leaders in La'ie decided to test the marketability of a Polynesian dance revue performed by students from the college. Faculty members trained the student troupe and staged them at various locations in Honolulu as the "Polynesian Panorama." After two years of shuttling students back and forth to perform in Honolulu, decision makers were convinced that a spirited, tourist-oriented Polynesian revue with a student cast was definitely marketable (Ferre 1988:26-33; O'Brien 1983:77).

Sanctified Materialism

Markets, profits, and commerce have a special sanctity in Mormon theology. Mormonism began as an amalgamation of colonial Puritan materialism and Jacksonian progressivism that some experts regard as distinctly American (Hansen 1981:82; Ahlstrom 1972:502-4, 509, 1021; O'Dea 1957:56). The Mormons' sense of errand, like that of the Puritans, encouraged them to prosper materially to build God's kingdom. O'Dea (1957:134) observes that the Mormons, by setting up the material kingdom of Zion on earth, expected worldly prosperity as part of their covenant with God just as Abraham, Isaac, and Joseph prospered under theirs.

Arguing that Mormonism is "the most typically American theology yet formulated," Hansen says that

> the American locale and historical framework of the Book of Mormon is perhaps the most obvious and yet least important reason why this is so. More typically American is the optimistic, progressive, "materialistic" nature of Mormon theology....perhaps most typical of all is its practical, nonutopian emphasis—not only in social thought....but also in its metaphysics. (1981:82)

He concludes (1981:116-17) that Mormonism promised an alternate route to social progress for those left behind in the otherwise progressive surge of Jacksonian laissez-faire America.

As Hansen implies, the Book of Mormon expresses this American composite. Mormonism's most sacred text, and most impressive cultural creation, was translated from golden plates by Joseph Smith, Mormonism's founder and the first in a succession of Mormon prophets. The plates were delivered to Smith in 1827 by an angel, and contained the history of an ancient American civilization. The book is replete with instances in which characters prospered when they kept God's commandments, and became enslaved when his teachings were disobeyed (e.g., Alma 1:29; Helaman 3:25; 4 Nephi 1:12-18).[3] Even its symbols—the angel, the gold—assert an enduring bond between the material and the spiritual worlds, and imply that Mormonism is chosen for religious and also worldly greatness. The Book of Mormon not only admonishes church members to subdue the earth, but expressly warrants the pursuit of material prosperity to build God's kingdom as part of one's spiritual progress. For example,

> But before ye seek for riches, seek ye for the kingdom of God. And after ye have obtained a hope in Christ ye shall obtain riches, if ye seek them; and ye will seek them for the intent to do good. (Jacob 2:18-19)

Other sacred Mormon texts also sanctify materialism. Doctrine revealed by God to Smith teaches that no duality exists between spirit and matter (D&C 29:34; 131:7-8). In Mormonism, the material world is only an extension of the spiritual, a stewardship (D&C 42:32), the wise management of which will lead to an eternal reward (D&C 51:19). God Himself, who is believed by the Mormons to possess a tangible body of flesh and bones, is evidence of the eternal importance of matter (D&C 130:22). According to Albanese,

> in Mormon teaching there was no pronounced dualism between spirit and matter. Things spiritual were a refined essence of the material world—all spirit was matter—so that God, as well as humanity, was testimony to the sacredness of matter...In an America which in the nineteenth century pursued material success and subscribed to the cult of worldly progress, Mormons taught their neighbors how important matter really was. (1981:43)

The emphasis on material prosperity was embodied in the Mormon economic system of the nineteenth century through which surplus produce from one settlement became a resource to exchange for more needed items in surplus in other settlements. According to Leone (1979), this practice assumed a sacred stature and contributed to the worldview that is the root of modern Mormonism, namely, that material adaptation and success constitute religious acts.

Arrington (1958) examines the "economic missions" sponsored by the church after the Mormon migration to Utah. Between 1850 and 1890, the church called great numbers of "missionaries" to perform gainful labors that were considered as sanctified as the evangelical missions. The laborers mined gold and lead, manufactured iron, raised silk, operated businesses, farmed cotton, milled textiles, and built factories as part of a deliberate plan to fulfill the Mormons' religious errand. As Arrington states,

> The performance of economic activity, under church direction, thus came to occupy a position of honor alongside evangelization. While some looked upon this adaptation as a materialization of religion, the Mormons were proud to regard it as the spiritualization of temporal activity. (1958:33)

La'ie itself had such a purpose. According to Brigham Young's plan, La'ie was to be an "agricultural mission" to produce cotton and sugar for the vast redistribution of goods that made up the early Mormon economic system (Spurrier 1978:17; Britsch 1986:129.) In La'ie the church built a sugar mill, dug wells, and cultivated sugar, but cotton proved fruitless.

Most PCC employees are not ritually ordained to serve as were the economic missionaries of the nineteenth century. But the Center's purpose of supporting the operations of the church through large-scale commercialization make it comparable to the church's economic enterprises of that period. Founded as an economic venture, La'ie now exploits tourism for the church as it once exploited natural resources.

In the early 1960s, when the hukilau and the Polynesian Panorama were both proving successful separately, the next logical step was to merge them at a facility designed and controlled by the church in order to provide income for a large number of students. Some still feared, however, that La'ie was too far from Honolulu to attract audiences large enough to make the undertaking profitable. But others pointed to the success of the hukilau as a demonstration that Laie could draw the market. The decision to move forward was made by David O. McKay, then president and prophet of the church (Ferre 1988:33-34). When it opened, the PCC combined the audience participation, cultural activities, and feast of the hukilau, with the staged spectacle of the Polynesian Panorama.

Despite its heritage of sanctified commerce, the PCC venture was not initially successful. In four years it lost $740,000, and some church leaders in Utah favored closing it (Ferre 1988:2, 75, 111). Instead, the management struck deals with tour companies to include the Center in their marketing and tour packages in return for 30% of all profits the Center made on their customers (Ferre 1988:74, 89-90, 99). Then the Center began to turn a profit. Initially, church leaders had refused such deals insisting that the Center would attract tourists without them. But in the face of financial disaster, that view changed. Thus, like the motivation behind the Center's creation, its eventual success was sealed by a shrewd "spiritualization of temporal activity."

Ancestralism

The Mormons' affinity for ancestors is unparalleled elsewhere in Christianity (see Ahlstrom 1972:506; Hansen 1981:103, 165; O'Dea 1957:56-7). *Ancestralism* as used here differentiates between ancestor worship and propitiation, which are common religious practices elsewhere, and the Mormons' devotion to ensuring the salvation of their progenitors. Mormonism maintains that those who die without receiving baptism and other ordinances must nevertheless receive these sacraments through the peculiar practice in which Mormons perform the ordinances vicariously for the dead.

Mormon ancestralism has its origin in a message received by Joseph Smith from the same angel who delivered the Book of Mormon. Three times in a single night, the angel appeared and recited a version of Malachi's prophecy that in the last days God "shall turn the heart of the fathers to the children, and the heart of the children to the fathers, lest I come and smite the earth with a curse" (Malachi 4:6). The angel's version was somewhat different:

> And he shall plant in the hearts of the children the promises made to the fathers, and the hearts of the children shall turn to their fathers. If it were not so, the whole earth would be utterly wasted at his coming. (Joseph Smith—History 2:39)

This pronouncement is interpreted by Mormons as a charge to perform vicarious ordinances for their ancestors (D&C 124:29-30), and is one of Mormonism's favorite scriptures. Of the two, the angel's version more closely describes the phenomenon of Mormon devotion to forebears. It is the sentiment that the departed have embraced the Mormon perception of salvation, but are languishing in the spirit world, denied further progress toward salvation until the vicarious rites are performed. In a manner of speaking, Mormon ancestralism likens past generations to the present one. Mormons re-create their ancestors in their own image.

At the PCC, the theme of ancestralism is pervasive. The employees don costumes supposedly like those worn by their ancestors; they perform songs, dances, and other simple cultural activities said to have been practiced centuries ago by their forebears; they tell the tourists about their ancestors in brief lectures and memorized dialogues; they play roles in a setting that simulates lifestyles of their progenitors. Because the employees themselves are Polynesian, their role-playing is deeply personal; because they are Mormon, their attitude toward their ancestors is overlaid with religious significance and fervent intensity. A Maori respondent stated,

> This piece of land, the building, and everything [the Maori village] belongs to our *tupuna* [ancestors], and we're upholding those principles in this latter-day. We're upholding the principles that they upheld, and this makes us feel good.

A Hawaiian village supervisor said he taught his student performers "to take pride in who you represent. We represent our *kapunas* [ancestors]. Our ancestors worked hard for us to be where we are."

Though the PCC is only a model of the past, it creates in its employees a filial attachment to their ancestors that is thoroughly Mormon.

The Book of Mormon and the Hagoth Figure

Fascination with Polynesia has been part of Mormonism almost from the beginning of the movement. Mormon scriptures refer repeatedly to unnamed "isles of the sea" in passages about God's promised gathering of scattered Israel. For example:

> But great are the promises of the Lord unto them who are upon the isles of the sea.... For behold, the Lord God has led away from time to time from the house of Israel, according to his will and pleasure. And now behold, the Lord remembereth all them who have been broken off, wherefore he remembereth us also. (2 Nephi 10:21-22)

The Book of Mormon recounts the history of a chosen group who secretly fled Jerusalem before its destruction by the Babylonians. Lehi and Nephi, leaders and prophets of this group, led their followers to the sea where they built a ship and sailed to the Americas, arriving about 600 B.C. This great but ill-fated people never returned to Israel. They have a share in God's promise to recover scattered Israel from wherever they have wandered.

Although the scriptural "isles" are nameless, Mormons consider them to be the Pacific islands because of the brief story in the Book of Mormon about Hagoth the shipbuilder. In about 55 B.C., Hagoth undertook a series of ocean voyages from which he and his followers ultimately did not return. The Mormon church contends that Hagoth sailed from the Americas to some Pacific island, and that his descendants migrated throughout Polynesia. Thus, Polynesians are literally Israelites.

Although the origin of this belief is unknown, it developed concurrently with the church's success in Hawai'i, and has been consistently reiterated by church leaders. In 1851, the first Mormon missionaries to Hawai'i were also the first on record to tell the Polynesians that they were descendants of Abraham (Britsch 1986:xiv, 97-98, 151). In 1865, Brigham Young sent a letter to Kamehameha V that acquainted the king with the Mormon account of Polynesia's inhabitation (Bock 1941:58). In 1913 Joseph F. Smith, then president of the church, said, "I would like to say to you brethren and sisters from New Zealand, you are some of Hagoth's people, and there is no perhaps about it!" (Quoted in Cole and Jensen 1961:388). In his prayer offered at the cornerstone laying of the New Zealand Temple in 1956, Apostle Hugh B. Brown said,

> We thank Thee, O God, for revealing to us the Book of Mormon, the story of the ancient inhabitants of America. We thank Thee that from among those inhabitants, the ancestors of those whose heads are bowed before Thee here, came from the western shores of America into the South Seas pursuant to Thy plan. (Quoted in Cummings 1961:63)

Apostle Mark Peterson said,

> The Polynesian Saints are characterized by a tremendous faith...because these people are of the blood of Israel. They are heirs to the promises of the Book of Mormon...As Latter-day Saints we have always believed that the Polynesians are descendants of Lehi...despite the contrary theories of other men. For that reason, from the beginning of our Church history we have had more than an ordinary interest in them as a people. (1962:457)

As a literary device, the Hagoth figure serves no purpose in the Book of Mormon story of the rise and fall of great pre-Columbian civilizations. But when the Polynesians are cast as Hagoth's descendants, Hagoth's journey replicates the book's premise, which is that God may lead people away from their homes to found new civilizations in promised lands. The Polynesians become a sacred race, Polynesia becomes a promised land, and the Hagoth story becomes an unwritten sequel to the Book of Mormon itself.

For its employees, the PCC completes the Hagoth fragment, and re-creates the sacred origins of Polynesia. One village manager routinely refers to Polynesia as "Book of Mormon Land." According to one night show dancer,

> Each practice is opened and closed with prayer. Right there, it's a comfortable feeling. And it's stronger. [The instructor] will get up and give a strong testimony and the relationship with the Hawaiian people and the Book of Mormon and with Christ. He knows a lot about Hawaiian genealogy, and he'll just [recite] the names that go all the way back to Book of Mormon times, and we'll just get goosebumps listening to him because he's got all the genealogy. He'll name Book of Mormon names, except it won't be like "Nephi," "Lehi." He'll name them in Hawaiian, and then say, "This is Nephi, this is Lehi." We'll just go "Wow!"

The Hagoth fragment gives the Polynesian Mormons a starting point for their own epic, and continues the Book of Mormon story in Polynesia. As such, their role playing at the PCC becomes an enactment and reinforcement of teachings from the Book of Mormon. The spectacular success of the PCC becomes an evidence of the truthfulness of the Book of Mormon and by extension all other precepts of the Mormon religion.

The PCC in Prophecy

The lore of La'ie is rich with accounts of visions and prophecies that have created an aura of holiness around the community. In 1865, a vision convinced missionaries to purchase La'ie as a Mormon gathering place (Cummings, 1965). And although its beginnings were hardly bountiful, prophecies of La'ie's eventual prosperity convinced the early settlers to endure (Britsch 1986, p:142). When prosperity did in fact ensue, it strengthened their faith and added to La'ie's aura of holiness.

La'ie's temple, the first Mormon temple outside the United States Mainland, was also prophesied by key figures in the history of the church in Hawai'i (Britsch 1986:150, 153-54). Likewise, construction of the Church College, later BYU-Hawai'i, is popularly linked to an apostolic inspiration that occurred three decades before its founding (Britsch 1986:180).

The PCC, too, has its prophetic origins. In 1955, President McKay made a prophecy at the College's groundbreaking:

> We dedicate our actions...that this college, and the temple, and the town of Laie may become a missionary factor, influencing not thousands, not tens of thousands, but millions of people who will come seeking to know what this town and its significance are. (Quoted in Law 1972:69)

To the Mormons of La'ie, the PCC literally fulfills McKay's prophecy by attracting a million visitors annually.

Another "prophecy," however, had a more tenuous fulfillment in the PCC. When completed, the La'ie temple drew Mormon Polynesians from around the Pacific to participate in its sacred ordinances. As early as 1951, knowing that the long journey to La'ie was costly, Mormon apostle Matthew Cowley proposed that each group of islanders—Maori, Tongans, Samoans, Tahitians, and others—construct traditional "little villages" in La'ie where they could stay during their temple visits (O'Brien 1983:73).

Unofficially known as "the apostle for the Polynesians," Cowley lived many years in Polynesia as a representative of the church. He believed that communal lodging in La'ie would make the stay there more economical for his beloved Polynesians. He further suggested that they perform traditional songs and dances for tourists who came to see the temple. This would provide the Polynesians with money for their return passage and also acquaint tourists with traditional Polynesian arts (O'Brien 1983:73).

Although the PCC was created by combining the hukilau and the Polynesian Panorama, many Mormons attribute to Cowley the inspiration behind the Center, and not to the community, church, and college leaders who played the actual founding role. Linking Cowley, an apostle, to the PCC guarantees its sacred stature. His simple plan to help Polynesians attend the temple thus became a prophetic vision, and the PCC became the fulfillment of his prophecy (Forester 1986:61). This raises the Center to a level equal to that of the temple and the university, each of which is considered a fulfillment of prophecy, and elevates the PCC above the hukilau, which was the result of local initiative, but which lacked any comparable claim to prophetic origin.

Cowley died before the college and the center were undertaken. Had he lived, he might have revised his vision, but his "little villages" do not sound much like the PCC. He envisioned dwellings, not replicas, to benefit those who came to attend a temple, not a college. The proceeds would have been modest, the performances simple; customers would have been tourists who came to investigate the temple. Cowley's plan contained no suggestion of a theme park on the order of the PCC. Nevertheless, Cowley is spoken of with great reverence as one of the "fathers" of the PCC.

The importance of these prophetic utterances to the Center's Mormon employees is indisputable. The words of one Maori village worker were typical of the interviews taken for this study. In a marvelous confusion of the spiritual with the material, he stated that the purpose of the PCC is

> to bring all the cultures together and to share with the rest of the world, with regards to the Polynesian culture. And to give students like myself an opportunity to explain my culture to the world and to give me the affordability to pay my way through school. I work here and I get paid for it. And I just pay my school account off. That's basically the purpose, the original purpose as thought of by the prophets with regards to having a school here, and especially to teach Polynesian culture, and so it can be affordable for us while we're doing it. We come up from our islands, down from different parts, and work our way through school. And the tourists come in and pay their money at the gate. The church has provided this for us. It's a fulfillment of a prophecy made by President McKay ... back in the fifties, and it's a reality.

The Manipulation of Religiosity

These religious precedents endow the Center with its quasi-religious stature. Virtually all the informants spoke of its importance as a missionary tool, as a link to the Book of Mormon, or as an extension of the church. In her personal journal, one villager recorded her feelings as she performed for the Maori queen visiting from New Zealand:

> I could really feel the spirit of God with us today as we performed. I think that if we had not asked Him for His presence and thanked Him for all He'd done for us, we would not have performed as well as we did. Everyone put their faith in Him. I felt as we were performing that I was actually back in the days of the ancient Maori. I felt fear as the trumpet was blown announcing strangers into our village. I felt proud of our Maori warriors as they challenged them, and I felt happiness when they made known to us that they came in peace and were welcomed into the village. I think everyone today performed at their best and really showed our queen that we are proud of our heritage and respect it.

This religiosity, typical of the Center's employees, is so essential to the Center's success that the administration manipulates it when necessary. Because the PCC is a business, it is considered an "auxiliary" of the church and not an official ecclesiastical organization. As such, it can engage in practices that would be otherwise prohibited. For instance, the Center serves coffee to the tourists although coffee drinking is proscribed by the church. The Center also allows its performers to wear costumes that are immodest by the church's strict dress standards. Also, the Center contradicts its own ancestralism by practicing an uneven faithfulness to authentic Polynesian tradition in its performances and exhibits (Ferre 1988:3-5, 188-89).

These practices often offend the employees, but interviewees report that when they question these inconsistencies, PCC managers respond that to be financially successful, the Center must cater to the tourists and therefore cannot always maintain the church's high ideals. But if this line of reasoning fails to satisfy the employees, management takes the opposite tack and squelches dissent by invoking the Center's prophetic origins, inspired leadership, and status as a church operation. One student employee stated,

> It's really hypocritical as far as I'm concerned, the business way of it. I just don't agree with the way that [the Center is] run. It's not a profit-making organization supposedly. And I'm sure it's not, because we have the apostles as the Board of Directors. But I don't think that [the PCC management] is channeling the money in the right directions. I think a lot of money could be used to put the rate up for the workers so that we wouldn't have to go on food stamps. [The general manager] always reminds us that this is a business. It's not church-oriented. Then when something goes wrong, he bears to us his testimony and always brings the gospel into it. And somehow it makes us feel guilty.

Another villager and night show performer said,

> The gospel is part of the Center. Sometimes we wonder, Isn't this being directed? Sometimes they'll tell us—our leaders there—"Well, this is the Lord's Center." We'll tell them, "Well, maybe it was established by the church, and it's for the purpose of the saints [i.e., the Mormons], and for the students. But are you sure it's being directed by the right inspiration? Business is business. You run the business, and sometimes you're at fault. And if we have a complaint, it's not against the Lord, it's against men." And sometimes they don't see that. They always use the connection, "I know [the unpopular decision] was inspired for the benefit of the students." They usually shut [complaints] down with that saying, "Well, this is the Lord's." And you're not supposed to go against them. Whenever I hear that I cringe.

To this tactic, faithful Mormons can barely offer any open rejoinder in good conscience. One village manager said,

> As soon as I mention the church [i.e., to the students], there's a tremendous response. There's a feeling. You can feel it. You mention the church, and they align all their [cultural and traditional] principles with the church.

Although Mormon doctrine unifies the material and the spiritual, conflicts occur, and the Center's leaders must occasionally resort to religious manipulation to maintain loyalty. As one veteran performer observed, "A lot of things happen, I know. You have to follow in the footsteps of the world as far as the economy is." When idealism fails to operationalize with pragmatism, only the Center's near-sacred stature preserves its success in the face of ideological inconsistencies.

The near-sacredness notwithstanding, ambivalence and in some cases outright hostility toward the Center were prevalent among those interviewed for this study. Although all were grateful for the cultural learning they had gained there, the inconsistencies of the Center's purposes and the management's manipulation of the employees' religious loyalty created for many respondents an unsettling ambiguity. They maintained an unwavering devotion to the principles that are the religious foundation of the PCC. However, this only intensified their resentment for the expediencies taken by the management, the superficiality of some of the cultural presentations, and the repetitious monotony of the routines and demonstrations.

Yet these same respondents, almost to a person, remained loyal to the church itself. They displayed the ability to dissociate their disapproval of the Center from the church that founded it, promotes it, and controls it through managers and boards of directors made up mostly of high church officials. These persons, and the church they direct, would seem to be the logical targets of the employees' dissatisfaction.

In fact, however, performing at the Center, with its internal contradictions and ambiguities, appears to encourage the performers to become even more faithful to the formal organizations of the church. Confronted by the logical and symbolic inconsistencies of the PCC, respondents indicated that activity in the official church programs was refreshing. There, the ambiguity, the commercialization, and the routinization were not present.

In this way, the PCC indirectly influences its employees to remain firm in the church as a result of the equivocations that the management must make to assure the Center's success. The employees expect the Center to be a sacred place. That much is clear from their responses. But they eventually feel a desire to shun the ambiguity of the place and return to the unequivocal motives of the church's official doctrine and sacraments. The church, whether shrewdly or unknowingly, set up the Center to be the target of the performers' deep conflict that inevitably resulted from catering to tourists. In this manner, the performers can rebound more strongly toward the church's more controlling influences within its official organizations.

The Consequence of Profit

Perhaps the inconsistencies in merging religion and commerce caused the center to become a victim of its own success. In any case, the PCC has come under close and repeated scrutiny of tax authorities. In 1974, the IRS began an action to revoke the income tax exemption granted the Center in 1965 under Section 501(c)(3) of the Internal Revenue Code, which exempts religious, charitable, educational, and certain other nonprofit organizations.

The IRS argued that, since its opening, the PCC had "sublimated" its cultural preservation and educational purposes, and had "evolved into an entertainment center to the extent that its exempt status should be revoked" (Corsi 1975:2). The IRS based its case on the Center's enormous marketing and advertising operations that were unparalleled among nonprofit organizations, but characteristic of a profit-oriented entity. The IRS offered as evidence the Center's inordinately high marketing budget of $1,000,000 for fiscal year 1973 compared to its much smaller budget of $100,000 for cultural research for the same period (Corsi 1975:4-5). The IRS also cited the exorbitant costs then projected for the expansion of the night show theater ($1,500,000) and that the theater is operated much like a commercial theater, using Hollywood consultants and professional-quality "lighting, costumes, sound effects, music, et al." as further evidence that the Center's main purpose had become entertainment (Corsi 1975:3, 9, 10).

The ten-year court battle ended in the Center's favor (see Ferre 1988:154-156, 187), but according to informants, the Center's gift shop and restaurant eventually lost their exemptions.

More recently, Judge Frederick J. Titcomb of Hawai'i's First Circuit Court ruled that the Center is a tourist attraction, and not a museum, church, or charity, as the Center contends, and is therefore subject to property tax (Titcomb 1992:9-11). Echoing the IRS arguments of 1974, Judge Titcomb stated, "It is not a museum; it's a tourist attraction . . . I agree with the City that the Polynesian Cultural Center is entertainment . . . It depends on the tourist trade, it seeks out the tourist business, it advertises for that business. They have an advertising agency, and they spend $700,000 to $900,000 a year in advertising" (Titcomb 1992:8-9).

It is likely that further litigation followed by appeals in this matter will go on for years. But Judge Titcomb's ruling is accurate; the PCC is clearly a tourist attraction, its claims of being a "living museum" notwithstanding. This, however, in no way lessens the importance of the peculiar relationship between religion and commerce that produced the PCC and made it an unexpected and unparalleled success. On the contrary, it illustrates that the elaborateness, scale, and profitability that set the PCC apart from other cultural tourism ventures in Hawai'i, and elsewhere, are directly attributable to the presence of fundamental tenets of Mormonism in the Center's themes and operation.

Conclusion

Materialism, ancestralism, and the lessons of the Book of Mormon are connected by more than their common angelic origin. They unify the material with the spiritual, and draw the ancient past and the eternal resolutely into the present. These same forces drive the PCC. It gathers wealth for the church's university. The employees gain income as well as the eminence of ancestral approval while forging a link to the Book of Mormon through the daily enactment of ancient ancestral behaviors.

The commercialization at the PCC is only one instance in a long historical series of Mormon entrepreneurial ventures arising from this spiritual-material, eternal-temporal unification. The PCC is unique in Mormon economic history, however, because it exploits the ethnic art and culture of Polynesia instead of natural resources.

Still, it thrives as a contemporary economic mission because Mormons and tourists share a fixation for Polynesia. For the church, it is a fascination with Polynesian origins. For tourists, the popular image of a tropical island paradise, peopled with beautiful "primitives," creates a powerful mystique and an invigorating tonic. The church capitalizes on this mutual fascination, but also employs the quasi-religious stature of the Center and the ethnicity of its employees to make the place successful. The tourists are grandly entertained. The employees, however, are steeped in Mormon lore and doctrines that overlay their involvement in the Center with a significance non-Mormon tourists cannot know, but in which they unknowingly participate. The employees are actually engaging in an approximation of a religious experience, and feel all the emotions attending such an occurrence. If any of these motivational elements were lacking, the PCC would not succeed.

According to Ferre (1988:186-187), the PCC is successful because there is a large, inexpensive, and willing work force at a highly desirable tourist destination site. He states that the student employees receive a low rate of pay compared to that of professional entertainers, but the Center allows them to attend college while learning about their cultural heritage. These incentives, he observes, make them more willing employees.

By itself, however, La'ie is not a highly desirable destination site. Its beaches are nondescript, there are no resorts or hotels, and La'ie is hardly picturesque. Only the Mormons' sanctified business savvy, their awareness of the susceptibilities of tourists, and their confederation with the tour companies make La'ie desireable. Furthermore, the willingness of student and nonstudent employees to work for the Center, despite its contradictions, is greatly enhanced by the fact that it holds a religious importance for them, and elicits a kind of enduring loyalty to their employment that would not be present in another work situation.

Notes

1. Speaking historically, religion and tourism are connected in several ways. Crusades, pilgrimages, conquests, and expeditions have been precursors to pleasure travel. Cathedrals and reliquaries promoted a cottage-level entrepreneurialism that foreshadowed the modern tourism industry. Drawing on Eliade's expositions of sacred time and sacred space (1959), Graburn (1989) proposes that tourism is "sacred" to modern individuals because it interrupts the routine of everyday life and provides the tourist with status and with social and personal refreshment the same way sacred ceremonies and festivals did for earlier and more secular societies. Also, tourism promotion often follows foreign evangelism. The most graphic example of this in Hawai'i is La'ie's Polynesian Cultural Center.

2. Scholarly opinion about the PCC is divided as well. Kanahele (1982:7) and Stagner (1985:22) accept it as a catalyst for the Hawaiian "renaissance" and give credit to its preservation of Hawaiian arts and crafts. Others have accused the Center of superficiality, commercialism, and anachronism (e.g., Graburn 1983:77; Stanton 1989:254).

3. References to Mormon scriptural works appear as follows: the component books of the Book of Mormon and Pearl of Great Price are named without abbreviation followed by chapter and verse; D&C indicates the Doctrine and Covenants, the divisions of which are sections and verses (e.g., D&C 76:31).

References

Ahlstrom, Sydney E. 1972. *A Religious History of the American People*. New Haven: Yale University Press.

Albanese, Catherine L. 1981. *America: Religions and Religion*. Belmont, CA: Wadsworth.

Arrington, Leonard J. 1958. *Great Basin Kingdom: Economic History of the Latter-day Saints, 1830-1900*. Lincoln: University of Nebraska Press.

Bock, Comfort Margaret. 1941. "The Church in the Hawaiian Islands." M.A. thesis, University of Hawai'i.

Book of Mormon.

Britsch, R. Lanier. 1986. *Unto the Islands of the Sea: A History of the Latter-day Saints in the Pacific*. Salt Lake City, UT: Deseret.

Chase, Lance. 1981. "Laie Life, 1850-1883." *Proceedings of the Second Annual Conference*, pp 91-102, La'ie HI: Mormon Pacific Historical Society.

Cole, William and Elwin W. Jensen. 1961. *Israel in the Pacific: A Genealogical Text for Polynesia*. Salt Lake City, UT: Genealogical Society.

Corsi, C. 1975 [Text of] Department of the Treasury, Internal Revenue Service. Report of Examination - Exempt Organization: Polynesian Cultural Center, Key District Office - Los Angeles, July 7, 1975.

Cummings, David W. 1961. *Mighty Missionary of the Pacific: The Building Program of the Church of Jesus Christ of Latter-day Saints, Its History, Scope, and Significance*. Salt Lake City, UT: Bookcraft.

_____. 1965. *Centennial History of Laie*. Laie, HI: ND.

Eliade, Mircea. 1959. *The Sacred and the Profane: The Nature of Religion*. New York: Harper & Row.

Ferre, Craig. 1988. "A History of the Polynesian Cultural Center's 'Night Show': 1963-1983." Ph.D. dissertation, Department of Theatre and Film, Brigham Young University, Provo, UT.

Forester, Rubina. 1986. "The Polynesian Cultural Center: The Realization Gone Far Beyond the Dream." Proceedings of the Seventh Annual Conference, pp 60-72. La'ie, HI: Mormon Pacific Historical Society.

Graburn, Nelson H. H. 1983. "Art, Ethno-Aesthetics and the Contemporary Scene." *Art and Artists of Oceania,* edited by Sidney M. Mead and Bernie Kernot, pp 70-79. Mill Valley, CA: Ethnographic Arts Publications.

_____ 1989. "Tourism: The Sacred Journey." *Hosts and Guests: The Anthropology of Tourism,* 2nd edition, pp. 21-36. Edited by V. L. Smith. Philadelphia: University of Pennsylvania Press.

Hansen, Klaus J. 1981. *Mormonism and the American Experience*. Chicago: University of Chicago Press.

Hooper, Susan. 1992. "Top 250." *Hawai'i Business* 38(2):43-180.

Kanahele, George S. 1982. *Hawaiian Renaissance*. Honolulu: Project WAIAHA.

Kawahigashi, Kehau. 1968. "The Hukilau Festival," January 31, 1948. Brigham Young University-Hawai'i Archives, La'ie, HI. Photocopy of unpublished manuscript.

Law, Reuben D. 1972. *The Founding of the Church College of Hawai'i.* St. George, UT: Dixie College Press.

Leone, Mark P. 1979. *Roots of Modern Mormonism.* Cambridge, MA: Harvard University Press.

O'Brien, Robert. 1983. *Hands Across the Water: The Story of the Polynesian Cultural Center.* La'ie, HI: The Center.

O'Dea, Thomas F. 1957. *The Mormons.* Chicago: University of Chicago Press.

Peterson, Mark E. 1962. "New Evidence for the Book of Mormon." *Improvement Era* 65:456-459.

Pierce, Bernard Francis. 1956. Acculturation of Samoans in the Mormon Village of Laie, Territory of Hawai'i. M.A. thesis, University of Hawai'i, Honolulu, HI.

Smith, Valene L. (ed.) 1989. "Introduction." *Hosts and Guests: The Anthropology of Tourism.* 2nd ed. pp 1-17. Philadelphia: University of Pennsylvania Press.

Spurrier, Joseph H. 1978. *The Church of Jesus Christ of Latter-day Saints in the Hawaiian Islands.* Honolulu: Hawai'i Honolulu Mission of the Church of Jesus Christ of Latter-day Saints.

_____. 1981. "The Life and Times of Early Missionaries to Polynesia." in *Proceedings of the Second Annual Conference* pp 41-48. Laie, HI: Mormon Pacific History Society.

Stagner, Ishmael. 1985. *Hula.* La'ie, HI: Institute for Polynesian Studies.

Stanton, Max E. 1989. "The Polynesian Cultural Center: A Multi-Ethnic Model of Seven Pacific Cultures." *Hosts and Guests: The Anthropology of Tourism,* 2nd edition pp 247-262, edited by Valene L. Smith. Philadelphia: University of Pennsylvania Press.

Titcomb, Frederick J. 1992. Court's Ruling. Circuit Court of the First Circuit, State of Hawai'i. In the Matter of the Tax Appeal of the Islands Foundation and Polynesian Cultural Center, Appellants. Tax Appeal No. 2653. Transcript.

Wiles, Greg. 1992. "HVB's New Chiefs: 'In-House' Slate for Tourism's Fate." *Honolulu Advertiser,* September 15: E1-3.

Traversing Inter-Ethnic Social Orders: Native Hawaiian Song Collections*[1]

Jeffrey J. Kamakahi
and
Albert B. Robillard

Introduction

The pervasiveness of political economic arrangements can be assessed through their influences upon the practices (praxis) of those linked to it. When, as in the case of Hawai'i, there has been a succession of political and cultural influences (cf. Kuykendall, 1938, 1953, 1967; Lind, 1936; Beechert, 1985; King, 1987), the efficacy of subsequent arrangements may be evaluated by the changes in practices that have taken place. In Hawai'i, one manifestation of such influence can be seen through the changes in the practices surrounding Native Hawaiian folk songs: from *mele* in the oral traditional Hawaiian culture to songs in a commodified market context.[2] This transformation informs us of the impact of the Europeanization of local culture upon Native Hawaiian poetic expression in folk songs.[3]

Native Hawaiian folk songs refer to those texts that simulate in form and content the poetic style of traditional mele, have lyrics written primarily in the Native Hawaiian language, and employ the structures of Western musical tonality and notation. The "double transcription" of Native Hawaiians folk songs, first by phonetic symbols and second by musical notation, makes them an interesting site for the study of social change in Hawai'i. Since it is text itself that is of primary interest, the concern focuses upon how the characteristics of the text inform readers of the relationship between Native Hawaiian culture and the reader.

Published collections of Native Hawaiian folk songs are treated as "inter-ethnic" texts.[4] Of primary interest is how textual representation is a site of inter-ethnic relations and how the coding of an ethnicity in a hegemonic discourse extrinsic to that ethnicity changes the perception that ethnic members have of themselves and the access they and others have to their own traditions. Our specific topic is the transformation of Hawaiian songs, from indigenous forms of composition, storage, transmission, and contexts of performance into Western scored, printed, copyrighted, mass-marketed, and commercially performed songs. We examine attributes of song collections to describe how political economic influences have altered Native Hawaiian folk song practices.

Texts within Context

This paper treats Native Hawaiian folk songs and song collections as sites that involve language as mediator, or as constructive of, and/or as purveyor of social orders in that the use of language involves the production and reproduction of social relations inclusive of political economic influences.[4]

A text is a positive, semiotic event that represents a substantively limited accomplishment that can be located within a set of broader relations (cf. Barthes 1981; Duncan 1962; Fish 1980; Foucault 1972). This broader set of relations includes existing published texts as well as "silent texts": the "unwritten literature," which is (un)produced through the inability of possible agents to provide adequate analogues (e.g., the absence of orthographies in oral cultures) in suitable form. Because traditional Native Hawaiian mele were not indigenously codified into written form, we refer to them as "silent" in the context of texts. As a traditionally oral production, positive artifacts of mele did not exist independent of their performance. It was not until the appropriation of phonetic writing to the Native Hawaiian language and the notation of Western musicality in the nineteenth century that texts of Native Hawaiian folk songs and song collections could emerge (divorced from performances). Only at that juncture could one speak of folk-song texts as sites of study. This is not to say that the oral tradition is extinct, but only that it is incongruent with and superseded by written texts within the processes of mass commodification. This paper concentrates upon the process of commodification and its relation to Native Hawaiian folk songs. In the following section, a general historical description of the political-economic circumstances within which the Native Hawaiian folk song and song collections emerged is presented.

Political-Economic Changes and Native Hawaiians

The impact of the late eighteenth-century Western expansion in Hawai'i was far-reaching. Sustained contact after 1778 brought knowledge of peoples with a metallurgical technology, a complex system of recording information, a capitalist mode of production, distribution, and consumption, vastly different cultural codes, and perhaps, most importantly at first, diseases to which the indigenous people had little or no immunities (cf. Stannard 1989; Handy and Pukui 1972; Blaisdell 1989).

Within the span of a few decades, the several principalities that had existed prior to sustained Western contact had been amalgamated into a Western-style political arrangement complete with a bicameral legislature, a judiciary system, an executive branch, and a legitimizing constitution (cf. Kuykendall 1938; 1953; 1967; Lydecker 1918). Christianity after 1820 was employed as the fulcrum for introducing literacy and Western world views to the indigenous peoples. Conversion to Christianity would transform many traditional Hawaiian chants, dances, and songs from sacred to secular. By the late 1800s—a little more than a hundred years after Captain James Cook happened upon Hawai'i on January 18, 1778— English superseded Hawaiian as the official language of government and commercial affairs. Hawaiian would be banned from being spoken in the public schools.

By the late nineteenth century, an oligarchy of Westerners (foreign-born or missionary families) and Hawaiian royalty (indigenous people, the *ali'i*, who had converted traditional high social position into wealth status) was installed in the archipelago. With the importation of contract laborers to work the sugar plantations, the Native Hawaiians found themselves to be one among many ethno-cultural groups in the islands. It was within this context that "Hawaiian" became an ethnicity, a differentiated group, in a Western-dominated but multi-ethnic society. The overthrow of the monarchy by Westerners manifestly working with United States Marines and the subsequent annexation of the islands by the United States, crystallized the incorporation of Hawai'i into the capitalist world-system (Blount 1893; Native Hawaiian Study Commission 1983).

During the early twentieth century, the sugar plantation economy was beginning to be supplemented by a concerted effort to encourage tourism. The Western mythic imagery of personal quest and redemption or renewal in sun-drenched exotic lands, especially the host of historical narratives about exploration in the Pacific, was used to open up and sustain the tourist industry. Concomitant with the notion of renewal in the exotic islands of Hawai'i, peopled by an attractive but naive Other, was the creation of Western-Hawaiian (e.g., *hapa haole*) music written in the English which reified the tourism imagery.[6] In Hawai'i they were not folk songs, but rather commodities produced in the service of tourism, like the aloha shirt (Robillard, 1991). On the mainland hapa haole music was both a demonstration of America's new acquisition of an underdeveloped brown people and the introduction of a new musical commodity or product line. Hapa haole music was also played in Europe (Buck 1985; Kanahele 1979). Hapa haole music took the biggest market share in the active recording and selling of Hawaiian 78-rpm records.

The idea of a primitive tropical paradise has given ground to the notion of a tropical resort in which people can get away while still enjoying all the amenities of big city entertainment. The varieties of leisure commodities far exceed the orbit of Hawaiian culture. The entertainment expectations of early twentieth century hapa haole Hawaiian music have yielded to contemporary Western entertainment in discos, dinner cruises, and floor shows. Honolulu has been integrated into the international entertainment market.

The scale and substance of Hawai'i's political and economic development through the twentieth century, especially after the explosion of the tourist industry in the 1960s, have exhibited a structural blindness about Native Hawaiians and their culture—as Native Hawaiians continue to identify it—except in the service of the commodification of cultural iconography for the tourist industry. While the tourist industry is in need of the Hawaiians as an exotic backdrop, providing the otherness of Hawai'i as a place for a vacation escape, actual Hawaiian people and their lived contemporary experience of being Hawaiian are practically irrelevant in the capital centers that program development in Hawai'i.

Native Hawaiian folk songs represent only a modest proportion of songs composed, recorded, and given air time on radio in the current milieu in Hawai'i. One is much more likely to hear rock-n-roll, Japanese language broadcasts, or talk shows than Native Hawaiian folk songs. Even radio stations that air Native Hawaiian folk songs (for example KCCN) are hosted by English speaking disc jockeys and play a substantial amount of local music in their programming.

Native Hawaiian Folk Songs

This sketch of the political-economic peripheralization of Native Hawaiians tells us little concerning the process of how Hawaiian culture was appropriated by the rationalities of a dominant Western social order. Ironically, the contemporary Native Hawaiian gains access to the artifacts of his ethnic identity through the texts written in the English language and for an audience presumably ignorant of all aspects of Native Hawaiian culture. Folk-song collections are examples of the processes whereby recourse to one's own minority code is readily accessible only through the dominant code. The complementary process is that text can only be voiced (with the disappearance of widespread indigenous language use, as is the case with the Hawaiian language) by transforming the artifacts of culture into the dominant code.

The accommodation of the Native Hawaiian folk song into the dominant code of textual representation is reflected in song collections. The commodified market, inclusive of universalistic expression and intellectual property, involves the use of such characteristics as copyright symbols and acknowledgements, Western musical notation, English translations of lyrics, and explications of traditional Native Hawaiian allusions. This study looks at the extent to which these signs of commodification are present (or absent) in song collections of Native Hawaiian folk songs. Their combined presence is indicative of folk songs being appropriated into the dominant code-English language, European musicality, and intellectual property ownership.

The data base is a selection of song collections published in the twentieth century. The songs in the collections are ancient, old, and new compositions. Fifteen such texts are used, spanning the period of 1902 through 1977. These texts represent a more than reasonable selection for the time span including the most well-known song collections. Included in our sample are the most referenced Native Hawaiian song collections: Almeida (1946), Cunha (1902), Elbert and Mahoe (1970), Henderson (1960), Kamaunu (1929), King (1948, 1950), and Noble (1929, 1931, 1935).[7]

Aspects of Textual Presentation

The song collections were written texts. The codification of Native Hawaiian folk songs into written text presumes at least two things. First, folk songs were translated into a form (i.e., writing) that was nontraditional, a foreign import transformative of the oral tradition. And second, the language of exposition was not the Hawaiian language but English. This study explores the folk song within the context of an inter-ethno-cultural asymmetry.

We are interested in the extent to which the texts inform us of inter-ethnic relations. How are the texts the site of the incorporation of Native Hawaiian culture into the Euroamerican codes? What aspects of textual presentation can be indications of the nature of inter-ethnic relations? The characteristics we looked at in the textual inscription of Native-Hawaiian folk songs were: (1) the explicatory prose prefacing the collection; (2) the political-economy of composition (e.g., the copyrighting of lyrics and/or music; "required" acknowledgment of such "rights");[8] (3) the presence of translations of lyrics into another language; (4) the identification of specific musical arrangements (e.g., musical notation); (5) comments regarding performance (i.e., pronunciation guides, phonetic spelling, chord diagrams); (6) the ethnic identification of the authors; and (7) the intended audience of the work. These aspects of textual presentation allow us to gauge the location of such productions with regard to the traversing of ethnic and inter-ethnic social orders. In general, the more of the characteristics present in a song collection, the more the text is assumed to be written for those ignorant of Native Hawaiian culture.

Note that it is less important who authors the texts or who performs the songs than how they are presented in text. The text embodies the features and characteristics of the relevant codes of the context within which it is written and the prospective readers for whom it is written.

Discussion of the Texts

We shall concern ourselves with the relative occurrence in the texts of the empirical indicators specified above. Discussion will focus upon the factors of internal consistency (i.e., reliability) of the texts as well as their comparative structural characteristics.

Internal Consistency - Reliability

The justification of scrutinizing the internal consistency of the folksong texts is the issue of whether the collections are texts written with a particular context and audience in mind, or are simply a hodgepodge of folk songs thrown together. In Table 1, the texts are listed by year of publication, collection author code, total number of songs within the collection, percentage of songs that are Native Hawaiian language folk songs, and the percentage of songs in the collection with explicatory prose, copyright, translations into English, musical notation, and performance instructions. As can be seen, each song collection exhibits high internal consistency. That is, all folk songs within the collection are likely to be presented to the reader in similar fashion—i.e., share the same characteristics. Song collections, then, can be construed of as being written for particular audiences. The following issue becomes: What audiences were texts written for? Were all texts written for the same audiences or were texts fashioned for several audiences?

In order to address the previous questions, the characteristics of the song collection texts themselves were investigated. If all characteristics of texts occurred in unison, then it could be argued that song collections are written for those both interested in and ignorant of Native Hawaiian folk songs as musical and cultural productions.

Five variables were created from the list of characteristics, which were applied to song collection texts: Prose (i.e., the percent of songs within collections providing English language explanations of songs); PolEc (i.e., the percent

Table 1.
Folk Song Collections

Year	ID	Tot	NH	Prose	PolEc	Trans	Mus	Perf
1902	Cunha	27	100	0	100	33	100	0
1909	Emerson	112	100	100	0	100	8	100
1917	Souvenir	30	37	0	100	18	100	100
1926	Roberts	152	84	100	0	0	100	100
1929	Noble 1	76	79	0	100	68	100	100
1929	Popular	9	100	0	100	0	100	100
1931	Noble 2	31	100	0	100	0	100	100
1935	Noble 3	32	31	0	100	0	100	100
1946	Almeida 1	26	26	0	100	100	0	100
1948	King 1	100	95	0	100	58	100	100
1950	King 2	100	85	0	100	26	100	94
1960	Henderson	31	97	0	100	17	100	100
1970	Elbert/Mahoe	101	87	100	100	100	0	100
1977	Himeni	237	18	0	100	0	0	100
1977	Almeida	2	80	90	0	3	0	100

Year = date of publication
ID = author or partial title of the collection
Tot = number of songs in the collection
NH = percentage of songs written by Native Hawaiians
Prose = percentage of songs having English prose explanatory material
PolEc = percentage of songs bearing signs of copyright
Mus = percentage of songs with standard musical notation
Perf = percentage of songs for which there are performance instructions
Trans = percentage of songs with translation of lyrics from Hawaiian to English

of songs within collections bearing signs of copyright); Trans (i.e., the percentage of songs within collections with English translations of Hawaiian language lyrics); Music (i.e., the percentage of songs within collections accompanied by standard musical notation); and Perf (i.e., the percentage of songs within collections in which performance instructions were provided). A matrix of phi coefficients with cut-off points at 50% for each variable were performed between all bivariate combinations of the five variables. The resulting correlation matrix is displayed in Table 2.

Table 2.
Correlations of Appropriation Variables

	Prose	PolEc	Trans	Music	Perf
Prose	1.00				
PolEc	-.58	1.00			
Trans	.35	.00	1.00		
Music	-.35	.35	-.40	1.00	
Perf	-.17	-.25	-.35	.35	1.00

The above values are unadjusted phi coefficients used when the values in Table 1 were dichotomized with 50% as the cut-off. Adjusted phi coefficients would have strengthened the relationships between variables. (Note: these figures should be interpreted with caution and are used for illustrative rather than for statistical purposes).

The covariance structure in Table 2 reveals two major clusters (i.e., variables positively correlated with one another) with regard to the five variables. The first cluster (involving the variables Music and Perf, phi=+.35) is composed of the nexi between the musical notation and performance variables. The second cluster (involving Prose and Trans, phi=+.35) contains the variables of explicatory prose and the presence of translations from Hawaiian to English. PolEc, the variable dealing with copyright signs, spans the clusters being directly related to prose (phi=+.35) and musical notation (phi=+.35), but not as strongly with performance (phi=-.25) and translations (phi=.00). In other words it seemed that song collections attempted to do one of two things as is indicated by the negative phi values between variables in different clusters. They either opted to concentrate upon aspects of performance, emphasizing musical notation and instrumentality (the first cluster of variables), or they opted to concern themselves with poetic form and content inclusive of translations (the second cluster of variables). But in either case, those variables associated most closely with composition of folk songs, musical notation and explanation of meanings, were associated with folk songs as a site for intellectual property.

Songs versus Meanings

A dialectical depiction of the folk song emerges. Musical notation, chord diagrams, along with performance acknowledgements, all aspects of the first cluster, are representational standards or methods that arise from the position of the folk-song text in a literate mass society where music is a commodity. As positive occurrences, this list of attributes serves to incorporate the folk songs into a modern social order (i.e., that of individual ownership and the exclusive right to convey possession) and the generalized distribution of the methods of expression (i.e., the particular manner in which the folk song is performed). However, general explanatory prose and translations of lyrics serve to reconstruct the layers of Hawaiian signification to an alien cultural code. The reconstruction produces relations of explication, i.e., legitimated mutual understanding between cultural memberships.

Explication in Folk Songs

Explication demonstrates at least two things: (1) the layers of meaning within the folk song are not apparent to the reader or are hidden and (2) the folk songs originate from a minority code (i.e., peripheral to the social context of the reader). In other words, the code is practically ephemeral and culturally irrelevant. The code of the song does not reproduce the social institutions of the dominant social order. The reader, then, is placed in the position of outsider, someone who needs an exegesis of the song to be brought into the presence of the song's signifieds.

Of the three texts that were primarily texts of explication, only one was expressly written for those unfamiliar with the folk songs as musical productions. Emerson (1909) introduces Native-Hawaiian performing arts, the "unwritten literature of Hawai'i," to the entirely uninitiated. He writes in the context of introducing the newly acquired Territory of Hawai'i to the rest of the United States. However, Almeida (1946) and Elbert and Mahoe (1970) are texts of explication written for both the neophyte and those technically familiar with the songs as musical compositions. But knowledge of musical performance techniques is somewhat independent of understanding the layers of significations of the lyrical form and content. Also suggested by the presence of explanatory material is the increasing transformation of Hawai'i's social milieu from knowledgeable to ignorant of the Native Hawaiian ethnic code, insofar as the song books have to be consulted by residents of Hawai'i to understand Native Hawaiian music.

Traversing Inter-ethnic Social Orders

The samples of twentieth-century, Native-Hawaiian folk song collections express the mixture of assimilation and peripheralization of Native Hawaiians.

The texts, as written documents in English, are inter-ethnic: that is, they inform the reader (situated within the dominant code) of a minority (peripheral) cultural code through the semiotic of the dominant cultural relations. The reader as well as the author situate themselves as members of the dominant code regardless of their affiliation with any other cultural group. Thus, a contemporary Native Hawaiian learning about his/her ethnic code through the textual materials of the song collections can do so only subsequent to being a member of the dominant cultural code; the rational access to indigenous Hawaiian codes in the songs is only through Western explanations for the majority of Hawaiians who do not have the resources of the Hawaiian language and the detailed family history of Hawaiian musicianship.

Table 3.
Authorship and Intended Audience

Year	Name	Domain	Author	Audience
1902	Cunha	music	local	western
1909	Emerson	prose	local	western
1917	Souvenir	music		
1926	Roberts	music	non-local	western
1929	Noble 1	music	local	mixed
1929	Popular	music		
1931	Noble 2	music	local	mixed
1935	Noble 3	music	local	western
1946	Almeida 1	prose	NH	mixed
1948	King 1	music	NH	mixed
1950	King 2	music	NH	mixed
1960	Henderson	music		
1970	Elbert/Mahoe	prose	local/NH	mixed
1977	Himeni	music	local	mixed
1977	Almeida 2	music	local	local

Traversing Inter-Ethnic Social Orders 223

The folksong collections arose mainly from the Territorial period (1900-1959). Their appearance at this time is not accidental. The monarchy had been deposed and no longer was available as a source of cultural support and an icon of cultural continuity. It was followed by a short-lived Republic (1893-1898), headed by a Caucasian oligarchy of commercial and plantation interests. The Territorial period opened up a vast market on the U.S. mainland for new musical products and brought in the early Waikiki tourists, who were entertained nightly by orchestras at hotels like the Moana and the Royal Hawaiian. It was also a time of increasing division of labor, culture became just one more commodity to be produced for exchange. Full-time musicians and singers could be employed. The expansion of the capitalist division of labor and Territorial education policies markedly reduced the role of the Hawaiian language. Most Hawaiians and Hawai'i local residents incrementally lost facility in the Hawaiian language and had to consult song-book texts to find out about Hawaiian music. Whereas both Hawaiians and Caucasian residents used Hawaiian up through the monarchy period, people became increasingly alienated from the social structural arrangements reproduced by the Hawaiian language and literally lost contact with traditional Hawaiian culture. The change in the intended audience of the folk song collections from "non-local" to "mixed" reflects the recognition of the demise of the indigenous code in Hawai'i and of the assimilation of the resident population, inclusive of Native Hawaiians, into membership in the dominant (Western) code. The Native Hawaiian folk song is, in a sense, an adaptation (simulated and modified toward the dominant code) of traditional Native Hawaiian lyric productions.

When the U.S. mainland market was opened up to the novelty of Hawaiian music, the U.S. music market more thoroughly penetrated the Hawai'i market, at the same time. Mainland musical innovations and fads, as well as bands and singers, came to Hawai'i. When the big band sound was displaced by radio, records, television, and the infinite permutations of rock-and-roll, the economy of scale of the mainland-originated music market pushed Hawaiian music off the airways of radio in Hawai'i. It was not until 1966 that KCCN radio started to broadcast Hawaiian music as its sole format. The penetration of Hawai'i by mainland music markets, as well as other forms of entertainment, left fewer social spaces for the performance and memory of Hawaiian music (cf. Bachelard 1969 on social memory). Published Hawaiian song collections became all the more consulted resources, the storage bins of an endangered culture.

The irony of the situation with Hawaiian folk song collections is that it reflects an internalization, by Hawaiians, of an English-based Western social structure and political economy. By having to accept the values of American social structure and political economy, while still identifying themselves as Native Hawaiians, the indigenous inhabitants of these islands actively participate in defining Hawaiians as peripheral and American social structure as the core.

Perhaps even more ironic is the role of this process in the rejuvenation of the Hawaiian Renaissance of the 1960s and 1970s. The dominant code became a means by which Native Hawaiians were able to recapture interest in their ethnic identity. This newfound resurgence in Hawaiiana, folk songs included, was approached through the dominant code. The transformation of folk songs is not the death knell of Native Hawaiian culture, but is an impetus for a rational (i.e., uniform) manner of approaching it. In the end, we can view Native Hawaiian folk songs as simulations of ancient mele adapted to the milieu of a non-indigenous dominant code and a commodity marketplace.

Conclusion

We have analyzed twentieth century Native Hawaiian folk song texts as a locus of larger societal relations. The texts materially are the hierarchical relationship between a dominant societal code and Native Hawaiians. The pervasiveness of the dominant code has infiltrated and suffused itself throughout Native Hawaiian culture and practices. Furthermore, the hegemony of the dominant code, supported by homologous institutional structures, continues to reproduce Hawaiian political-economic and socio-cultural marginality.

The study of Hawaiian folk song collections has demonstrated that the larger, overarching societal rationalities were homologically reproduced in the microcosm of the folk song texts, in the ways the songs were represented and explained. The objectivity of the inter-ethnic relations has been reproduced in the subjectivity of ethno-cultural expression and then again objectified as text. This is the non-recursive cycle of a social semiotic of inter-ethnic relations.

Lest it be believed that folk songs leapt from a state where songs were really chants to an abrupt form of commodification, we need to enter a qualification. Soon after the arrival of the missionaries in Hawai'i, printing presses were brought in to print religious materials in Hawaiian. These were followed by government and commercial presses. Spoken Hawaiian was reduced to print long before the first commercial song-book. Furthermore, songs were written, printed, and widely circulated for 40 years before they became a commodity.[9]

Among the song authors for the print medium were members of the royal family. The commodification of Hawaiian songs was built on a foundation of prior literacy.

The Native Hawaiian folk songs and song collections have acted as enabling devices for the resurgence in Hawaiiana. It is important to note, however, that this resurgence was made possible through the socialization of Native Hawaiians into the dominant code. As this study has pointed out, the folk song is an extension of traditional Hawaiian culture, but it is an extension constrained by the milieu of the widespread absence of traditional Native Hawaiian cultural practices, the presence of a commodification of that culture, and the accommodation of practices to the parameters of the dominant code (i.e., English language, Euroamerican musicality, and intellectual property).

Notes

* This is a revision of a paper presented in a Sociology of Culture session at the American Sociological Association Conference, Cincinnati, Ohio, 1991.

1. We appreciate the comments of various friends and colleagues including Karen Watson-Grego, Gene Kassebaum, Peter Manicas, Beverly Keever, and Katie Kamakahi.

2. The term *mele* refers to indigenous forms of songs, chants, and poems. We use the term folk song to emphasize the transformation of mele (indigenous forms of construction and performance specific to Native Hawaiian culture and performed intraculturally) to folk songs (a generic category used to classify various ethnic, melodic constructions fitted to intercultural standards of linguistic and musical notation).

3. The authors make a distinction between Native Hawaiian culture and local culture. We use the former, which refers to the practices of the indigenous peoples of Hawai'i prior to Western contact; while the latter refers to the amalgam of practices that emerged through the interaction of the various ethnic and cultural groups residing within Hawai'i. The Native Hawaiian folk song is seen as an ongoing extension of the former, while the hapa haole (see note 6) and locally produced music is construed as part of the latter.

4. For a more complete statement of intertextual relations see Derian and Shapiro (1989). The first application of Barthes' (1981) idea of intertextuality to Hawaiian music was made by Buck (1984).

5. There is a central place in the history of sociology regarding the relationship between language and social order including: the structuralist/post structuralist's "order of things" (Lyotard 1984; Giddens 1983; Baudrillard 1981; 1975; Foucault 1979; 1972; Durkheim 1970; Saussure 1966), the symbolic interactionists' "negotiated orders" (Denzin 1989; Couch 1984; Strauss 1979; Duncan 1962; Mead 1934), the Frankfurt School's study of mass communication (Habermas 1984; 1974; Gadamer 1975; Marcuse 1964), or the

enthnomethodologists' concentration on talk and the structure of conversational interaction (Boden 1990; Garfinkel 1988; 1967; Lynch 1985; Mishler 1984; Sacks, Schegloff, and Jefferson 1974). This is, obviously, only a partial listing of orientations to the issue.

6. Hapa haole means half-white or half-Caucasian. Here it is used with regard to hapa haole music, which is an admixture of local (sometimes Native Hawaiian) words and English lyrics. It should be noted here that these songs were expressly geared to non-local audiences.

7. The samples included represent almost the entire list of such published song collections for the time period in the University of Hawai'i at Manoa's Hawai'i Pacific Room in Hamilton Library.

8. Copyright ownership is of great import with regard to the appropriation of Native Hawaiian folk songs into the capitalist commodity system—analogous to the introduction of private land ownership in Hawai'i with the Great Mahele of 1848. The importance of private ownership with regard to music beyond the context of our paper has been discused by James (1988) and Kaplan (1987).

9. Both Peter Manicas and Beverly Keever have raised the issue as to whether hymns were to be considered Native Hawaiian folk songs. The position of the authors is that they are not because the former were primarily non-Native songs in which the lyrics were translated in the Hawaiian language, rather than being Native Hawaiian mele that were modified into folk songs.

References

Adams, R. 1927. *The Education and Economic Outlook for the Boys of Hawai'i: A Study of the Field of Race Relations.* Honolulu: Institute of Pacific Relations.

_____. 1933. *The Peoples of Hawai'i.* Honolulu: Institute of Pacific Relations.

_____. 1936. "Race Relations in Hawai'i: A Summary of Statement." *Social Process in Hawai'i* 2:56-60.

_____. 1937. *Interracial Marriage in Hawai'i.* New York: Macmillan.

Almeida, J. (ed.) 1977. *Songs of Hawai'i.* Honolulu: Almeida Music Publishing.

Almeida, J.K. 1946. *Na Mele Aloha.* Honolulu: John Kameaaloha Almeida.

Austin, J.L. 1975. *How To Do Things With Words.* Edited by J.O. Urmson and M. Sbisa. Cambridge, MA: Harvard University Press.

Bachelard, G. 1969. *The Poetics of Space.* Translated by M. Jolas. Boston: Beacon Press.

Barthes, R. 1981. "Theory of the Text." In *Untying the Text*, edited by Robert Young. Boston: Routledge and Kegan Paul.

Baudrillard, J. 1975. *The Mirror of Production.* Translated by M. Poster. St. Louis: Telos.

_____. 1981. *For a Critique of the Political Economy of the Sign.* Translated by C. Levin. St. Louis: Telos.

Beechert, E. 1985. *Working in Hawai'i: A Labor History.* Honolulu: University of Hawai'i Press.

Blaisdell, R.K. 1989. "Historical and Cultural Aspects of Native Hawaiian Health." *Social Process in Hawai'i* 32:1-21.

Blaisdell, R.K. and N. Mokuau. n.d. "Kanaka Maoli (Indigenous Hawaiians)." Unpublished manuscript.

Blount, J. 1893. "Report to U.S. Congress: Hawaiian Islands." In *Executive Document No.46, 53rd Congress.* Washington, DC: U.S. Government Printing Office.

Boden, D. 1990. "The World as It Happens: Ethnomethodology and Conversation Analysis." In *Frontiers of Social Theory*, edited by George Ritzer. New York: Columbia University Press.

Buck, E.B. 1984. "The Hawai'i Music Industry." *Social Process in Hawai'i.* 31:137-153.

Connor, S. 1989. Postmodern Culture: An Introduction to Theories of the Contemporary. Oxford: Basil Blackwell.

Couch, C.J. 1984. *Constructing Civilizations.* Greenwich, CT: JAI.

Cunha, A.R. 1902. *Songs of Hawai'i.* Honolulu: Bergstrom Music Co.

Denzin, N. 1989. *Interpretive Biography.* Newbury Park, CA: Sage.

Derian, J.D. and M.J. Shapiro, (eds.). 1989. *International/Intertextual Relations: Postmodern Readings of World Politics.* Lexington, MA: Lexington Books.

Duncan, H.D. 1962. *Communication and Social Order.* New York: Bedminster Press.

Durkheim, E. 1970. *Suicide.* Translated by J. Spaulding and G. Simpson. London: Routledge and Kegan Paul.

Elbert, S.H. and N. Mahoe. 1970. *Na Mele o Hawai'i Nei.* Honolulu: University of Hawai'i Press.

Emerson, N.B. 1909. *Unwritten Literature of Hawai'i.* Washington, DC: Bureau of American Ethnology.

Fish, S. 1980. Is There A Text in This Class? The Authority of Interpretive Communities. Cambridge, MA: Harvard University Press.

Foucault, M. 1972. *The Archaeology of Knowledge.* Translated by M. Sheridan-Smith. New York: Vintage.

_____. 1979. Discipline and Punish: The Birth of the Prison. New York: Vintage.

_____. 1980. *Power/Knowledge: Selected Interviews and Other Writings 1972-1977*. Edited by C. Gordon. Translated by C. Gordon, L. Marshall, J. Mepham, and K. Soper. New York: Pantheon.

_____. 1990. *Politics, Philosophy, Culture: Interviews and Other Writings, 1977-1984*. Edited by L.D. Kritzman. Translated by A. Sheridan et al. New York: Routledge.

Gadamer, H. 1975. *Truth and Method*. Translated by G. Barden and J. Cumming. New York: Seabury.

Garfinkel, H. 1967. *Studies in Ethnomethodology*. Englewood Cliffs, NJ: Prentice-Hall.

_____. 1988. "Evidence for Locally Produced, Naturally Accountable Phenomena of Order, Logic, Essential Quiddity of Immortal Ordinary Society, (I of IV): an Announcement of Studies." *Sociological Theory* 6:103-9.

Giddens, A. 1983. *A Contemporary Critique of Historical Materialism*. Berkeley: University of California Press.

Glick, C.E. 1980. *Sojourners and Settlers: Chinese Migrants in Hawai'i*. Honolulu: University of Hawai'i Press.

Habermas, J. 1974. *Theory and Practice*. Translated by J. Viertel. London: Heinemann.

_____. 1984. The Theory of Communicative Action, Volume One: Reason and the Rationalization of Society. Translated by T. McCarthy. Boston: Beacon Press.

Handy, E.S.C. and M.K. Pukui. 1972. *The Polynesian Family System in Ka'u, Hawai'i*. Rutland, VT: Tuttle.

Harvey, D. 1989. The Condition of Postmodernity: An Enquiry into the Origins of Cultural Change. Cambridge: Basil Blackwell.

Henderson, R. 1960. *Music of Hawai'i*. Boston: Boston Music Co.

Hormann, B.L. 1965. "Hawai'i's People in Transition." In *The Kamehameha Schools 75th Anniversary Lectures*. Honolulu: Kamehameha Schools Press.

Howe, K.R. 1984. Where the Waves Fall: A New South Sea Islands History from First Settlement to Colonial Rule. Honolulu: University of Hawai'i Press.

James, D.E. 1988. "Poetry/Punk/Production: Some Recent Writing in L.A." In *Postmodernism and Its Discontents: Theories, Practice*, edited by E.A. Kaplan. London: Verso.

Kahananui, D. 1965. "Influences on Hawaiian Music." *The Kamehameha Schools 75th Anniversary Lectures*. Honolulu: The Kamehameha Schools Press.

Kamaunu, R. 1929. *A Collection of Popular Hawaiian Melodies*. Honolulu: Hawai'i Sales Co., Ltd.

Kanahele, G.S., ed. 1979. *Hawaiian Music and Musicians: An Illustrated History*. Honolulu: University of Hawai'i Press.

Kaplan, A.E. 1987. *Rocking Around the Clock: Music Television, Postmodernism and Consumer Culture.* Madison: Coda Press.

Kent, N. 1985. "Straws in The Wind." *Social Process in Hawai'i* 31:183-186.

King, C.E. 1948. *Hawaiian Melodies.* Honolulu: Charles E. King.

———. 1950. *Songs of Hawai'i.* Honolulu: Charles E. King.

King, P.N. 1987. "Structural Changes in Hawaiian History: Changes in the Mental Health of a People." In *Contemporary Issues in Mental Health Research in the Pacific Islands,* A.B. Robillard and A.J. Marsella, editors. Honolulu: Social Science Research Institute.

Kuykendall, R.S. 1938. *The Hawaiian Kingdom: Volume 1.* Honolulu: University of Hawai'i Press.

———. 1953. *The Hawaiian Kingdom: Volume 2.* Honolulu: University of Hawai'i Press.

———. 1967. *The Hawaiian Kingdom: Volume 3.* Honolulu: University of Hawai'i Press.

Lind, A. 1936. *An Island Community: Ecological Succession in Hawai'i.* Chicago: University of Chicago Press.

———. 1954. "Changing Race Relations in Hawai'i." *Social Process in Hawai'i* 18:1-9.

———. 1955. *Hawai'i's People.* Honolulu: University of Hawai'i Press.

Linnekin, J. 1985. *Children of the Land: Exchange and Status in a Hawaiian Community.* New Brunswick, NJ: Rutgers University Press.

Lydecker, R.C. 1918. *Roster Legislatures of Hawai'i: 1841-1918.* Honolulu: Hawaiian Gazette Co.

Lynch, M. 1985. *Art and Artifact in Laboratory Science: A Study of Shop Work and Shop Talk in a Research Laboratory.* London: Routledge and Kegan Paul.

Lyotard, J. 1984. *The Postmodern Condition: A Report on Knowledge.* Translated by G. Bennington and B. Massumi. Minneapolis: University of Minnesota Press.

Marcuse, H. 1964. *One Dimensional Man.* London: Routledge and Kegan Paul.

Mead, G.H. 1934. *Mind, Self and Society.* Edited by C. Morris. Chicago: University of Chicago Press.

Mishler, E.G. 1984. *The Discourse of Medicine: Dialectics of Medical Interviews.* Norwood, NJ: Ablex Publishing Corporation.

Native Hawaiian Study Commission. 1983. *Report on the Culture, Needs, and Concerns of Native Hawaiians: Volume 1.* Honolulu: Native Hawaiian Study Commission.

Noble, J.N. 1929. *Royal Collection of Hawaiian Songs.* Honolulu: Johnny Noble.

———. 1931. *Collection of Ancient and Modern Hulas.* Honolulu: Johnny Noble.

_____. 1935. *Book of Famous Hawaiian Melodies.* Honolulu: Johnny Noble.

Richard, N. 1987/8. "Postmodernism and Periphery." *Third Text* 2:5-12.

Roberts, H.H. 1926. *Ancient Hawaiian Music.* Honolulu: Bishop Museum Press.

Robillard, A.B. 1991. "Where is Social Change in Hawai'i: The Reyn's Aloha Shirt." *Social Change in the Pacific Islands.* London: Kegan Paul.

Sacks, H., E. Schegloff, and G. Jefferson. 1974. "A Simplest Systematics for the Analysis of Turn Taking in Conversations." *Language* 50:696-735.

Saussure, F. 1966. *Course in General Linguistics.* New York: McGraw-Hill.

Sayre, H. 1983. "The Object of Performance: Aesthetics in the Seventies." *Georgia Review* 37(1):169-88.

Senior Citizen Clubs. 1977. *E Himeni Kakou (Let's Sing): Book 2.* Honolulu: Department of Parks and Recreation.

Shiach, M. 1989. *Discourse on Popular Culture: Class, Gender, and History in Cultural Analysis, 1730 to the Present.* Stanford, CA: Stanford University Press.

Spanos, W.V. 1979. "De-struction and the Question of Post-Modernist Literature: Toward a Definition." *Par Rapport* 2:107-22.

Stannard, D. 1989. *Before the Horror: The Population of Hawai'i in the Eve of Western Contact.* Honolulu: Social Science Research Institute.

Stillman, A.K. 1988. *Hawaiian Music: Published Songbooks.* Pacific Collection - Hamilton Library, University of Hawai'i.

Strauss, A. 1979. *Negotiations.* San Francisco: Jossey-Bass.

Trask, H.K. 1983. "Cultures in Collision: Hawai'i and England, 1778." *Pacific Studies* 7:91-117.

_____. 1985. "Hawaiians, American Colonization, and the Quest for Independence." *Social Process in Hawai'i* 31:101-136.

_____. 1991. "Natives and Anthropologists: The Colonial Struggle." *Contemporary Pacific* 3:159-167.

Wong, K. 1965. "Ancient Hawaiian Music." In *The Kamehameha Schools 75th Anniversary Lectures.* Honolulu: Kamehameha Schools Press.

Contributors

Ibrahim G. Aoudé is Associate Professor at the University of Hawai'i Ethnic Studies Program. His research areas include Hawai'i's political economy and Middle East politics.

Joyce Chinen is Assistant Professor of Sociology at the University of Hawai'i - West O'ahu. She has taught sociology within the University of Hawai'i system for about fifteen years, at Leeward and Honolulu Community College, and the University of Hawai'i at Hilo, before joining the faculty at the University of Hawaii - West O'ahu. Her areas of specialization are Women and Work, Race and Ethnic Relations, and Social Stratification and Inequality. She has published several articles on Asian American Women, and is currently collecting oral histories of Women of Color who have been activists in Hawai'i's labor, peace, and community movements.

Paul A. Herbig is Professor in the Marketing department at the College of Commerce and Business Administration of Jacksonville State University of Jacksonville, Alabama. He has previously published in such journals as Journal of Business Research, Industrial Marketing Management, Asian Journal of Marketing, and Journal of International Marketing. His research interests include reputation and signaling, innovation and culture, Japanese marketing practices, and industrial trade shows/distributors. His first book, the Innovation Matrix, is due out summer 1994 by Greenwood Press.

Jeffrey J. Kamakahi, Ph.D., is Assistant Professor of Sociology at the University of Central Arkansas. His interests include the socio-cultural transformation of Hawai'i focusing upon Native Hawaiians, comparative methodologies, and the metatheoretical foundations of social research.

Marion Kelly is Associate Professor, University of Hawai'i at Manoa, and has taught in the Ethnic Studies Program, since it began. She was born and raised in the Islands, lived on a sugar plantation and attends the University of Hawai'i. The focus of her research is the history of land tenure and use in Hawai'i.

Noel Jacob Kent is Professor at the University of Hawai'i Ethnic Studies Program since 1972. His study, *Hawai'i: Islands Under the Influence*, is widely used as an analysis of modern Hawai'i's development. Kent was a Fulbright lecturer at the University of Aaruhs (Denmark) in 1986-87 and has written extensively on the linkages between the United States political-economy, racial structures, and racism.

Karl Kim is Associate Professor of Urban and Regional Planning at the University of Hawai'i at Manoa. He is a graduate of Brown University and the

Massachusetts Institute of Technology. His research interests include planning and development in the Asia-Pacific region.

Hugh E. Kramer is Professor at the University of Hawai'i at Manoa since 1969. He is chairman of the Department of Marketing where he teaches international marketing strategy and entrepreneurship. His specialization is in high tech industry and the role of marketing in economic development.

John K. Matsuoka is Associate Professor of Social Work at the University of Hawai'i at Manoa. He teaches courses in human behavior, community organization, mental health, and research. In terms of research, Dr. Matsuoka has conducted numerous socio-cultural impact assessments in rural Hawai'i and other Pacific Island communities.

Davianna Pomaika'i McGregor is Assistant Professor of Ethnic Studies at the University of Hawai'i at Manoa . She is a historian of Hawai'i and the Pacific. She has documented the persistence of traditional Hawaiian cultural customs, beliefs, and practices in rural Hawaiian communities. Her research endeavors focus on protecting rural Hawaiian communities from the negative impacts of tourist, commercial, and industrial development.

Luciano Minerbi, Dr. Arch., MUP, AICP, AAIA is Professor in the Department of Urban and Regional Planning at the University of Hawai'i at Manoa. His research includes neighborhood and community based planning, planning with indigenous people and the Native Hawaiians, island environmental and land use management, and ecologically sustainable development.

Jonathan Y. Okamura is a researcher in the Office of Student Equity, Excellence and Diversity at the University of Hawaii at Manoa and also teaches occasional courses in the Ethnic Studies Program. A social anthropologist by training, he has conducted research with cultural minorities in the Philippines and on ethnicity and ethnic relations in Hawai'i.

Albert B. Robillard, Ph.D., is Associate Professor of Sociology at the University of Hawai'i at Manoa. His research interests include postmodern Hawai'i, the Pacific Islands, medical sociology, and ethnomethodology.

Ira Rohter is Associate Professor of Political Science at the University of Hawai'i at Manoa. He regularly teaches courses in alternative futures, the politics of Hawai'i, politics and media, Green politics and philosophy, and political ecology and development. He is a founding member of the Transformational Politics section in the America Political Science Association, and initiated the Hawai'i Research Program for Sustainable development.

T. D. Webb, Ph.D., is Associate Professor and Head Librarian at Kapiolani Community College. He has written three books and several articles on library management and automation and a number of articles on the anthropology of tourist art.